BYRON: ROMANTIC PARADOX

BYRON
ROMANTIC PARADOX

BY

WILLIAM J. CALVERT

Chapel Hill
The University of North Carolina Press
1935

COPYRIGHT, 1935, BY
THE UNIVERSITY OF NORTH CAROLINA PRESS

PRINTED IN THE UNITED STATES OF AMERICA BY THE SEEMAN PRINTERY, DURHAM, N. C., AND BOUND BY L. H. JENKINS, INC., RICHMOND, VA.

THIS BOOK WAS DIGITALLY PRINTED.

ACKNOWLEDGMENTS

TO my mother; to those friends who helped in small but significant ways; to Robert Kilburn Root, who, quite unknowing, influenced my view of the eighteenth century; to Irving Babbitt, who stung all his students, even through violent disagreement, into thought; to the members of the University of North Carolina Press; to George Coffin Taylor; and above all to John Livingston Lowes, master and friend, a great debt is owed and with gratitude acknowledged.

WILLIAM J. CALVERT

Jacksonville, Alabama
November 25, 1934

FOREWORD

EVERY popular poet is accepted by his time as much for his weaknesses as for his strength. If he is popular enough, he is made the standard-bearer of his age. He must symbolize what it wants, or what it thinks itself to be, and he rises and falls with public opinion. As the mood of the next generation contradicts that of his own, he suffers a period of neglect or recrimination, during which his popularity is recollected and wondered at by the critics, although it persists for a time among those unaware of critical standards. If there is stuff in him, however, he must eventually re-arise. Gradually here and there an enthusiast takes up his cause. Where he has been only tolerated, he is acclaimed and studied, and books are written about him. Reasons are found for his greatness. He is appointed his peak in the mountain range of poets. He is recognized as the pinnacle of a culminating tradition. He becomes legitimate.

Such a course is not to be regretted. The poet, dying usually before the decline of his fame, is not hurt by the neglect. His few remaining friends form a minute, indignant minority. Succeeding poets are saved from the tyranny of his name, or have the privilege of revolting against him. His resurrection is like the delayed entrance of a stage heroine: he is the more noticed for having kept his audience waiting. By being so long a wraith, he has become more god than man. And posterity, having recovered its breath and regained its perspective, may settle down to the acceptable task of judging. It perceives, and excuses, the flaws. It seizes upon the undeniable virtues, emphasizing them by repetition, by common consent, by critical discussion. It recommends the poet's works as ornaments for a library of uncut leaves. It teaches him critically, historically, textually, in its schools.

But posterity, though it is in many ways to be felicitated, has nevertheless one almost insuperable disadvantage: it must see its object in perspective. Having, in the meantime, sharpened and defined its critical terms, discovered schools, traced movements, and assigned to individuals their proper niches and labels, it regards the past as a map or panorama, and finds it difficult to regain past prejudices, or even to recall, for the occasion, a former bias. It is hampered by the paraphernalia of its scholarship. It discovers judgment to be easier than sympathy, explanation than description, and intellectual understanding than imaginative reconstruction. It is alien, and increasingly so, to the period it attempts to comprehend.

The fame and the after-fame of Byron offer an excellent case in point. His popularity, sudden and overwhelming, soared, even in its heyday, above a strong, croaking sub-chorus of suspicious disapproval. Its meteoric decline threw him into the hands of the Philistines. He became, throughout the Victorian Era, a bogey man to fright the young with from the lurid paths of vice. Of all English poets, perhaps, he still remains, certainly for the English and the American critic, the hardest to treat objectively, without adopting a decided bias for or against. The formerly compelling temptation, when writing of him, either to join the chorus of disapproval or to reply to it, grows smaller, however, with each succeeding year, as the problems connected with his life recede further into the background—until an *Astarte* is published, and the whole vicious round must be made again.

The very nature of Byron's work is deceiving. In its sweep, its lack of subtlety, its vivid clarity, there is an apparent promise of simplicity that is not borne out on examination. Where Keats is autumn haze and Shelley pure ether, Byron is rock—and the hard outcroppings may indicate geologic epochs or hot underflows of lava that are worth noting and understanding. From whatever angle we approach him, he is highly complex. A complex personality, he lived in a complex era, and formed his artistic aims and inspirations from complex, even contradictory sources.

It would be well if, recognizing the danger of modern chitchat biographical criticism, of forgetting the work in the man, or of obscuring the soul by an overplus of flesh, we could ignore biographical events altogether. It is not always well to dwell upon an artist's life, especially as affecting his creation, or upon the stages in the production of a masterpiece. We may very easily come to overlook the beauty and worth of the product in discovering how it has come to be made. There is a larger and truer perspective from which to view a hero than that of his valet.

Nor can we, as serious ponderers and investigators, avoid that other danger of presenting the poet merely as a projection of his period, and so losing the man, or his work, in the times. Times do not make the man, certainly not the great man, though they may have much to do with bringing out greatness that might otherwise have been undeveloped. Life to the poet is an opportunity or a lack of opportunity for expression, and though he may seek in the contemporary scene his materials or the sources of his inspiration, his particular poetic flair remains his own. Byron, a restless individual, attained to greatness in a particularly restless epoch, when mankind, balanced between two worlds, was in the throes of producing a new. He was himself both a Georgian dandy of the Regency and a romantic, Wordsworth's junior and Shelley's contemporary, an inheritor and worshiper of the preceding century's renown and a vacillating disciple of new fashions in poetry and thought.

Thus the crux of any critical approach to Byron must always be the oft recalled paradox: Why, as one of the great romantic poets, did he yet pay lip-service to Pope and the school of Pope? The present volume, though it has borrowed its title from this old problem, considers it not so much a paradox and Byron's defense of it not so entirely whim or perversity as has usually been assumed.

To portray the literary life-history of a genius, to understand and integrate him, first as man and thinker and then as self-critic, and finally to estimate his worth in terms of his own self-knowledge must be this volume's final aim. It presupposes, as a fundamental thesis, the existence in every significant artist of a life-in-work, distinct from his daily living, and dependent upon it only as the spirit waits upon the flesh, a life with a rationale, an inner urge, a growth of its own, an interaction between aspiration and accomplishment wherein each achievement helps to determine, if only through revulsion, the achievements to follow. While such a study must make allowance for the person, its true concern is with the *act and principle of creation*, which forms the basis of the artistic personality and differentiates the creator from the journeyman.

The obsession of the criticism of Byron during the past decade, the problem of *Astarte*, has consciously been fought shy of for two main reasons. First, though the case for the prosecution has been made exceedingly plausible, and indeed is more probably true than not, it rests too utterly for its direct evidence upon the testimony of one person, Lady Byron, who, whatever her character, was hardly a disinterested witness. Secondly, for the purposes of this study, Augusta is unnecessary in the explaining of Byron. There is enough, it is believed, in the early chapters of the book to indicate that Byron was, by forces outside his power, destined for torture. How, as poet, he coped with his fate, is the theme of the later chapters.

TABLE OF CONTENTS

CHAPTER	PAGE
FOREWORD	vii
I. THE MAN	3
II. THE AGE OF REASON	21
III. THE MAN OF SENSE	38
IV. THE PRACTICAL POET	74
V. ESCAPE	104
VI. REBIRTH	123
VII. DRAMA AND PROPAGANDA	152
VIII. ACHIEVEMENT	181
NOTES	211
SELECTED BIBLIOGRAPHY	226
INDEX	229

BYRON: ROMANTIC PARADOX

CHAPTER I

THE MAN

BYRON had the fortune, good or ill, to be observed and reported by many persons; and it was by the external aspects of his personality that his acquaintances were mainly impressed. Women saw, not only the dark, mysterious, imperious genius whom they had been led to look for in reading *Childe Harold,* but also a man with a beautiful, pale, vividly intelligent countenance, and with a slight limp, of which he was acutely conscious. The beauty, the intelligence, the lameness, people saw in varying perspective and proportion; but all three they always saw and retained in memory as the realization of the poet. Those foolish women who were a-titter over his possible past, who claimed to recognize the evidences of sin in his countenance, and who interpreted his shy reserve as satanic pride, may conveniently be ignored. To those who knew him best, Byron was not a perverted Apollo. He was, in the main, an ordinary human being, with an uncertain temper, a baffling mixture of vanity, modesty, petulance, repentance, aristocratic pride, and democratic sentiment—the whole glossed over with affectations that Peacock ridiculed and Lady Hester Stanhope found occasion later to mimic.[1] There is reassuring unanimity in the pictures of Byron we have inherited from so many and such different people. They disagree in emphasis and interpretation, but, taken all in all, they depict an essentially noble nature, striving against petty weaknesses of temperament and temper and sometimes all but submerged in foibles.

The Byron familiar to his intimates was not the self-tortured hero portrayed by European criticism, but that other side, the wayward, charming, well-meaning person who captivated the society of the Regency for a season; a Byron dim or obscured in most of the books written about him, shining more clearly in his letters than in his conscious art. The poet was not altogether the stuff of which heroes are made. Like most highly sensitive natures he was strongly affected by his environment; he very readily took on the stamp of his associates, accepted their opinions, aped their manners. He was too conscious of the world's gaze, too eager for the world's suffrage, too concerned with what others thought of him, too uneasy as to his own good station, too easily hurt and turned aside by the hostility of the mob. "Nothing so completely serves to demoralize a man," in his view, "as the certainty that he has lost the support of his fellow creatures."[2] Byron was obsessed, to his own handicap in action, with the fear that the world, his English world, might turn, or had turned, against him. His very rebellion was apt to be a gesture of desperation. He had to help him a hot instinct-for-action and a sense of the truth that rendered him intolerably restless in the face of sham.

Byron's want of assurance was, to his acquaintances—to those at least who came to know him after his reputation had been won—his most remarkable characteristic. "He had no address," complains Leigh Hunt. "He hummed and hawed, and looked confused, on very trivial occasions; . . . he could much more easily get into a dilemma than out of it, and with much greater skill wound the self-love of others than relieve them."[3] A character somewhat like Crampton in Shaw's *You Never Can Tell*, embarrassed by the conflict between *savoir faire* and his own impetuous good intentions, between a lack of self-assurance and a sensitive uncompromising pride, making a confidant of every first comer, out of pure loneliness, dismay, or restlessness. It is impossible —though for some of his contemporaries it proved far too easy—to ignore in Byron, however deeply it is overlaid, a native kindliness, like that of Swift, a kindliness preëminently protective. He was, like Swift, one of those people who are much more popular with their valets, their house-servants, and the poor, than with their peers. Supersensitive and affectionate, he gathered a menagerie about him because he could not be sure enough of the regard of his fellows.

The "Byronic pose," in the main, may be traced to a tendency to accept the opinions of others. Byron's flair for the aristocratic style, his penchant for swaggering as a lord, was the natural heritage from Newstead and from student days at Harrow and at Cambridge. Superficially, in his imagination, he saw life as an aristocrat is supposed to see it— looking at others always a little haughtily, a little aloofly, at once despising them and distrusting them; accepting only his immediate fellows in high isolation. Byron's reverence for the old, in the abstract, was either instinctive or early acquired and never quite lost, although his dislike for particular manifestations of survivals from the past lent him the rôle, during his Italian days, of an *enfant terrible* on the grand scale. "Respect for age is the natural religion of childhood; it becomes in man a sentiment of the soul. An obscure melancholy, the pathos of human fate, mingles with this instinctive feeling. The fascination of the sea, the sublimity of mountains, are indebted to it, as well as the beautiful and solemn stars, which, like them, the mind does not distinguish from eternal things, and has ever invested with sacred awe. It is the sense of our mortality that thus exalts nature."[4] The third canto of *Childe Harold* is summed up in that worship of the old and the eternal; the fourth canto is but the transference of such an emotion to the relics of man's power, mellowed, transformed, or overcome by time and nature; loyalty, which in its way is an acquiescence, struggled in Byron for mastery with the impressionable mobility which he admitted as his greatest weakness.

The aristocrat in Byron was but one facet of a many-sided individual. The young lord had benefited but little from his rank. He lacked the money, in his youth, to live up to his position. He was coldly received in the House. Lord Carlisle, for pardonable reasons, was hardly kind to him. He was essentially an outsider, even in the days of his triumph, for then he was accepted as a poet and a romantic figure; he was a temporary fashion, a fad; he was aware that his day as lion would soon be over. His insistence on his rank, which brought down on his head the ridicule of the *Edinburgh Review*, increased in the face of a world which, in the main, liked him little the better for it. To his literary imagination, his family history made him a solitary, an outlaw. This vision of himself was rooted in the feverish past of his race; Lara was the projection of the youthful Byron grown aged in this world of woe and given his chance. Fate had granted him a name notorious rather than famous, an honor rooted in estrangement, and Byron was enough of a fatalist to feel the obligation of living down to his family's reputation. From the start, he led a double life within. His early training was Protestant, Presbyterian, moralistic, and gloomy; family tradition gave him an impetus toward adventure, contention, not overscrupulous pursuit of not too disinterested ends. His paganism was of the Berserker type, his Christianity was northern, manly, and violent.

Carlyle has been likened to Byron, and rightly. The strict Calvinistic training of both was similar, and each nature craved imperiously a solution. That in the poet's case this religious residuum was unconscious, we may conclude from the fact that Calvin is mentioned only once in his poetry and not at all in his *Letters and Journals*. Consciously, Byron leaned toward Catholicism, admiring its elegance of worship, its "incense, pictures, statues, altars, shrines, relics, and the real presence, confession, absolution," which gave one something tangible to grasp, and finding in dogmatism an answer to the troubled uncertainty of his soul. The Catholic ritual, furthermore, offered the beautiful in religion, which Calvinism lacked, and seemed to satisfy a longing in his soul that beauty and goodness should go hand in hand. But this was no more than longing. Byron must have felt a speciousness in Catholicism, as he felt it in whatever else had promised to satisfy an ideal. Certainly the total effect of his works is not that of a successful union of the beautiful and the good.

In the depths of his mind the tenets of original sin were immovably intrenched. *Manfred* was but a defiance of the doctrine, a not very convincing defiance. *Cain* was an exposition of its minor premises; and though the more vivid impression upon contemporaries, radical and conservative alike, was made by the heterodox speeches of Lucifer, Byron was correct in his contention that he had caused his rebel to speak in character. The two dramas, together with *Heaven and Earth*, may be considered as giving Satan's side of the high argument in Heaven which resulted in the fall of man and as protesting against the punishment of man for acts committed through no fault of his own will; but they do not bring into question the dogma of the Fall. The character of Cain is an unsuccessful attempt to trace the inevitable causes of crime to outside forces. But although as a study of character the drama is a failure, the expression of religious determinism in unforgettable verse conveys the meaning of the work in spite of obvious flaws of technique. The deliberate anticlimaxes of *Don Juan* are again the expression of a soul that could not look upon earthly matters with the calm, cheerful acceptation of the conventional pagan, but that decried every foible and folly of mankind as a mortal fall from grace.

There is something in Calvinism that seems to suit the northern nature. From the point of view of the humanist, there was never a crueler religion. Its purpose is to make man ill at ease in Zion. It denies the full, healthy, rich life. It destroys a sense of beauty and proportion in conduct, by isolating these qualities from the moral order. By ascribing natural instincts to the malevolence of the Devil, it makes suffering inevitable, creates a morbid sense of sin, as in Bunyan or Cowper, suppresses or dams up in man those very emotions that are precious to the catholic artist. It divides one being from another, each in his own cell of torment and trial; it stresses the competitive out of all compass; it multiplies tenfold man's native loneliness. Its cruelty is, above all, spiritual rather than physical, and for that reason all the sharper. Yet, like science, which is in its own way cruel, it has added to the individual's power. It has withdrawn man's thoughts from soft beds and still waters of comfort. It has necessitated hard thinking and action. Frustrate emotions, denied other outlet, have demanded relief in ceaseless activity, wherein man plunges to forget, or benumb, not to express, himself.

Upon Byron its action had this twofold result. It exaggerated his melancholy and sufferings; it denied him ease. Only a Puritan conscience, plus a taste for literature, was needed to transform the son of "Mad Jack" Byron into a major poet. It did not create a strength of will and a sincerity that were already there. But it granted suffering to aid the poetic flame, and made the ordinary outlets in sensual indulgence uncomfortable if not impossible.

Between Byron's Calvinism and his passion for liberty existed a more intimate relationship than might be apparent at first glance. The two supplemented rather than contradicted each other. Fretted by the shackles of a religion basically fatalistic, he developed a horror of being confined or ruled, an impatience of check, an obsession with liberty, which was abetted by the romantic dogmas of the time, stimulated by the French Revolution and the career of Napoleon with his European wars, and raised to fever pitch by the Holy Alliance and its atrocities. Joined to this was a love of disagreement and of fighting, with however little success—the ancient Berserker spirit translated incontinently into terms of the nineteenth century. Byron was happy only in action; but literature and his imagination offered the sole vent to his inherited corsair nature. His eccentricities, inconsistencies, and violent passion may be traced largely to the fact that, essentially a man of action caught in inactivity, he floundered about like a whale in a puddle, until the Greek Revolution presented him with his chance for relief.

In one other aspect of his life, paradoxically, Byron was deeply affected by his Calvinistic training. Puritanism has ever looked askance at sex. Victorian prudery was but the emasculated climax of generations of bad conscience. Byron's sense of guilt was, in large measure, responsible for his notoriety. He was hardly by nature wickeder, though more violent, than other men, but he boasted openly of those things it is prudent not to admit; he had to relieve his conscience by talking of his sins.

Byron, we can very well believe, expressed to Lady Blessington all the commendable and sane views on marriage that she reported. The young man Byron might well have been capable of a happy marriage, had not his springs of life been poisoned from the start by his unlucky romance with Mary Chaworth, a school environment favorable to his reaction into cynicism, his anxiety to be fashionable, and the looseness of morals that was still *comme il faut* in the English upper circles. "I could have left or lost the world with or for that which I loved," he soliloquized long after; "but, though my temperament was naturally burning, I could not share in the commonplace libertinism of the place and time without disgust. And yet this very disgust, and my heart thrown back upon itself, threw me into excesses perhaps more fatal than those from which I shrunk, as fixing upon me . . . the passions. . . ."[5] His view of love was either naïvely sentimental or naïvely cynical, essentially romantic and essentially male. He dreamed always of his ideal woman, though quite willing to admit that she possibly did not exist. He was conscious ever of the *besoin d'aimer*,[6] of the necessity of some ideal object of affection, who should exist if only to be worshiped. But his native laziness made him incapable of lengthy courtship against odds, which might have made him appreciate woman as an attainment. His life was a series of conquests—*by* women, too often easy women. But the kind of woman he needed was apart somewhere. "He said [to Lady Blessington] that most people had *le besoin d'aimer*, and that with this *besoin* the first person who fell into one's way contented one."[7] Love with him was a constant effort to escape from morbidity; it was a fever, a disease, and women were his medicine.

Excess of desire, inflamed by the imagination and never held in check, threw Byron into a fatalism of passion, which he was forever, unsuccessfully, justifying to himself. "I cannot exist without some object of love."[8] "I could never live for but one human being at a time, (and, I assure you, *that one* has never been *myself*, . . .)"[9] "We must love something."[10] He used to throw himself upon the floodtide of his passions, shirking responsibility, as if moved by some universal blind power too great to be resisted. Afterwards would come satiety, and disillusionment, and a sense of guilt. Marriage, he told himself, was the sole satisfactory status for man. Even the relatively respectable relation with La Guiccioli was too much for his stomach. "I feel . . . that this Cicisbean existence is to be condemned. But I have neither the strength of mind to break my chain, nor the insensibility which would deaden its weight."[11] So he wrote to John Cam Hobhouse.

Wherever we start, we are brought back to one note in Byron, the drone bass of his life—the sense that not he was acting, but some greater force through him. Such fatalism forms part and parcel of the charm of his correspondence: "Like the fly in the fable," he said of himself, "I seem to have got upon a wheel which makes much dust; but, unlike the said fly, I do not take it all for my own raising."[12] Lady Blessington observed the quality, and ascribed it to indolence, or to an abandonment to his destiny, beyond the understanding of commonplace people. It was Shelley's complaint that his friend had no decisiveness of character and could never make up his mind on any subject whatever. And Galt had once remarked, during a social evening in Greece, that his fellow traveler appeared to be "actuated by no purpose—he spoke no more of passing 'beyond Aurora and the Ganges', but seemed disposed to let the current of chances carry him as it might."[13]

This judgment of his friends finds ample echo in the words of Byron himself. His correspondence and conversation are full of *apologiae*, all insisting on his greatest defect: "I am not famous for decision."[14] "I look upon self-command as a positive virtue, which I have not the courage to adopt."[15] "It is not eagerness of new pursuits, but that nothing impresses me sufficiently to *fix*; neither do I feel disgusted, but simply indifferent to almost all excitements. The proof of this is, that obstacles, the slightest even, *stop* me. This can hardly be *timidity*, . . ."[16] "I seem to have *two* states of existence, *one* purely contemplative, during which the crimes, faults, and follies of mankind are laid open to my view (my own forming a prominent object in the picture), and the other *active*, when I play my part in the drama of life, as if compelled by some power over which I have no control, though the consciousness of doing wrong remains."[17] "It appears to me, just from my own reflections and experiences, that I am influenced in a way which is incomprehensible, and am led to do things which I never intended. . . . I have . . . contented myself with believing that there is a predestination of events, and that the predestination depends upon the will of God."[18] "Like Sylla, I have always believed that all things depend upon Fortune, and nothing upon ourselves."[19]

There is some significance in the fact that nearly all of these are the pronouncements of the later, disillusioned, self-distrustful Byron, of him who wrote *Don Juan*. We must not hold our conclusions too belligerently. The effect in the main, however, of Byron's personality on those who came to know him was one either of utter will-lessness, or at least of a vagueness and vacillation of intention and a skepticism of results. In his later days, certainly, he presented a front of fatalistic lethargy, which let him float with the stream or in still waters, and allowed him to be moved only through circumstances or before the blast of passion—never, like Freedom's flag in the famous metaphor of *Childe Harold*, *against* the wind. His soul was in its essence stationary, as André Maurois has called it;[20] it resisted all change, not giving way till the last minute—and then, as with the ultraconservative, the change was more spectacular and more devastating for having been delayed. Byron, conscious of his defect, acknowledged it, characteristically did nothing about it, and shifted the responsibility to a theory of life—fatalism, or, to speak more accurately, as linked with his childhood religion, predestination.

It was Byron's unhappiness to extract the maximum of irritation and the minimum of comfort from each circumstance of his life. Though his religion, in this case, held him caught as in a vise, all was not to the bad with predestination. It presented life on a grand scale: the devotee, dwarfed in his individuality, was nevertheless a unit in the universal warfare of God and Satan; behind his actions cosmic forces were outlined; once enlisted on the side of righteousness, he could expend his will and his ingenuity on outwitting the Powers of Hell; his stage was the universe, and he had the consolation of the tragic actor—a sense of importance, and the verve of the play. But Byron was both a Calvinist and not a Calvinist—unfortunately in both cases. "He was a Christian by education; he was an infidel by reading. He was a Christian by habit; he was no Christian upon reflection...."[21] "On the gloomy and narrow religion taught by his first Scottish masters, there had been superimposed, but without destroying the first, the Voltairean deism of the Cambridge undergraduates, and on the ingenuous sentimentalism of adolescence, a strongly ironical humor."[22] Calvinism presented an enigma, but it offered a way out; skepticism denied the solution. The divine curse was left in all its rigidity as a residue, but the voice of God had departed from the waters. The imagination and the emotions have laws of which articulate reason is unaware. Rationalism mocked at imagination and emotion, though it could not destroy them; it strangled Byron's religious hopes and purposefulness, but it could not prevent imaginative terrors, nor could it get at implanted prohibition. The new, disrupting the old, brought with its sense of liberation the curse of chaos—and of an old promise, or command, unfulfilled.

With no backbone of belief and with a wavering taste, Byron, in all verity, could not hope to escape the charge of inconsistency and mobility which he was quite ready to lay at his own door. He performed, according to Emerson's dictum, each day what that day commanded him. There was something in him, too, characteristically English in this acting at a moment's notice, something in his hatred of formal philosophy and of dependence on experience akin to Dean Swift, or Bacon, alien alike to the logical Frenchman or the methodical German. He indulged himself in a hatred of system *per se* that baffled Shelley. "I have not had time nor paper," he wrote Leigh Hunt, "to attack your *system*, which ought to be done, were it only because it is a *system*."[23] He was suspicious of mankind's tendency to reduce everything, even Divinity, to a formula, however incongruous with or unrelated to observable realities. Men of a more logical nature he unquestionably impressed as being unintellectual. "His Lordship was so poor a logician," in Leigh Hunt's view, "that he did not even provoke argument. . . . He did not care for argument and . . . was too easily convinced at the moment, or appeared to be so, to give any zest to disputation. . . . He was moved to and fro, not because there was any ultimate purpose which he would give up, but solely because it was most troublesome to him to sit still and resist."[24] There is a sketch of Leigh Hunt, as well as of Byron, in that comment, and much to explain the relations of the two. The gazetteer liked to convince; the poet, intellectually too lazy to resist, nevertheless doubted that argument in the abstract could prove anything. His method of argument was to marshal an array of facts wherewith to crush his opponent; or to seize on a minor issue and, by harping upon it, emphasize its absurdity; or to confine himself to one major contention and state it with clear but unconvincing logic. "Not completely non-moral," says Mr. Symon, "but prone to run exactly contrary to any promptings of an ever lively conscience, Byron could see no reason at all why his opinions should be consistent. Consistency, in his view . . .

was one of those so-called virtues which of right belonged to the humdrum."[25] His philosophy is more theoretical than practical, he admits of himself, and never at hand when he has need of it; he is "constancy in the abstract, . . . more faithful to people on the 'high seas' than if they were on shore."[26] His tendency, in the face of a problem, is not to think it out, but to forget it in boxing, fencing, or making love. "Philosophy would be in vain—let us try action":[27] that is a cry from his heart. His practical philosophy is the spontaneous expression of himself—cynicism, common sense sometimes contorted by passion, and certain realizable ideals, like freedom and the possession of beautiful women.

In a more happily situated individual such a bent would have saved from pedantry and added to the savor and richness of life. "The difference is fundamental between the man who looks for rationality and strict causal connection in [life], and the man who seeks primarily adventure and surprise,"[28] and the odds for happiness are not altogether in the former's favor. But spiritual opportunism, to a man already on the rack of doubt, could but add to the preëxistent chaos of mind. Shelley gained much of his strength from his simplicity and consistency, from his lack of a sense of humor; his philosophic preconceptions guided his life in the face of all discouragement. There was nothing in Byron to take the place of will. He saw and reacted to the part, not the whole; the immediate, not the distant—causes and results of a purposelessness that gained direction only from blind propulsions of the ego. Never seeing an idea through to a logical conclusion, neither could he pursue a dilemma to its ultimate source. He attempted self-consolation by artifice, not by solution.

Everything combined, in him, to produce discomposure. He fell heir to a nature that made normal existence intolerable and abnormal existence hardly less difficult. Besides a naturally violent temper, he had an inherited "rush of blood to the head," which gave him fears, reminiscent of Swift's, for his future sanity. A miserable childhood, with a mother whose alternate rages and caresses were equally intolerable; an unhappy youth, in which natural shyness was exaggerated by his status of impecunious nobility; a whole life obsessed by the realization of his lameness—there was no period when he could mingle easily with the crowd. Nor could he ever find his way out. Caught between a religion which explicitly condemned the physical as an instrument of the Devil, and a new emotional morality which made madness charming; looking on marriage as a convenient approach to a fortune and free love as attractive but damned; and having no sufficient means of exercising a very vital energy, he was condemned to a permanent suffering which led him to doubt not only the goodness of God but the possibility of any final reconciliation between the soul and the senses.

Concealed in society, but admitted in solitude and vented in his writings, his depression was constitutional. His early letters complain insistently of either dullness or melancholy, often of both. Lady Byron considers him, even in his high spirits, the most melancholy of mortals. His gaiety in society is a mask, or it rises out of his depression; he speculates much on the relation between morbidity and the comic genius. The latter third of his life seems in retrospect but "eleven long years of bitterness."[29] And he is carried out of himself only when debate or persecution gives a fillip to his mood.[30]

The fact is, that in all the facets of his personality he was a man of quick feelings and impatient temper, of a constant irritability that amounted to disease, of what we have come to look upon, with severe reservations, as one aspect of the poetic temperament. His intelligence, which impressed so vividly all who saw it play on his countenance and light up his eyes, was not the calm, inquiring intellect of the philosopher, scientist, or analyst, but quick, colorful, and in itself almost an emotion. Excessive emotionality, emotional instability, lack of poise, and uncertain taste are almost a single characteristic of the poet's. Acted on almost as by a mechanical outside force, "like Galvanism on a dead body, or the muscular motion which survives sensation,"[31] he is but infrequently capable of long periods of steady application; he works, plays, and talks feverishly, and loses even his resentments when the immediate cause is removed.[32] Difficulties in love bring on spells of depression which are nearly convulsions, and these are punctuated by outbursts of hysterical laughter, at nothing that he is conscious of.[33] He is fatigued by the slightest exertion,[34] yet violent exercise fails to tire or even to satisfy him. He gambles with a kind of frenzy, without coolness or calculation, for the delight of hearing dice rattle and dash in the box.[35] He seeks relief in the difficult study of Armenian, as something craggy to break his mind upon, to torture him into attention.[36] He prefaces an English-Armenian grammar by his instructor, Father Aucher, makes proposals for its publication, translates part of Paul's Epistle to the Corinthians from the original Armenian, and then leaves it on the discard of his past endeavors. He has difficulty, when in company, in controlling his temper.[37] He obtains relief from *ennui* only when under the sway of violent passions.[38] He is indeed most thoroughly at ease in a life of sensation; passions appeal to him as his normal element, as man's sole escape from mere vegetating, and he gives himself up to them feverishly,[39] however regrettable the aftermath.

Perhaps his superstition, made so much of by late commentators,[40] is best comprehensible when linked with his temperament as well as with his religious training. He had before him the precedent of his mother, who impressed on him the idea of fetches and forewarnings, and astonished her sober English friends with strange tales of the wonders of second sight.[41] So incited, he surprised his bride with similar fancies: "Every coincidence was a miracle; he believed in omens; to wear a black gown was dangerous; a bat flying into the room brought ill-luck. One night, standing in the snowclad garden, they watched a wooly wisp of cloud come close to the moon. If it crossed the moon, he declared, he would be ruined; if it didn't all would be well. . . . The cloud crossed the moon."[42] Superstition may be cultivated as well as imbibed. Such bets as these with fate are the result of deep unhappiness, nervous apprehension of the future, and a feeling of individual helplessness. Byron, as in other cases, was shirking and shifting responsibility.

The clash of this nervous excitability and need for action with uncertainty of intention, each aggravating the other, gave us the character that is Byron. Emotion, to him, made action essential—and skepticism made it, except fitfully, impossible. Neither was there anything in the "high-strung cult of feeling and intuition" (Norman Foerster's definition of the romantic movement, of which Byron was emotionally and imaginatively a part),[43] to allay or alleviate his misery. In Byron converged the romantic longing for the impossible, the restlessness and flux of his times, an inherited instability and emotionality, the inhibitions of a religious creed which he could understand neither from the outside nor from within, until it is a wonder that his emotional frame was not racked apart. Driven by this fever called living, by Carlyle's thirst for excitement, and yet spiritually stagnant or stationary, he appears to the imagination like Jonathan Edwards's spider, suspended over chaos and old night, turning "this way and that like sick men trying to find coolness in movement, yet never finding it because their fever comes from within."[44]

If insanity may be defined as a state of mind that prevents one from living, in the language of the world, a happy and wholesome life, then Byron was, on one side of him, insane. To that extent, he fitted into his conception of the poetic genius.[45] But fighting this insanity, dominating it in crises, curbing it and appraising it, was his English common sense: two yoked coursers, pulling in opposite directions, sometimes made to work in harness, though always rebellious, sometimes allowed their heads, one or the other, with the reins flung over their flanks.

Byron's inner contradiction was his greatness and our difficulty. The one half of him was a normal enough man, with a lucid, logical mind and simple emotions. The other half was possessed of a devil, not the ordinary demon, but the prince of devils, Lucifer the lightbearer and Mephistopheles the sayer of nay. The result was a constant warfare; the result was also his poetry. To such a nature, never at one with itself, calm and continued thought, the steady light of a philosophy consistently arrived at, was impossible. His criticisms were matters of enthusiasm, prejudice, or personal hate. His ideas burst out in flashes and died down, as the need for them arose or departed, or as they proved insufficient to utter the emotion of the moment. He, in whom life was stronger than any theory of life, was at the mercy of life as he was forced to live it. He had to accept a disposition inherited, a childhood not of his own choosing. He seized upon what materials life offered him and adapted them to his poetry.

What was the man's misfortune was the world's gain. Suffering calls up profound powers in brave spirits. Passionate misery that paralyzed or derailed or thwarted Byron's will and made every action a reaction to immediate stimulus, too powerful often to be governed by a scruple, nevertheless intensified his vision of what was at his hand. As man and thinker, he was as superficial as, and no more sincere than, the rest of us. He perversely refused to look steadily at the truth, to see both sides of a question at the same time, to admit mere facts when they were unwelcome to him. But the profound, bubbling up from his depths, surprised the merely human with the divine fire of the daemonic. Byron's genius was responsible for his terrible sincerity.

Into this frenzied life, poetry fitted as a needed supplement to daily existence. Byron, in the words of Professor Garrod,[46] was always seeking to get free of himself, and his poetry is "a kind of frightened logic." It is more than that. It is his confessional, or one of his confessionals, freeing his heart, for the moment, from an "ineradicable taint of sin." Perhaps, had he been a Catholic, we might have had less of his verse; certainly it would have been of a different character. But Byron, barred by circumstances from a father confessor, turned his tortured conscience into rhyme. So did Pepys report another kind of conscience in a quainter confession. Byron, however, did not bear his heart upon his sleeve merely as an actor in a European pageant. What was later to become the common property of a sensation-loving public, was poured out at first in the privacy of his chamber. The fashion was to look for sensations. Here the searcher, after long experience with the mystery-mongers and the false analysers of passion, found sincere emotion frankly expressed. Byron, by living his inner life so openly, so straightforwardly, turned on himself a more insistent spotlight of literary curiosity than had any man since, perhaps, Montaigne. He was to enjoy its glory and to suffer for it.

CHAPTER II

THE AGE OF REASON

THE BYRON we have been describing wrote *Manfred*, *Childe Harold*, and the romances, adventurously toured the Mediterranean, scandalized British society, aided and abetted the Greek Revolution, and made "Byronic" a household word in half the languages of Europe. It was this Byron who, being more spectacular and confiding, impressed on the nineteenth century the pageant of his bleeding heart, so dazzling the eyes of mankind that it has been hard, since, to perceive another Byron, quieter but more insistent, behind the glare. As Byron was the child of two centuries, so was he the meeting place of two personalities, the one immediate, spontaneous, emotional, partly self-conscious and partly naïve—in a word, contemporary—and the other rational, sophisticated, conservative, partly naïve and partly self-conscious—a man of traditions to which he must sometimes, even by force of will, return. In that mass of contradictions which made up the poet-lord's character, no other contradiction has nearly the importance, in respect to his work, of this. He was the battle ground of two opposing forces, eternally at war, of which now the one was victorious and now the other.

Nor is it sufficient for our purposes to consider the eighteenth century as a conglomeration of prejudices or even as a cold body of theory. For four generations and more persisted a point of view, held by a never large group of intellectuals, which had the power to appeal to imaginations and mold personalities. Jealously kept, it had many of the qualities of a cult, giving to its votaries that sense of aloofness and moral superiority of which no amount of mere adventuring could take the place. It produced, in Melbourne, Victoria's prime minister, a near-perfection of the type of the eighteenth-century gentleman, and led, in Byron, to *English Bards and Scotch Reviewers, The Vision of Judgment,* the Bowles letters, and, through conflict, to *Don Juan.* To be understood, it must be stated as a personality, incorporated in a small continuing group, the arbiters of taste to each generation, and potent to absorb lesser personalities. Byron, though it could not absorb, it could at times lead, and often modify.

Whether introduced or merely encouraged by Charles II's returning prodigals, there is in England, after 1660, a predominance of those principles of literary taste and aims usually associated with the classic age of France. Bacon and Gabriel Harvey had gone back to Aristotle and the classics as authority for their opinions. But in place of Bacon's free paraphrase of Aristotle[1] or Ben Jonson's independent adaptation of the Unities, there exists, after 1660, a rationalistic, dogmatic bent that was but embryonic in either of the earlier men. Of the French literary influence there is strong evidence in both translations and imitations. A thesis of Bossu's was prefixed to the Popean translation of the *Odyssey*, and Pope himself was highly flattered to be likened to Boileau, "the greatest poet and most judicious critic of his age and country."[2] Certainly this analytical and rationalistic bent was the strongest single influence in the century following 1660. Rymer accepts it entire, and Dryden and Johnson, even when protesting against its deductions, adopt its method. Parallel to this, there were a growing orderliness, precision, and purity of diction, and an increasing respect for the critic and the analytical philosopher.

That this belligerent rationalism was no slavish mimicry of the classics is well illustrated in the case of Rymer. Rymer attacks each poem bluntly, sensibly, vigorously, intent upon answering two questions: Does the poet describe nature and life exactly as they appear to the reasonable man, and, incidentally, with what poetic artifice has this been done?[3] He does not wish to consider the Rules, which are "beauties" but not essentials of composition. Neither, in his view, are learning and knowledge of critical theory, even experience, necessary to the critic; *"common sense suffices."*[4] His "poetical justice," the center of his criticism, is Platonistic, not Aristotelian,[5] and he reconciles it to the theory of pleasure by remarking the delight of the mind in contemplating the orderliness of nature.[6]

Rymer, not altogether the pedant that he has been painted, was provocative and liberating. The doctrine of common sense, at its inception, threw the brunt of judgment upon the individual. The latter must apply standards, it is true, but standards rather implicit than specific, which left him the freedom of their vagueness. The critic must depend upon his own mind for discovering those principles by which he may judge each work; he must examine without prepossession how each writing affects himself, without considering the past, or contemporary sycophants and ignoramuses. "When the reading of a book elevates the mind," said La Bruyère, "and inspires brave and noble sentiments, seek no other rule by which to judge it; it is good."[7] Self-dependence, the writing with one's eye on the object, remained an important though unexpressed quality of later criticism; Samuel Johnson but implies it in his sarcastic reference to "those who judge by principles rather than perception."[8]

The turn of the century brought a shift in horizons. It was a soberer and sedater England that welcomed Addison, than had flocked to see the plays of Wycherley and Congreve.

Collier, for all his bigotry, was not a lone voice crying in the wilderness. Whether the change was due to the influence of Anne and her intimates, to the growing power and consequent seriousness of political writers, or to the final triumph of a public opinion that had long disapproved, or whether it was but a symptom of a gradual slowing down from the madcap days of Charles, is not absolutely clear. It was most likely due to all of these causes. There was an unmistakable, aggressive protest against what the preceding generations had represented—license in art and life, the language of the Elizabethans, the imagination of the metaphysical school, and the morality of the court of Charles II. Of this sentiment Addison is the logical spokesman. His own placidity led him to emphasize the principle of taste, and his didactic bent to insist upon the moral purpose of art. Taste and moralizing are the moving forces in literature for the next two generations, in criticism, poetry, the essay, the drama, the novel. Divergent tastes and divergent interpretations of morality make it sometimes difficult to perceive this underlying kinship among individuals. But the bias remains.

"Prudence and Justice are virtues and excellences of all times and of all places; we are perpetually moralists, but we are geometricians only by chance."[9] This saying of Johnson's might be taken without great modification, as the motto of the literary century in which it was spoken. For from the time that Addison "broke loose from that great body of writers who [had] employed their wit and parts in propagating of vice and irreligion,"[10] articulate England was, at least superficially, a didactic England. Poets wrote epics to instruct. Richardson displayed Pamela as the model housewife, and Fielding undertook *Joseph Andrews* as a refutation of Richardson. Steele crusaded against dueling. Addison corrected manners. Pope wrote the *Dunciad* to rebuke the morals of his enemies, and "at last, in 1734, . . . avowed the fourth [edition of his *Essay on Man*], and claimed the honor of a moral poet."[11] Dennis placed the *Rape of the Lock* below the *Lutrin* because of the lack of a moral.[12] It was in the spirit of Addison that Pope denounced precedent immorality in his *Essay on Criticism*.[13] And he merely followed the genius of his age when he renounced Fancy, "stooped to Truth, and moralized his song."[14]

To the protest against reckless unrestraint in living corresponded another protest against all excess in art and manners. The ideal of eighteenth-century England was the man of the world, mingling freely with his fellows, seeing facts as they are, and differentiated by no foolish extravagances. Club and coffeehouse alike had encouraged social intercourse among the élite. In club or coffeehouse gathered the wits and with their ridicule enforced its decrees. There was yet one distinction from the salons in France—the presence of women was not permitted. With the decline of these gathering places, and after the suburbanizing of the upper clique, as of Pope at Twickenham, the English upper classes retained their fashionable contempt for women's intellect, though mingling more freely in feminine society. For this reason their taste is more uncertain, their language coarser, but their prose more masculine and vigorous than that of their French contemporaries.

The literature of the century, above the subcurrent of middle-class sentimentalism, is largely the expression of an upper dominating caste. Hatred of pedantry and enthusiasm, which the gentleman was likely not to distinguish, led to an emphasis upon life as it was lived in the world, to discomfort in the presence of abnormal manners and expression. The gentleman desired what he could believe in as sincere,—

> Something whose truth convinced at sight we find,
> That gives us back the image of our mind.

Incredulus odit. To him literature was something to be read and enjoyed without undue exertion; beyond moral instruction and acceptable information, he could not appreciate ulterior metaphysical excuses for writing. "The end of poetry is pleasure." "The purpose of a writer is to be read."[15] Johnson, in his supreme common sense, was but echoing the opinions of those he dominated. To the eighteenth-century gentleman, *Paradise Lost,* great poem though it might be, was dull,[16] Spenser was foolish, Chaucer was quaint but antique, Shakespeare was given to exaggeration. But though he disliked enthusiasm, the gentleman equally disliked writing by rule and compass; he asked that his author should be first a man and only secondarily a writer.

> But in such lays as neither ebb, nor flow,
> Correctly cold, and regularly low,
> That, shunning faults, one quiet tenor keep,
> We cannot blame indeed—but we may sleep.[17]

He objected to the starched critic, drily plain, who wrote "dull receipts how poems may be made."[18] Horace, in whom he found a closely kindred soul, he accepted as master.

The critics that ministered unto this society, while retaining their individual independence, strove to emphasize and heighten its merits. The moving principle of the period was taste, a reaction, such as we have described, from lawlessness and excess. The eighteenth-century gentleman had much justification for his attitude that the Elizabethan age was barbaric and that its tradition needed improving and correcting. The critics, admiring individuals within the former era, felt that its general tone was low. Dryden, Addison, and after him his literary admirers and personal enemies, strove to raise the tone of their own age by a wise contemplation of the ancients, the sole "correct" writers, and, by distilling from them the essence of their virtues, to set up for contemporary and later writers standards by which excellence might be judged. They did not accept entirely the rules of Aristotle, because they wished to base their judgment upon the whole body of classic literature.[19] Their taste, which they emphasized, was not so much imitation of the ancients as it was propriety, a fitness of language to the subject, and, in poetry, an avoidance of the low. Applying this principle, Johnson criticized Milton for making his Adam speak out of character, and Addison deplored the broad humor of Homer's Thersites, as injurious to the epic tone of the *Iliad*. In accord with it, Addison criticized the ancients themselves, for "trifling points and puerilities . . . in Ovid, . . . epigrammatic turns of Lucan, . . . swelling sentiments . . . in Statius and Claudian, . . . mixed embellishments of Tasso . . . which were, indeed, the false refinements of later ages."[20] Much as they disliked what they considered barbarities in thought and language, they disliked still more the signs of a decadent, effete civilization.

This criticism, in other departments than taste, was far from being a mass of dead precepts. Its doctrine of imitation approaches more nearly the classic doctrine than what we now condemn as "neoclassic." The school of Pope and Johnson approved the general principle that "every art is best taught by example."[21] But they placed spirit above technique. Imitation, even to the mild Addison, was perfect only when "one great genius . . . catches the flame from another, and writes in his spirit without copying servilely after him."[22] Virgil is at his greatest when he is aflame with Homer, and all succeeding poets have been inspired and uplifted by the noble example of the first, primeval bard.[23] Poetic imitation is, to use a classic simile, the torch in the race, handed on from runner to runner.

Addison, and with him Pope and Johnson, with all their admiration for the great work of the past, did not advise an inspiration "drawn from books and systems";[24] they had no conception that rules could make a poet, any more than that a formula could make a tree. But they did demand, with perhaps an over-great seriousness, and not too great an ability always to detect the true from the false, that the inspiration should be sincere. It was this stress upon the sincerity of inspiration that cut them off from so much of the literature of the past, since its style seemed to them unnatural and therefore affected. *Lycidas,* to Johnson, was "not to be considered as the effusion of real passion; for passion runs not after remote allusions and obscure opinions. . . . 'Where there is leisure for fiction there is little grief.' . . . Its inherent improbability always forces dissatisfaction on the mind."[25] In Addison's view, Aeschylus, Sophocles, Claudian, Statius, Shakespeare, and Lee had all been guilty of "swelling to a false sublime."[26] The ideal of both critics was inevitability of expression, which we still look upon as the one absolute in poetry. For a somewhat parallel reason, the *honnête homme* had suspected enthusiasm as a false affected emotion. But in each case, though both objections were based on the best intended principles, the effect was to discourage the finest enthusiasm and the highest poetic inspiration.

It was the misfortune of this self-consciously classic criticism to suffer from the vices of its virtues. In the first case its emphasis upon the moral purpose of art tended to minimize the importance of beauty as an essential in artistic expression. Such an emphasis placed too great a burden on those poets who were not by nature earnest moral teachers. "The Epic Poem is a discourse invented by art, to form the Manners, by such instructions as are disguised under the allegories of some one important action, which is related in verse, after a probable, diverting, and surprising manner."[27] So proclaimed Bossu, and was followed at no great distance by the great Doctor.[28] Such an analysis is hardly a thoroughgoing description of the attitude of a Homer, if it be that of a Virgil or a Milton.

In the second place, the effort at a more exact, judicious standard, and the emphasis upon reason as the surest means of arriving thereat, result in the accentuation of analysis and logic at the expense of the synthetic imagination. "The art of uniting pleasure with truth, by calling imagination to the help of reason," is Johnson's definition of the poetic impulse.[29] There was a minute division of literature into categories, and these categories were capable of indefinite subdivision. Plots, or "fables," for instance, might be divided into "the *probable*, the *allegorical*, and the *marvellous*."[30] Analysis, furthermore, brought in its train a host of terms, "fancy," "sense," "machinery," and the like, which soon lost all color and gained a purely technical significance. What could not be covered by ordinary terms, was included under the *je-ne-sais-quoi*, a term first raised to critical importance by Shaftesbury in 1711, to denote aesthetic enjoyment.[31]

In the field of the novel, the conception of form, at least in the case of Fielding, brought forth the most splendid result. But in another field, the analytical approach led to poems which seem more a joining together of parts than organic wholes. Pope, always aware of the Rules (which we might modernize to "requirements"), even when disobeying them, produced his most spontaneous work in mock heroic or other mocking poetry, when he used the Rules with conscious condescension and parodied them in his preface. The introduction by "Martinus Scriblerus" to the *Dunciad* is a burlesque of the more pedantic trends in the criticism of the day. Scriblerus postulates for Pope's authority an unprocurable poem of Homer's, antecedent to the *Iliad*, whose "hero was no less *obscure*, and his understanding and sentiments no less quaint and strange . . . than any of the actors of our poem." The title, "Dunciad," is framed after the ancient Greek manner. The power of the goddess Dullness is to be exemplified "in some one, *great, and remarkable action*." A person is fixed upon to support the action, the fable is made one and entire, and branched into episodes, "each of which hath its moral apart, though conducive to the main end." The characters are justly drawn, the diction pure and chaste, "yea, and commented upon by the most grave doctors and approved critics." Bearing the name of epic, it is subject to "severe indispensable rules . . . a strict imitation of the ancients; insomuch that any deviation, accompanied with whatever poetic beauties, hath always been censured by the sound critic." Again, in the arguments of the several books, Pope burlesques epic machinery, speaking of hastening "into the midst of things," and giving *Odyssey*, XXIV, as his authority for the use of games. There was perhaps an intentional sting at the point of the poet's humor. He had no love for critics, especially those who disapproved of his own productions. And his reference to Rymer, in the same introduction, since the latter is put into company with Dennis, can hardly be complimentary.

Indeed, dissatisfaction with strict classic canons was part of the eighteenth-century tradition. Sturdy independence and a love of paradox were involved in Johnson's sweeping modifications of accepted opinions. Pope revolted as a matter of temperament, and Swift hated dogmatists as pedants. Each author, inasmuch as he was human and allowed to be human by the fundamental common sense of the day, held to his own views tenaciously. There was much dislike, also, of critics as critics, as in the case of the tender-skinned Pope; and in the bitter inky wars of the period, there was much calling to account of dogmas. That the discontent, however, was deeper than a surface rash, was due to the emotion opposite to hate—reverence. The canons of taste, being strict and exclusive, damned too readily those great writers that had not lived up to its requirements, and who were sincerely admired, nay worshiped, during the period. The reaction was not, as it might have been, to make the canons more flexible and more inclusive. Taste, being infixed within a class, and inbred within the individual, could admit no exceptions. The tendency rather was to deny its importance in the face of another quality which worked outside and in spite of taste. This quality, under the influence of Longinus, appeared first as the Sublime, as in Addison's famous review of Milton in the *Spectator*.[32] But in many cases, where the epithet could obviously not be applied, what was admired was a sort of higher and intenser *je-ne-sais-quoi*, which the critic, unable to place it in the accustomed categories, could find no name for. How comfortable or how daring the individual may have felt in his heterodox enthusiasms, we have no means of determining. Pope admired Homer above Virgil, loved Shakespeare, Milton, Chaucer, and Spenser, and was accounted no fool, nor ignoramus. The place of the greatest preceding English poets in the eighteenth century was little different from what it is today—it was assured, if indeterminate. It was in the temper of the gentleman to honor the Rules, but to honor them lightly. What justification he needed he might have discovered in a passage in the very *Ars Poetica* of Horace, which found its echo in the *Essay on Criticism*:

> Great wits sometimes may gloriously offend,
> And rise to faults true Critics dare not mend;
> . . . .
> From vulgar bounds with brave disorder part,
> And snatch a grace beyond the reach of art.[33]

But it is doubtful whether he felt the need of justification.

This worship of the fault, as we may almost call it, must not be taken as an anticipation of romanticism, in the sense that it intended to anticipate anything. A necessary corollary of the classic criticism, as a complement to the more rigid Rules, it may be discovered in nearly all the eighteenth-century criticism of great poets. Though digressions should not exist in an epic poem, says the usually phlegmatic Addison in speaking of *Paradise Lost*, "I must confess there is so great a beauty in these very digressions, that I would not wish them out of his poem."[34] That is the tone of a lover of literature, who admires facts before theories. "We love him with all his faults" is little different, as a sentiment, from "We love him because of his faults." Surely the two came close together in the eighteenth century.

The artist or critic of this time may best be compared to a gardener. Though his duty consisted in cultivating his garden, and though he felt thoroughly at home only when within it, he was not prevented by the high wall of taste from seeing the beautiful and the rare outside. The great individual enthusiasms of the eighteenth century were for the supreme masters of poetry who cannot be bounded by taste. Among these, of the English poets, the most firmly established were Milton and Shakespeare. Pope, idolized as he was during his lifetime, had yet a feeling akin to reverence before Shakespeare and Homer. The criticism of the great, in the nature of justification, amounted to a cult of the untaught genius, a normal outgrowth of the criticism of taste. Of the promulgators of such a doctrine Pope was the supreme offender. His prefaces to his translation of the *Iliad* and his edition of Shakespeare, discount as much as we may the necessity for praising incumbent on an editor, present a curious adjunct to his own expressed intentions. To him both Homer and Shakespeare are original geniuses and, as such, the greatest poets of the world.

His prefatory manner was not original with Pope. By his time it had been well established in criticism, and definitely anticipated both in structure and in spirit, by Addison's review of Milton. One statement from his friend-and-rival may be taken as equally a motto for the two: "I have seen in the works of a modern philosopher a map of the spots in the sun. My last paper, of the faults and blemishes in Milton's *Paradise Lost*, may be considered as a piece of the same nature."[35] Pope is quick to admit the faults of his idol; but though he does not deny the canons of taste, his whole attitude toward Shakespeare's contemporaries is disparaging: "[Shakespeare's] works, in comparison of those that are more finished and regular [are as] an ancient majestic piece of Gothic architecture, compared with a neat modern building. The latter is more elegant and glaring, but the former is more strong and more solemn."[36] The great poets, furthermore, have had to triumph over the handicap of their environment. Shakespeare's reputation has suffered from errors in the text of his plays, insertion of bombast by players, and the like. He has been led, by his connection with players, to follow ephemeral fashions. He has been betrayed, by the theatrical conditions of his time, into "strange, unexpected, and consequently most unnatural, events and incidents; the most exaggerated thoughts; the most verbose and bombastic expression; the most pompous rhymes, and thundering versification," and in comedy, into "mean buffoonery, vile ribaldry, and unmannerly jests of fools and clowns." He has composed without knowledge of the best ancient models, which might have inspired him to emulation. Homer, likewise, has been exposed to the manners and morality of his age, "when a spirit of revenge and cruelty, joined with the practice of Rapine and Robbery, reigned through the world; when no mercy was shown but for the sake of lucre." To overcome such a disadvantage, the poet had need of an extraordinary natural force and originality, which gentlemen associated romantically with earlier, or cruder, ages. Homer is remarkable for "the extent and fecundity of his imagination," for "impressions taken off to perfection, at a heat." Of Shakespeare, it is happy and extraordinary that "so many various (nay contrary) Talents should meet in one man." The talents are not due to conscious cultivation, but the result of a strong native urge and capacity. The two poets, being unsophisticated, are likewise more natural than those of later cultivated ages; they gain their power from their affinity with the primitive emotions, the mainsprings of life. "The poetry of Shakespeare was inspiration indeed; he is not so much an imitator, as an instrument, of Nature; and 't is not so just to say that he speaks *from her*, as that she speaks *thro' him*."

The result of such an idea was a broadening and weakening of the older, stricter standards. Once it was admitted that there was a higher court than mere good taste and common sense, taste, as it had been conceived, was doomed to a gradual decay. It makes no difference for our purposes that the idea is latent throughout the Age of Reason, and that the germs of it may be traced to the accepted Longinus. With Pope the unsophisticated genius had become a cult, or at least a vividly imagined conception that was easily transformable into a cult. The praise of originality and genius at the expense of taste, of nature at the expense of art, of invention at the expense of imitation and tradition, of Homer at the expense of Virgil, was a subtle denial of whatever the eighteenth century held peculiarly its own. These principles and sentiments, also, were not confined to the enthusiasm of a single poet, but became increasingly dominant in the accepted criticisms of the latter half of the century. The Great Cham himself, who was not given to romanticizing, did not entirely escape the enthusiasms of Pope.[37] His preferences are far richer and less exacting than those of Addison. He makes the Elizabethan age the golden age of English poetry and offers Shakespeare and Spenser, in his introduction to his *Dictionary*, as models of correct English. His preface to his edition of

Shakespeare, though systematically critical of the dramatist's moral insufficiencies, the looseness of construction of his plots, his anachronisms, his violations of propriety in diction, his "tumor, manners, tediousness, and obscurity," is markedly friendly, and more respectful than his life of Pope. Pope's extreme thesis, that "to judge, therefore, Shakespeare by Aristotle's rules, is like trying a man by the laws of one country, who acted under those of another,"[38] he does not concede, but he does inveigh against those critics who, by applying "rules merely positive" cavil against the greatness of the dramatist. His portrait of Milton, finally, for all its political prejudice and impeccable good sense, is a sturdy bow to the original and superhuman genius: "The English poems . . . have this mark of genius, that they have a cast original and unborrowed."[39] "Milton . . . overlooked the milder excellence of suavity and softness: he was a 'Lion' that had no skill in 'dandling the Kid'."[40] "He had accustomed his imagination to unrestrained indulgence, and his conceptions therefore were extensive. . . . He sometimes descends to the elegant, but his element is the great. He can occasionally invest himself with grace; but his natural port is gigantic loftiness."[41]

The problem of why the eighteenth century, while admiring the greatest unrestrained geniuses of the past, had itself so little of the "liberty of license," has been partly answered by the foregoing. The man of taste, after all, was busy cultivating his garden, and though he might stop to admire, he did not follow. Homer and Shakespeare to him belonged to an alien culture. They were great because they were inimitable; and he preferred to do what he felt capable of doing well. Milton should "be admired rather than imitated,"[42] is the verdict of Johnson, in the midst of a critique that is largely eulogy. "But though the Ancients thus their rules invade, . . . Moderns, beware!"[43] The note of the time was caution in action, and apathy toward the profound and painful probings that had distressed the Elizabethans.

> Trust not yourself; but your defects to know
> Make use of ev'ry friend—and ev'ry foe.[44]

This was the spirit of the age. There was as much modesty as complacency in such a renunciation of the heights; the writer of taste was timid, unsure of himself, sceptical of his own powers. He was kept so by the prevalence of criticism and the fear of ridicule. But his timidity was due in as large part to a self-consciousness that he had imbibed from current critical conceptions; he was too conscious of possible flaws and absurdities ever to indulge his emotions uncensored. And consequently his emotions, except in satire, are awkward and stumbling when not superficial.

It is well to remember, however, that the classic poet was restrained not so much from principle as from an inability to let himself go. One with sufficent self-confidence might have defied the canons of taste and raved as a Timon, assured of being a great unregulated genius. But such supreme self-dependence did not exist. Instead, these men wrote excellent satire, charming whimsical pastorals after the manner of Shenstone, commendable topographical verse, curt epigrams and graceful *vers de société*, or, when they turned lovers, unconvincing, stiff, affected lyrics. The voice of eloquent passion is close to nonsense; Lear in the storm, or Romeo adoring, does not speak the voice of *la raison pure*. Robert Burns broke the fetters of the school. Apart, and unaffected by the wits, he sang his love, as no gentleman need be ashamed to sing his own, with the frank glowing passion of a man. And so he was accepted by the élite as something more than a rustic divinely inspired. In spite of humble birth, he was received and admired as much as mere literary genius can recommend one to good society. By the time of his death he was an accepted classic to gentlemen of taste. His sense of inferiority, on the other hand, was an indication of the social system on which the classic school ultimately depended, and intimated that Burns, while meeting its standards and continuing its traditions, was not thoroughly within its fold. He was both the culmination of the eighteenth century in poetry, and a product of that new complex fervor which was to result in romanticism. Like Byron, though in a different sense, he was a divided spirit.

CHAPTER III

THE MAN OF SENSE

THE change from the spirit of the eighteenth to that of the early nineteenth century is so gradual that it is impossible to draw accurate dividing lines. The so-called forerunners of romanticism were in good standing in their neoclassic day. The Preface to the *Lyrical Ballads*, which bulks so large in our later estimation, is but one of a succession of landmarks among which must be placed critiques by both Johnson and Warton. The great and living art of the century had been satire, which persisted in the prose of Lockhart after it had ceased to thrive in verse. It carries with it a tradition of finality, of bitter personalities, of shrewdness and hard-hitting that pretended to judiciousness. It had acquired its own forms and mannerisms, its own vocabulary of bitter invective. It made habitual use of the heroic couplet. It warred valiantly on the side of common sense.

The last strong satirist of the eighteenth century demands a share of our attention out of proportion to his historical importance. William Gifford, a respected man of letters in his day, has suffered a century of scorn; but to the youthful Byron he appeared a seer and a prophet. References to him, even in the most flippant passages of Byron's correspondence, are always profoundly respectful. The latter modeled his *English Bards and Scotch Reviewers* largely upon the *Baviad* and the *Maeviad*. And later he sent the proof of many of his poems to Gifford for final criticism and correction. Byron undoubtedly admired Gifford for his bluff, blunt, forceful manner, his masculine style, and his belligerent common sense —all aspects of a personality closely similar to one side of his own. He "was happy to regard Mr. Gifford as a wonderful old gentleman, not indeed a born gentleman, but the more honest in his patricianisms on that account, and quite a born critic; 'sound,' as the saying is; learned and all that, and full of 'good sense'."[1] His deepest admiration for Gifford was for him as the proponent of a school, a tradition, an attitude to which Byron, too, owed his conscious allegiance. Gifford perhaps first of all crystallized the young man's prejudices and natural predilections into the one literary loyalty of his life—his loyalty to the school of Pope and Johnson.

Gifford is interesting both as a man and as a writer. His early life had been hard, he had attained his position by energy and force of character after bitter struggles, and like Samuel Johnson he hated shilly-shallying, dilly-dallying, and all signs of an effete dilettanteism. The man is aggressively present in whatever he wrote; and he may perhaps be best described by a hasty summary of his loves and hates as he expressed them in the *Baviad* and the *Maeviad*. The style of the two satires, no more affected than the license of wit allowed, is pungent, direct, virile, if harsh; but it is neither musical nor imaginative. What originality the satires show is one of tone; their language draws in great measure upon the *Dunciad*, the *Epistle to Dr. Arbuthnot*, the *Essay on Criticism*, and the general eighteenth-century vernacular of vilification. "A linsey-woolsey song," "vacancy of thought," "unmeaning dash," "fustian," "flippant trash," " catchword," "idiot line," "shag-lane cant," "Moorfields whine," "mope-eyed dolts"—all are but fixed epithets of abuse in the satiric tradition. Self-conscious vigilance and dogmatism are everywhere apparent. The standards are those of the Age of Reason: common sense, "the critic's laws," "the sober verdict found by truth and sense," "truth's imperious light," nature improved by art. Gifford looks definitely backward to "our ancient vigor," "the plain tale trusted to the heart," "Burns' pure healthful nurture";

> Verse! that's the mellow fruit of toil intense,
> Inspired by genius, and inform'd by sense.

Much is the anger of a thoroughly masculine man directed against affectation and sentimentality, against the "sickly taste" of the times. But over the whole presides the genius of an earlier age, breathing in its soul and informing its mortal parts. Even in denunciation there is thorough consistency: "bloated pedantry," "preposterous fustian," "truth sacrificed to letters, sense to sound, false glare, incongruous images," "noise and nonsense," "modish strain," "prurient ears," "namby-pamby madrigals of love," "motley fustian, neither verse nor prose," are the many heads of the same monster that Gifford has gone forth to subdue.

As satire, the *Baviad* is hardly unjust toward the Della Cruscans. Gifford, conscientiously, has seized upon weapons already forged and at hand, which can be passed readily to a successor. The satiric terms gain point when we remember to what they are applied. The satirist is not merely playing with words or ideas but performing a necessary function in his community; and it is as a self-confident and assured personality that he appeals mainly to us. The criticism achieves its impressiveness not by aimless castigation, but by exposing its objects against a background of the greatest poetry. Pope, Milton, and Burns are introduced as the sure models of English; and though Shakespeare is not mentioned in the text, he is quoted profusely in the notes. Gifford is sincerely respectful to the master poets and an enthusiast over Pope. In a worshiping apostrophe to the latter, he, "the humblest of the tuneful train," desires only that he may

> With glowing heart, yet trembling hand, repay,
> For many a pensive, many a sprightly lay!
> So may thy varied verse, from age to age,
> Inform the simple, and delight the sage.

His modesty is almost as belligerent as his dogmatic criticism; yet his renunciation of the higher flights of poetry, has the ring of sincerity:

> PHOEBUS: What though thou canst not claim
> The sacred honors of a POET's name,
> Due to the few alone, whom I inspire
> With lofty rapture, with ethereal fire?
> Yet mayst thou arrogate the humble praise
> Of reason's bard, if, in thy future lays,
> Plain sense and truth (and surely these are thine)
> Correct thy wanderings, and thy flights confine.

In at least this case, the knowledge of his limits, both the finest and the most fatal of the virtues he affirmed, was fortunate for the artist. We have only to read the lyrics appended to the *Maeviad*, to conclude that in satiric writing he had discovered a surer outlet for his capacities.

Gifford's satires, in addition to denoting the slowly congealing vitality of classic principles, are so closely the ancestors of *English Bards and Scotch Reviewers*, that we are constantly reminded of the later satire while reading them. Many of their phrases—"To stagger impudence and ruffle vice," "To hunt the clamorous brood of Folly down"—might serve easily as mottoes for the latter. The use of notes—to explain, to forestall criticism, to vent personal opinions, and to display learning—the questionable humor of the "Printer's Devil" addenda, are characteristic of both. The habit of reproducing the text imitated at the foot of the page is not copied in the *English Bards and Scotch Reviewers*, which imitates nothing directly, but it is reproduced in the *Hints from Horace.*

Byron's first satire, considered in the light of the eighteenth-century tradition and of its immediate inspiration, gains a unity of purpose and result not in accord with the popular conception of the poet as a man immoderately enraged, slashing about him violently and blindly, hurting friend and foe alike. That Byron was thoroughly angry is unquestionable; but the bulk of the satire is directed against those who had not offended him except artistically; and besides, it was in the best tradition of satire to be bluntly and coarsely personal. It is not unprecedented for a poet to take advantage of an individual spite to compose a vigorous poem. *English Bards and Scotch Reviewers* is important, not as the first memorial to Byron's wrath but as extending beyond a petty expression of vexation to the broad basis of a critical thesis. The individual applications of this theory were not always fortunate. Byron had never a tolerant or sympathetic appreciation of qualities unlike his own, and was likely still less to have it under the goad of passion. But even the misjudgments have a sort of consistency; a standard was being conscientiously if awkwardly applied. The single difficulty with the standard is that it cannot be expressed in a short and comprehensible definition. Byron had no theory, but a body of theories, or rather, an impression. His ridicule of Erasmus Darwin, that "mighty master of unmeaning rhyme," who has sometimes been considered the embodiment of neoclassicism, was quite consistent with his ridicule of Wordsworth, Southey, and Coleridge, the avatars of romanticism. The principle of the golden mean and of common sense could not sanction extremes.

In form the poem is what we expect, or should expect, from a continuer of the classic satiric tradition. It is longer than either of Gifford's satires, but hardly more violent or

THE MAN OF SENSE

more loosely constructed. In conception it is simple; and its execution leaves room for the insertion of second thoughts or newly invented matter. The best synopsis is given in full by Byron himself, as an intended argument to be prefixed to the poem, but omitted for some unfortunate reason—perhaps Dallas—from any of the editions. Its own excellence, as emanating from the poet in one of his most delightful moods, must be offered as excuse for reporting it in full. Our other excuse is that it gives the proportions of the satire in shortened form and in mellower, ironic spirit, and reflects the plan as it had finally shaped itself in Byron's mind:

Argument Intended for the Satire: The poet considereth times past and their poesy—makes a sudden transition to times present—is incensed against book-makers—revileth Walter Scott for cupidity and ballad-mongering, with notable remarks on Master Southey—complaineth that Master Southey had inflicted three poems, epic and otherwise, on the public—inveigheth against William Wordsworth, but laudeth Mister Coleridge and his elegy on a young ass—is disposed to vituperate Mr. Lewis—and greatly rebuketh Thomas Little (the late) and Lord Strangford—recommendeth Mr. Hayley to turn his attention to prose—and exhorteth the Moravians to glorify Mr. Grahame—sympathizeth with the Rev. ——— and deploreth the melancholy fate of James Montgomery—breaketh out into invective against the Edinburgh Reviewers—calleth them hard names, harpies and the like—apostrophiseth Jeffrey, and prophesieth.—Episode of Jeffrey and Moore, their jeopardy and deliverance; portents on the morn of the combat; the Tweed, Tolbooth, Frith of Forth, severally shocked; descent of a goddess to save Jeffrey; incorporation of the bullets with his sinciput and occiput.—Edinburgh Reviewers *en masse.*—Lord Aberdeen, Herbert, Scott, Hallam, Pillans, Lambe, Sydney Smith, Brougham, &c.—Lord Holland applauded for dinners and translations.—The Drama: Skeffington, Hook, Reynolds, Kenney, Cherry, etc.—Sheridan, Colman, and Cumberland called upon to write.—Return to poesy—scribblers of all sorts—lords sometimes rhyme; much better not—Hafiz, Rosa Matilda, and X.Y.Z.—Rogers, Campbell, Gifford, etc. true poets—Translators of Greek Anthology—Crabbe—Darwin's style—Cambridge—Seatonian Prize—Smythe—Hodgson—Oxford—Richards—Poeta loquitur—Conclusion.

The satire, with few minor variations, is consciously and conscientiously in the conventional mould, and echoes, more intimately than its argument, established mannerisms. Pope and Gifford are offered as predecessors and models. There is an apostrophe to the author's grey goose-quill, an attack on critics, much after the style of the opening of Pope's *Essay on Criticism*, with the text that all contemporary criticism is bad, and a justification of his attitude, reminiscent of a passage in the *Epistle to Dr. Arbuthnot*. Eccentricity, turgidity, folly, immorality, obscurity, obscenity, confusion of *genres*, insipidity, sentimentality, are attacked in the accepted breathlessly inclusive fashion. The author, sighing for the good old times and despising the new, gives vent to his hopes, emotions, and prejudices. Scott he blames for taking money for his poems; Lewis and Little are attacked half-heartedly for their obscenity and immorality; Wordsworth, in being dull, and Hayley, in being insipid, have much more greatly offended. The author is revolted by opera, whereas gambling dens and bawdy houses have seized his imagination but mildly. When he moralizes, he grows apologetic and admits himself to be more immoral than he is. His wrath is tempered by modesty, and his modesty is contradicted by his wrath. He lacks sufficient assurance to be thoroughly successful in satire.

Byron's particular version of English classicism is largely borrowed from Gifford and modified by his own reading. He offers Milton, Dryden, Pope, Homer, Virgil, Tasso, Camoëns, as standards of poetry, and Shakespeare, Otway, Massinger, and Sheridan as England's great dramatists. He is enthusiastic over Pope, who sums up for him all the attainable poetic virtues, who has claimed the praise of a polished nation and increased its fame, who has charmed the rapt soul with a pure strain, yet erred with grace successfully—not merely a poet, but a man, "whose fame and genius, from the first, have foiled the best of critics," and have aroused the envy of his editor, Bowles, one who has dared to raise his hoof against the lion dead. The eulogy, extended throughout the satire, is continued in *Hints from Horace*, less extreme and more critical, an echo of the adulation in the preceding satire. In this Pope remains the model of elegance and polish, the one standard whereby to raise his country's taste. But his pastorals, though supreme, are overrefined. His satire, great as it is, has arisen from selfish anger. He is called, in the notes, an illustrious precedent, "a better poet than Boileau, and at least as good a scholar as Sevigné." A sincerer and more continuous tribute is the constant echoing of Pope in the style. The first line is reminiscent of the *Epistle to Dr. Arbuthnot*, and there is sufficient to indicate that Byron was writing under the spell of Pope's metre and diction and had him consciously in mind as a model.

We have to consider, concerning this second work, that the poet was imitating, and therefore largely translating, the *Ars Poetica* of Horace. He was confined by his purpose to reproducing the latter poet's separate opinions and the main structure of his thought. Byron could never be utterly confined to anything, as the long interpolated attack on Jeffrey witnesses. But it is significant that the poet consciously adopted these opinions of another and advanced them arrogantly as his own. He had no love for Horace the poet, having been drilled too thoroughly in him at school. But he was caught, apparently, by the impulse to profess his poetical creed and by some loyalty to the school of Pope and by a dislike of new upstart poets. The imitation, of which

Byron remained obstinately proud, was intended as a sequel to *English Bards and Scotch Reviewers* and was applied to "our new school of poetry." Whatever of satire there is within it is directed against tailor poets, cobbler laureates, and Wordsworth, Southey, and "Fitzscribble," and this is confined mainly to the notes. Scott has already been forgiven, and he and Campbell are approved. The young poet, in no satiric mood, but content and self-confident, from the success of the *English Bards and Scotch Reviewers*, resorts to laying down the law for the reading public—an occupation always thoroughly congenial.

Any significance other than that he laid down Horace's law, and felt afterwards that he had done so very well, must be inferred from his additions to his original and from shifts of emphasis. Horace's excellent but sketchy common sense Byron swallowed entire, without any apparent realization that the poem was a very practical letter to a very definite young man. Its principles of Judgment, Order, Lucidity, Common Sense, he copied dutifully, and often repeated its figures of speech. His applications to immediate conditions, however, are more interesting. He admits the dispute between rhyme and blank verse to be "as puzzling as a Chancery suit"; and decides, judiciously, that blank is well suited to tragedy, and prose to comedy. He returns to Pope as the model of models, to Milton as a great epic writer, adopts Swift and *Hudibras* as the standards of wit, and commends Scott for his use of iambic tetrameter. Shakespeare he accepts as the model for the rising dramatist, as one who has adapted his language to the state of his hero, has created the most alive of all characters, and has kept decorum by killing Banquo off-stage to save the audience's feelings. We may suspect that Byron chose Shakespeare, not because he intended to approve, but because he was most familiar with his dramas. He mixes reproof with commendation: Hubert has gone beyond the limits of dramatic endurance, and in the drama, "since our Shakespeare's days, there's pomp enough, if little else."

The poem, at best, is dull. If it were not variegated by bits of the poet's personality, it would be difficult reading. The inserted apostrophe to Jeffrey is entertaining, if not appropriate. Bits of unnecessary scholarship relieve the notes. Byron waxes actually wrathful upon one critical point which he has not borrowed from Horace. He is uneasy and suspicious before the new refinement of the stage, which bars frank subjects and strong language. He is resentful toward the Methodists, whom he considers chiefly responsible, and condemnatory of the Licensing Act, which is at the root of the evil. He voices some love for past poets who had not shrunk from expressing themselves, "Chaucer and old Ben." But in the main he is following his instinct for vigorous, manly, coarse expression, his hatred of overnicety, and his impatience of restraint. His feeling that refinement by expurgation is insipid has been restless in his mind since he first experienced the need for literary self-expression. It juts up in likely and unlikely places, as in an ambiguous passage in his earliest dramatic prologue:

>Since the refinement of this polish'd age
>Has swept immoral raillery from the stage;
>Since taste has now expunged licentious wit,
>Which stamp'd disgrace on all an author writ;
>Since now to please with purer scenes we seek,
>Nor dare to call the blush from Beauty's cheek;
>Oh! let the modest Muse some pity claim,
>And meet indulgence—though she find not fame.[2]

This rough place in Byron's mind was never thoroughly smoothed over. His plea for free and frank speech was perhaps his first original contribution to the critical theory of his age, and it would probably have been the reaction of a Swift or a Fielding to the time.

The unity of tone between the satires of Gifford and of Byron is complete. Gifford, given the other's wrath and genius, might have written *English Bards and Scotch Reviewers* and *Hints from Horace* without blotting a line. Minor points of difference, such as Byron's fuller list of standards, is a question of the times and of reading and is not at all fundamental. The second of these satires is Horatian only in theme; its coarse, blunt address, its crude precision, is the manner of one who could love Horace and Virgil only on principle,[3] but who accepted Gifford as a kindred soul. Too much, of course, should not be made of Gifford's influence. Byron was ready for a literary prophet and saviour, and he took what was closest to himself and his views. His own brand of classicism was largely that of his master, essentially a matter of caste and tradition, a stout defense of an accepted code against increasing infringements, a patriotic bias that excluded Boileau and his art—"that whetstone of the teeth—monotony in wire"[4]—while it held up Pope as its supreme pattern. His admiration for the latter was not borrowed, as we may judge from constant early imitations, but it was strengthened into an enthusiastic discipleship.

Byron's classicism is native enough to follow unaware the main outlines of the eighteenth-century classic tradition and yet to be distinctly individual. He placed Fielding above Richardson, reversing the somewhat inappropriate judgment of Johnson, loved *The Vicar of Wakefield,* and had moments of revulsion from Swift.[5] He admired Johnson as "the noblest critical mind which our country has produced,"[6] but preferred reading Boswell's biography to the *Lives of the Poets,* which he so loudly lauded. His approach to the past was largely a love for personalities and for particular landmarks. His conversation shows occasionally the reflection of classical critical terminology, as when he complains that the vast quantity of books which he has been receiving has "neither amused nor instructed."[7] The classical attitude—for it was an attitude rather than a theorem or a body of rules—had entered into the warp of his mind, but it limited neither his reading nor his preferences; it was but one thread, perhaps the strongest. Byron theorized little and read much, and did not avoid inconsistencies. But when he was called upon for theory, he reverted to the canons of taste and reason. His *Drury Lane Address,* worked at so conscientiously, is remarkable chiefly for its utter sincere lack of originality in reflecting neoclassic ideals. Not once did the poet call these ideals into question. And when he made fun of the Rules and classic terminology, he did so after the accepted manner of Pope.

In at least one phase of his personality, he follows instinctively the main lines of eighteenth-century critical thought. Any body of critical opinion, taken as scattered excerpts from his poems, letters, and journals, may be fitted easily into the classic tradition. It does not matter that his interpretations are sometimes new; his emphasis is always upon taste and morality, and he contradicts these only to allow for the higher quality, genius. He is always conscious of the opinion of such men as Gifford and Jeffrey and pays it due respect in his notes by citing authorities for his innovations. These innovations are always tentative, or guiltily defiant.

In the matter of taste Byron is perhaps closest to his mother century. His taste, the opposite of squeamishness, consists in a visible respect paid to the principles of common sense, fitness, and reason; an awareness of the Rules; and a dislike of the exaggerated and the low. He confides to La Guiccioli that the philosophy of common sense is after all the truest and the best.[8] He apologizes for a pun, offering Homer as his precedent: "Even Homer was a punster—a solitary pun."[9] He writes easily for Murray a mock Aristotelian critique of a play of Polidori;[10] or introduces the Rules into *The Blues*[11] in the same ironical vein as that of Pope in his preface to the *Dunciad*. His admirations are for polish and elegance; he considers himself Rogers's illegitimate son and marvels at the latter's elegance, "really wonderful—there is no such a thing as a vulgar line in his book."[12] He is, modestly speaking, illegitimate, but he retains his respect for legitimacy.

Byron's moral sense, again, is the dominating background of his poetry. In his letters, poems, and conversations, he was ever the preacher, lecturing others and justifying himself. His admiration for Johnson, besides his love of the man, was largely a moral admiration,[13] for with the latter's esthetic judgments he usually disagreed. His preface to *Childe Harold* is the pretext of a bad conscience: "[The Childe] never was intended as an example, further than to show, that early perversion of mind and morals leads to satiety of past pleasures and disappointment in new ones."[14] We are justified in doubting the genuineness of the excuse; but about the other side of his didacticism, sincerity, and truth to life as it is, we can have few misgivings. Byron's sincerity and personal directness are always complicating factors in his criticism; he could seldom judge a work of art without going behind it to the artisan, and his judgments are too often on the man rather than on the creative artist. To this violently sincere nature, the inhibitions of taste in the newer school of poetry were but euphemisms for cowardice and cant: "The subject is hardly refined enough for this immaculate period, this moral millennium of expurgated editions in books, manners, and royal trials of divorce."[15] "Nothing provokes me so much as the squeamishness that excludes the exhibition of many such subjects from the stage;—a squeamishness the product, I believe, of a lower tone of the moral sense, and foreign to the majestic and confident virtue of the golden age of our country. All is now cant."[16] Byron had been inclined by his experiences to doubt morality beneath the surface, and his vigorous masculine temperament detested sentiment as something effeminate and weak. "Learning, labour, research, wrath, and partiality. I call the latter virtues in a writer, because they make him write in earnest."[17] In every point, it must be granted, he lives up to his creed.

In his own composition the principle of sincerity took a somewhat exaggerated and sometimes unfortunate turn. On the one hand, it guarded him from inflated and meaningless expression, much more than did his own uncertain taste; but on the other it clipped the wings of his imagination by committing him to a loyalty to the unpoetic truth. "There should always be some foundation of fact for the most airy fabric, and pure invention is but the talent of a liar."[18] "In my mind the [ethical] is the highest of all poetry, because it does that in *verse*, which the greatest of men wished to accomplish in prose. If the essence of poetry must be a *lie*—banish it from your republic, as Plato would have done."[19] The principle is essentially healthy but, applied in excess, it befits the scholar better than the poet. We must hold it responsible for the poet's theory of translation, which certainly he inherited from neither Pope nor Johnson. "*Ricciardetto* should have been *translated literally, or not at all.*"[20] We might claim, on the contrary, that anything is preferable to the translation of Pulci's *Morgante Maggiore*, "which is word for word, and verse for verse."[21] The effect of such "pretensions to accuracy,"[22] was to make the poet highly exacting of accuracy in others, critical of inaccuracy in Voltaire and in Hunt's description of "old Ravenna's clear shewn towers and bay."[23] The instinct of scholarship was always close to the surface in the poet; but scholarship to him meant devotion to fact, not Shelley's desire for comprehension and insight.

Byron's critique of Homer—"I still venerated the grand original as the truth of *history* (in the material *facts*) and of *place*. Otherwise it would have given me no delight"[24]—is the *reductio ad absurdum* of this phase of his critical leanings.

His sympathy with the classic tradition is not difficult to explain. His temperament, on its nonpoetizing side, was closely akin to that of Samuel Johnson, in its rough common sense, its devotion to the past, its hatred of shrill-voiced radicals and impostors, and its ingrowing scepticism, which tortured his religious longings. In his common sense he was close to the spirit of the dying age. He was not, in Goethe's phrase, a child when he reflected; he was no seer, but he was a man—not far removed from the ordinary man of his day, except in the high diet of passion and religious probings that fed his reflections. It was but normal for this fundamentally conservative nature to accept a tradition that so well satisfied his scruples. Classicism, furthermore, though moribund under the surface, displayed still many vigorous signs of life. At its worst the Augustan tradition ran to an artificiality and negativeness that were deep-seated in timidity, it generalized the manners of a class into absolute standards for mankind, and it encouraged a complacent provinciality. But at its best, it produced an elevation of tone, an ease and sophistication of expression that are rare in the later more plebeian days of Victoria. It reflected the self-assurance and conscious self-mastery of a ruling class used to the sense of control, and offered to the artist an intelligent, critical audience, sympathetic to qualities like its own. There is one sort of convention, says Professor Ker, in which "the literature and arts of the eighteenth century are strong. It is the convention of a school or a tradition, such as keeps the artist from eccentricity, vanity, and 'expense of spirit', the convention which makes an understanding between them as to what is worth doing, and sets them speedily to work, instead of wasting their time considering what they ought to do next. It is this that makes an understanding also between the artist and his customers, and leads to *hilaritas* on both sides, to activity both in production and appreciation."[25]

This tradition appealed to Byron as much by its defects as by its excellences. Its very provincialism, as the monopoly of a single class in the little island England, was the provincialism of Byron himself, who longed most ardently to belong to that class. Seeing through its hypocrisies, he could, notwithstanding, never free himself from its prejudices; his attacks upon it were from within, the protest of a part against a whole. He despised the professional poet: "I thought that poetry was an *art*, or an *attribute*, and not a *profession*"[26]— in his eyes more an attribute, we suspect, than an art. He detested French poetry as much as Johnson disliked all things Scotch; "it was discordant to his ears."[27] He disdained the crowd while feeding it with his verses. "Drummond's works . . . are too good to be popular . . . [William Spencer's verses were not] calculated to please the *canaille*, which made me like them all the better."[28] He disliked pedantry as he despised professionalism: "Mr. Rogers . . . is a poet, nor is he the less so because he is something more."[29] He deplored the "systematized Sophistry of many men, etc., about London . . . false pretensions and nauseous attempts to make learning a nuisance and society a Bore."[30] He refused to make extravagant claims for the poet, as his contemporary poets were inclined to do. "The end of all scribblement is to amuse,"[31] he asserted in a Johnsonian vein, and this sentiment he echoed frequently.

The feeling of class prejudice was mixed with other elements of a more literary character. He borrowed from his acquaintance with satire a respect for legitimacy: "As to the poetry of [Francis Hodgson's] Newfangled Stanza, I wish they would write the octave or the Spenser; we have no other legitimate measure of that kind."[32] His love of the past, which forms the undertone of his satires, is the basis of his love for Greece. But more profound than either of these was his love for purity and distinction, "that certain proof of superiority—simplicity of manner and freedom from affectation."[33] He praised "the simplicity—the classical simplicity" of Dante's poetry.[34] He disliked affected simplicity, prettiness, "the flowers of poetry."[35] In criticizing the Lake School, he was the aristocrat considering *parvenus* who, afraid "of aught that approaches to vulgarity . . . are always superfine. . . . Birth . . . saves one from this hypocritical gentility."[36]

The classic strain in Byron, it must be reiterated, is but one element in a complex personality. Its importance cannot readily be minimized; but it is well to recall other elements which were also important and influential. The indelible impression the poet leaves upon us is that of a sharply contradictory spirit, divided against itself. "Byron affects to be unfeeling, while he is a victim to sensibility; and to be reasonable, while he is governed by imagination only":[37] this is Lady Blessington's analysis, and perhaps this interpretation of Byron as a thinker desiring to be sane but thwarted by the fever of his disposition and his environment is the surest guide to his character. His common sense was early colored by a strong sentimentalism, which can be most readily traced back to Little.

> I hate you, ye cold compositions of art . . .
> I court the effusions that spring from the heart,[38]

is but too truly an explanation of much in the *Hours of Idleness*. This weaker emotionalism was gradually sloughed off, under the constant mockery of a strongly realistic sense of humor. But the profounder, more violent emotions remained.

It would be incautious to draw too many conclusions from

Byron's criticism of books. The only general rule that can be offered is that he commended those he liked and disapproved when he mentioned those he disliked. He turned instinctively to authors like Crabbe, Burns, Campbell, and Scott, who were of his own manly disposition. But in his youth he had admired and imitated *Ossian*, and his admiration of *Christabel* was never qualified—"a wild and singularly original and beautiful poem," he assured Medwin.[39] Some things he was partial to, most likely, because of the mood in which he read them, or perhaps he saw more in them than was there; it is hard otherwise to explain his commendation of Sir William Drummond's *Odin*.[40] Shelley's poetry he could not understand or appreciate; his taste did not run to the ethereal, to beauty light as air; his judgments on Shelley are never predictable, except as, liking the man, he tried to like his poetry and seldom succeeded. His best word for a contemporary was for Scott, "the superlative of my comparative," who fulfilled most of his ideals, and was a gentleman and a friendly critic to boot. Another passion was Alfieri,[41] who had moved him to pity and terror in the theatre, and had similar tastes and pursuits. The assertion that Byron lacked that enthusiasm for books which has been displayed by most authors, is a distortion of the facts; his extensive readings, his constant quotation of lines and passages that pleased him, are sufficient refutation of any such thesis. His taste was less catholic, perhaps, and more mixed with baser matter, than Shelley's; he loved learning, possibly, for the sake of displaying his knowledge of the fact as well as for learning's own sake. But he loved books, he loved the authors of books, he took his pleasure in reading and exercise, and he had a fondness for reviews. He is apart from his contemporary poets only in his attitude toward his enthusiasms. He had always that other half of his personality which stood aside and criticized his likings; he was possessed by that Augustan conscience which apologized for its eccentricities. He reacted to, then he reacted against, the more unhealthy of his affections. He criticized Little and Rousseau while he praised them, and his final opinion of the former was fondness for the man and suspicion of the author.[42] *Ossian* to him was of undisputed merit only in spite of its faults—turgidity and bombastic diction.[43] Even Scott, whose novels were a new literature in themselves and whose poetry was as good as any, if not better, followed an erroneous system.[44] The latter note is the mark of a later period, after Byron had become the self-constituted champion of another school. But as one voice in the fugue of his mind, usually a lower voice, runs the neoclassic refrain: "In blank verse, Milton, Thomson, and our dramatists are the beacons that shine along the deep, but warn us from the rough and barren rock on which they are kindled."[45] That is entirely in the spirit of Pope.

There is little in Byron the critic and Byron the satirist in verse to explain his early apostasy from his ideals. This can be explained only if we remember that he was but slightly the critic and very much the artist driven constantly to write. His most general definitions of poetry have in them little of school or theory, but very much of the man. "Like paintings, poems may be too highly finished. The great art is effect, no matter how produced."[46] "Anything is better than weakening an expression or a thought."[47] "The passions [are] the food and fuel of poesy."[48] There speaks the orator, who desires to sway, and the artist, who seeks the impression. It is useless to ask of the poet that he shall live in his theories. In Byron, at least for the time, classic principles were relegated to the position of his conscience—basic, but subdued. His classicism, as he had acquired it, was after all but the negative side of his artistic character: it could correct others, but himself for a time at least, it could not inspire.

It did not want to be written, and he could not force his Pegasus.

We must also recall the specific conditions which made his default comprehensible. Classicism, by this time, its primary urge, improvement, gone, had lost its vitality; and its prophet, Gifford, was but the upholder of a tradition rapidly passing and the echoer, in his language as in his thought, of the major prophets gone before. The verve of the *English Bards and Scotch Reviewers*, a child of passion, was satiric; but thereafter Byron, well received, waxing mentally fat and well fed, had no occasion to be discontented. He lacked the subtlety and finesse of Pope, which could make of repetitions delicate variations on a theme; and so he had no delight in repeating. Besides, the demand of the time was against him. While his *Hints from Horace* could not obtain a hearing, his *Childe Harold*, written to beguile his melancholy, made him the cynosure of the nation's eyes; and the poet, the restive slave of public opinion, gave himself up to his fate and floated on the current of his popularity.

Parallel with his defection, he suffered a revulsion from the bitterness of his *English Bards and Scotch Reviewers*. With the diminution of his passion, he became ashamed of his extreme and unjust criticisms and of the spirit that had instigated them: "I find, on dispassionate comparison, my own revenge more than the provocation warranted. It is true, I was very young—that might be an excuse to those I attacked —but to me it is none."[49] He also came into contact with his victims, became friendly with Moore, Scott, and Jeffrey, reverenced Wordsworth, aided Coleridge, and admired Southey's "epic" head. In a series of marginal jottings in a copy of the *English Bards*, he recanted and reversed his individual criticisms, and repented the spirit of the whole. "The tone and temper are such as I cannot approve."[50] Yet he retained some lingering fondness for his earliest masterpiece, enough to consider it, in comparison with his later works, the best—"bating the malice."[51]

The reaction from the *English Bards* was against a mood and its consequences, not against a principle. Byron's apostasy was neglect, not renunciation. During these years of busy popularity, meaningless amours, dabblings in politics, and fitful immersions in society, his conscience was asleep, but it remained his conscience. Never, as now, was the fatalistic character of the man so apparent—his willingness to drift downstream, his goodnatured opportunism, complicated by desultory sacrifices to the ideal, his uncomfortable consciousness of unutilized strength, the old restlessness of indecision. These years, perhaps, might best be passed over in silence. But we cannot ignore the fact that while the poet was slumbering or dashing off productions below the level of his greater powers, the man was enjoying, suffering, gaining a first-hand knowledge of men and of a certain kind of woman, increasing in worldly wisdom, and deepening his cynicism. Further comment on those years immediately following the hegira, passed at a high intensity of inspiration and, under the influence of Shelley, stimulative of philosophical probings of the ideal, must, however, as not yet to our purpose, be postponed.

Had Byron been left to himself, and had all gone well with his personal as well as his poetical affairs in Great Britain, the matter might have been left indeterminate. But with his departure from England, though not immediately, he entered upon a reaction from his former practices. The change, we must admit, was not altogether an affair of conscience. He had been thrown, during the years of his popularity, into intimate contact with the rising local poetic lights of England. His retraction of the criticisms in *English Bards* was partly the result of a growing admiration for

Christabel and for bits of Wordsworth's verse, but it was even more the result of acquaintance with the authors and respect, if not friendship, for their personalities. The influence of Wordsworth, under the encouragement of Shelley and the romantic scenery of the Alps, even increased during the first year of the exile; *Childe Harold* in its last two cantos owes much to the older poet in theory and practice. But gradually, because of suspected personal grievances, disagreements on politics, and scorn for acts which he could explain only as political apostasy and timeserving, Byron's enmity for the Lake School had its birth and its increasing. From personal dislike to critical carping was for him but a single step. "It is difficult . . . when one detests an author, not to detest his works. There are some that I dislike so cordially, that I am aware of my incompetency to give an impartial opinion of their writings."[52] This honest confession explains the stimulus but neither the form nor all the ramifications of his reaction. His lengthy attack on the Lake School in his suppressed preface to the first canto of *Don Juan*, associating the group with Castlereagh, his arch aversion, consists mainly of a direct, vigorous but unconvincing assault on its literary self-sufficiency. Along with the carping, however, are echoes of his first satire, a harking back to its mood and sometimes to its phraseology; some of the turns of wit might be moved bodily from one work to the other, and the final couplet of the stanza has often the ring of the heroic couplet, the rather brassy ring characteristic of Byron and Gifford: Coleridge, for instance, is said to have been

> Explaining metaphysics to the nation—
> I wish he would explain his Explanation.

And to Southey,

> You, Bob! are rather insolent, you know,
> . . . you overstrain yourself, or so,

> And tumble downward like the flying fish
> Gasping on deck, because you soar too high, Bob,
> And fall, for lack of moisture quite a-dry, Bob!

Wordsworth

> . . . in a rather long "Excursion"
> Has given a sample from the vasty version
> Of his new system . . .
> 'Tis poetry—at least by his assertion.

Even here, however, the tone is different and the note is that of a later period, shown in the fondness for the feminine and the double rhyme, which prevents the snap and crackle of the couplet.

But to leave the matter here is to accuse of hypocrisy a man who was the antithesis of the hypocrite. Behind the about-face that so surprised or amused his contemporaries and has furnished material for many a subsequent monograph, was a long and steady if unexpressed development of a literary philosophy. The Bowles letters have too often been accepted as mere hoaxes of the poet in a rampant, devastating mood, or as the fruit of a sudden petulant irritation, or as another proof of his instability and inconsistency. They are rampant, devastating, and petulant, if you will, but they have reference to Byron's very center of stability.

It is easier for us than for some of his contemporaries to understand and sympathize with his defense of Pope and his school, and even easier than for Leslie Stephen, who could see in the business no more than a "rather wayward mood of Pope-worship."[53] Knowing Byron intimately from his letters, diaries, and journals, we may doubt that the mood of Pope-worship was as extreme as it struck contemporaries, and we may claim that Byron had great justification for his spirited defense. At the end of a century of shifting poetical horizons, many lovers of literature have come again to feel that Pope is a great, if not a greatest, English poet, or that if not a poet he is certainly a great writer and cannot be denied a sure place in the library of English literature. Too much energy has been expended in defining what a poet or what poetry is, and any man of strong common sense may object to the regrettable aimlessness of a pigeonholing criticism. Of course the romantic attack upon Pope was not regrettable nor was it aimless. It was the symptom of a change and the sign of a new vitality. The romantics built anew, and it was necessary, as they advanced, to clear away the débris left by the past. The assault on the classic school, sweeping and unjust as it often became, united under a common standard a school that was otherwise widely diverse. The refutation of the classic theory was in itself stimulating to the promulgation of new theories, which in their turn stimulated the production of a great new literature. Byron himself, in the whole range of his poetry and particularly in the latter half of *Childe Harold*, absorbed and used the fever of the time. But with the contemporary revolt and its depreciation of the past he had never associated himself, holding, even in the extreme of his romantic dissipation, an aloof neutral attitude, or no well defined attitude at all.

In this static condition of soul, he was more and more irritated by the upstart criticism of the time, with the disparagement of a great poet and a great tradition by men who were themselves in many ways inferior to both. Perhaps the earliest indication of the change is a passage in a letter to Murray, written in September, 1817: "Scott, Southey, Wordsworth, Moore, Campbell, I . . . are upon a wrong revolutionary system . . . from which none but Rogers and Crabbe are free. . . . I am the more confirmed in this by having lately gone over some of our classics, particularly Pope, whom I tried in this way—I took Moore's poems and my own and some others, and went over them side by side with Pope's, and I was really astonished . . . and mortified at the inevitable distance in point of sense, harmony, effect and even *Imagination*, passion and *Invention*, between the little Queen Anne's man and us of the Lower Empire. Depend upon it, it is all Horace then, and Claudian now, among us; and if I had to begin again, I would model myself accordingly."[54] It is reassuring that in this first sign of reaction Byron included himself among the offenders and rather confessed a fault than exposed the faults of others. Later he modified this burst of modesty: "We [Scott and I] keep the *saddle*, because we broke the rascal, and can ride. . . ."[55] "I *have* been among the builders of this Babel, attended by a confusion of tongues, but *never* amongst the envious destroyers of the classic temple of our predecessors."[56] And this, we feel, he had a perfect right to say. He had been guilty of no deliberate disloyalty, he had sinned more through negligence than through intent, and his sins, at least, were good sins—it was the poetry of his imitators that was bad; Cantos III and IV of *Childe Harold* were sufficient excuse for any theory. "Is not the vulgarity of these wretched imitations of Lord Byron carried to a pitch of the sublime?"[57] wrote Shelley in a slightly different context. The sentiment may be applied in the large to Byron's imitators.

The onslaught upon contemporary criticism followed in the main two genuine lines—a defense of Pope and a denunciation of the lower tone in poetry that was resulting from new schools, new systems, and the lack of good and assured models of taste. "The great cause of the present deplorable state of English poetry is to be attributed to the absurd and systematic depreciation of Pope, in which, for the last few years, there has been a sort of epidemic concurrence."[58] Pope, with Goldsmith, is the only perfect English poet,[59] and therefore the only safe foundation upon which any self-respecting school can be built. In all of the new schools, Byron feels, there has not appeared "a single scholar who has not made his master ashamed of him. . . . Now, it is remarkable, that almost all the followers of Pope have produced beautiful and standard works."[60] "Pope little suspected that the 'Art of Sinking in Poetry' would become an object of serious Study, and supersede not only his own, but all that Horace, Vida, Boileau and Aristotle had left to Posterity, of precept, and the greatest poets in all nations, of example."[61] Allowance must be made for the exaggeration of the crusader. Byron evidently did not mean all that he asserted in its unmodified form, beyond the heat of the moment and the delight of battle; he was amused as well as irritated. But he was irritated, particularly by any pretense to system on the part of the rebels: "I was not the last to discover its beauties," he writes of *Rimini*. "Even then I remonstrated against its vulgarisms. . . . Mr. Hunt's answer was, that he wrote upon principle; 'they made part of his *system*!!' I then said no more. When a man talks of his system, it is like a woman's talking of her virtue. I let them talk on."[62]

To understand Byron's revulsion from the poetry of his day, we must keep in mind that poetry itself, and put ourselves in his place, exiled in Italy, communing with Shelley, La Guiccioli, and the highest ideals of poetry, and not inclined, by the force of circumstances and of his own experiences, to be charitable toward his countrymen. There is a passage among the letters of Shelley so closely like several statements of Byron that it may be a reflection of the latter's mood, which paints vividly the situation of both the exiled poets: "Procter's verses," he complains, "enrage me far more than those of Codrus did Juvenal, and with better reason. Juvenal need not have been stunned, unless he had liked it; but my boxes are packed with this trash, to the exclusion of what I want to see."[63] Cut off from England and mostly out of touch, because of their remoteness, with the intimate gossip of the time, both men were more conscious of main tendencies and less lenient toward common foibles than if they had been in the thick of the warfare. They could afford to be exacting about what they received. Byron's dissatisfaction, apart from his love of classicism and his naturally pugnacious independence, was largely a dislike of certain trends in style. The romantics, by and large, claimed to do great things, and when they failed their failure was the more ignominious. On the one hand, their cry was for the greater passions of man, and, on the other, in their nature poetry they put too many trees into their forests and described the leaves too minutely. Byron's criticism of Cowper's lines "To Mary" and his choice of the needles as most effective from being "a simple, household, '*indoor*,' artificial, and ordinary image,"[64] is acutely discerning criticism. The weaker poetry of the day, that is, the mass of it, was essentially vulgar, in a manner utterly foreign to Byron's own type of vulgarity. This may be seen more readily by comparing his compositions with those he attacks than by reference to any of his stated conscious opinions. His poetic virtues, at their greatest in the latter part of *Childe Harold*, are sincerity, directness, clarity, the clean-cut strength of an athlete stripped for an encounter. Goethe expressed this well, when he remarked that there was no padding in Byron's poetry[65] and compared the clearness and brilliancy of his style to a metal wire drawn through a steel plate. Not romantic sincerity but romantic pretentiousness is objectionable; we cannot protest that a man speaks highly, but that he speaks highly when he has nothing to say. "The grand distinction of the under forms of the new school of poets is their *vulgarity*. By this I do not mean that they are *coarse*, but 'shabby-genteel'. . . . It is in their *finery* that the new under school are *most* vulgar."[66] Mrs. Hemans's "false stilted trashy style, which is a mixture of all the styles of the day, which are *all bombastic* . . . is neither English nor poetry."[67]

Byron is careful to distinguish in his reply to Bowles between the greater romantics, Burns, Chatterton, Wordsworth, "the upper Lakers," and "the new under school." The main objects of his critical distaste were really Bowles himself, Hunt, and Keats, the latter of whom bore the brunt of the attack. He disliked the "Cockney" elements in the newer verse; comparatively his other objections were incidental. Leigh Hunt unconsciously gives away his case, in a passage on Byron: "His brother Horace was delicious. Lord Byron used to say that this epithet should be applied only to eatables; and that he wondered that a friend of his . . . that was critical in the matters of eating should use it in any other sense."[68] It does not matter that the word, as Hunt claimed for it, has classical precedents. The poetry of Hunt, Bowles, and Keats in his less fortunate spells, was only too "delicious." *Rimini*, as is generally recognized today, is an inferior production; it is a "trash of vulgar phrases tortured into compound barbarisms," and not, as its author believed it, old English.[69] Much of the new style truly is either stilted and affected, or *"very, very*—so soft and pamby."[70]

The tendency has been, on the other hand, to overlook similar offences on the part of Keats. He is undoubtedly one of the greatest of English poets, and his temporary vices may be pardoned in view of his surpassing virtues. But Keats's poetry, in the years of his apprenticeship, suffered from the same weakness as that of his guide and philosopher, Hunt. Even *Endymion*, while prefiguring the magnificent odes and later narratives, displays nevertheless excessive and sometimes maudlin sensibility, which was always Byron's aversion,[71] and an over-ornamentation of style against which he most deeply protested. The two poets, at their respective ages, were not made to appreciate or to tolerate one another.

Keats, furthermore, had erred in criticizing Pope and his school in "Sleep and Poetry." Byron could forgive the younger poet neither his opinions nor his poetical obliquities, and the result was a series of recriminations, second in violence only to the recurring attacks upon Southey: "There is such a trash of Keats and the like upon my tables, that I am ashamed to look at them."[72] "Johnny Keats's *p-ss a bed* poetry."[73] "No more Keats, I entreat:—flay him alive; if some of you don't, I must skin him myself: there is no bearing the drivelling idiotism of the Mankin."[74] Any later retraction, as in the several references in the first Bowles letter or in the skit "Who killed John Keats?" was due partly to the enthusiasm of Shelley, but as much to the death of the young poet. Byron, by his own statement, was "always battling with the *Snake* about Keats . . . that idol of the Cockneys,"[75] and Shelley did not entirely win him over. Byron's recantation was condescending, the result of an obvious effort to be kind. "My indignation at Mr. Keats's depreciation of Pope has hardly permitted me to do justice to his own genius, which, malgré all the fantastic fopperies of his style, was undoubtedly of great promise. . . . He is a loss to our literature; and the more so, as he himself before his death, is said to have been persuaded that he had not taken the right line, and was reforming his style upon the more classical models of the language."[76] Shelley, on his own part, was largely led, whether by his own critical judgment or by the reasoning of his friend, to an almost identical conclusion: "*Hyperion* promises for [Keats] that he is destined to become one of the first writers of the age. His other things are imperfect enough, and, what is worse, written in a bad sort of style which is becoming fashionable among those who fancy they are imitating Hunt and Wordsworth."[77]

Along these two lines mainly Byron reacted against the poetical drift of his time. On the whole there is little to condemn in his attitude. It may be claimed for him that, as well as any of his contemporaries save perhaps Shelley, he kept his sense of values under the trying circumstance of being in a minority. He did not attack his greater contemporaries, except upon their weaker side. He modified his more violent statements, though the latter, through the pungency of his expression, are more memorable than their modifications. He turned the searchlight of his conscience upon his own poetry, and admitted its flaws: "I *have* been amongst the builders of this Babel, attended by a confusion of tongues."[78] He depreciated the field in which he had proved himself a master.[79] His manner, however, betrayed him into many misunderstandings. Allowance has seldom been sufficiently made for his sense of humor. He preferred not to say exactly what he meant if he could be more emphatic by exaggerating. His habit of baiting his audience, displayed before Medwin, Trelawny, and, we suspect, Lady Blessington, he extended and applied in his published criticisms with equal success. It is impossible not to take Byron seriously, and it is disastrous to take him literally. These must be the cardinal points upon which to base an investigation of the Bowles letters.

The *Invariable Principles of Poetry* in itself was hardly severe enough on Pope to warrant the outburst which it precipitated. Byron used it as an excuse to express what had long been brewing in his mind. The reply was written in the greatest good spirits. He was both angry and amused, and the amusement formed the exhilarating outlet for the anger; the whole circumstance, in many of its features, parallels the composition of *The Vision of Judgment*. Master of his subject and of his mood, he produced one of the most readable critiques in the language. He wrote "offhand, without copy or correction,"[80] and annotated, but never revised. Indeed, the effect would be marred by revision. The purpose is "to make fun of all those fellows."[81] The appeal of the reply is in neither its logic nor its structure, but in its humor, its rhythm, its irresistible verve. Though Byron can hardly be right in all his contentions, we feel, as he makes each point, that he is. He was justified in his claim to Medwin that he had "set Bowles and his invariable principles at rest."[82]

Byron evidently took his main purpose seriously. His letters, before and after the composition of the reply, are full of his high purpose. "I have at last," he wrote in one instance, "lost all patience with the atrocious cant and nonsense about Pope, with which our present blackguards are overflowing, and am determined to make such head against it as an Individual can, by verse or prose; and I will at least do it with good will. There is no bearing it any longer; and if it goes on, it will destroy what little good writing or taste remains amongst us. I hope there are still a few men of taste to second me; but if not, I'll battle it alone, convinced that it is in the best cause of English literature."[83] He contemplated, just before composing the reply, the production of another *Baviad* and *Maeviad*, to castigate the "villainous cant"[84] of "the Cockneys, the Lakers, and the *followers* of Scott, and Moore, and Byron."[85] As a preparation for his effort he studied Johnson intensively,[86] and perhaps underwent some purging of soul. But in the heat of composition, though he kept his objective constantly in view, he was carried away by his sense of humor and by the keen zest of battle. The first Bowles letter was probably not exactly what he had intended. If not, it was the better for the change.

The second letter is distinctly inferior to the first. With his inspiration evidently subsiding, he resorts to personalities and would-be clever hits that do not ring true. He gives the impression of trying to repeat a success, rather than of having anything new to say—or anything at all to say, for that matter. His whole case must rest upon the first letter, which is strong enough indeed to stand for both. Its certain critical weaknesses, evident upon analysis, are not obvious to the rapid reader. The letter—essay, article, critique, or what you will—is of the compound nature of a refutation of Bowles's strictures, a satire upon contemporary poetics, and an ebullient humorous composition. Byron was out to get Bowles wherever the latter, intentionally or unconsciously, had dropped a gauntlet. The introductory portion is hardly a reply to the *Invariable Principles,* but harks back to Bowles's 1806 edition of Pope, in which he had cast aspersions on the earlier poet's morality, and to which Byron had referred at length in his *English Bards and Scotch Reviewers.*[87] The refutation is hardly more than a categorical denial of Bowles's contentions. The latter is accused of bad taste, bad judgment, and a distortion of the facts of life that borders close upon cant. His artistic judgment is likewise challenged. His main thesis, that human manners are inferior to the passions or to nature as a theme for poetry, discredits the art of Pope, though the poet may not be directly attacked. Byron's confutation of this is in his most characteristic vein. On the one hand he claims for ethical poetry, which he has managed to confuse with the poetry of manners, that it is *"the very first order* of poetry"; and on the other, he holds up Pope as the supreme ethical and didactic, the great *universal* poet, "the most *perfect* of our poets, and the purest of our moralists,"[88] "the greatest moral poet of any age or in any language."[89] On the side he has a dig at his contemporary barbarians, who have dared raise a mosque beside a Grecian temple of the purest architecture,[90] and baits the Shakespearolators: "I shall not presume to say that Pope is as high a poet as Shakespeare and Milton.... I would no more say this than I would assert in the mosque . . . that Socrates was a greater man than Mahomet."[91]

The remainder of his confutation is in much the same vein. Bowles has claimed that to be a great descriptive poet one must be first an accurate describer of external nature; Byron replies that the result of the theory is usually a forgetting of the forest in the trees, an overemphasis of the unessential and meaningless detail. Bowles has placed nature poetry, indeed all other poetry, above the poetry of manners; Byron retorts that it is not in the branch of art, but in the execution, that greatness lies, and again, inconsistently, that in his mind, "the highest of all poetry is ethical poetry, as the highest of all earthly objects must be moral truth."[92] And finally, since he is actually irritated by the title of Bowles's article, "I do hate that word 'invariable.' What is there of human . . . which is 'invariable'?"[93] Around such reactions the whole argument revolves.

For the soundness of one contention, however, Byron has never been given sufficient credit. At the end of the *Invariable Principles*, Bowles had expressed, as the crowning conclusion of his article, the dictum which must be taken as its motto and its guiding principle: "Artificial manners are *human,* but *'human manners'* ARE NOT SO ADAPTED TO POETRY OF THE HIGHEST KIND AS HUMAN PASSIONS."[94] To introduce and prove this theorem, he had shown that "artificial" images or passages in the works of Milton or of Shakespeare are ennobled only through connection with man and with nature, that a ship is poetic only in association with the sea and that even in the drama, as in the plays of Sophocles, nature alone may be introduced to the best advantage. Byron's immediate retort was to take Bowles's illustrations one by one, and to prove by each the opposite dictum, that it is only in conjunction with the works of man that nature gains its profoundest poetry. Art, he asserted, must not merely borrow,

THE MAN OF SENSE

but heighten the poetry of nature; the true artist culls nature and paints her idealized; the sculptor and the painter must surpass their model; poetry is written for men and about men, nature is only a background and an environment, and the passions are great only so long as they are human; "nature is not lavish of her beauties; they are widely scattered, and occasionally displayed, to be selected with care, and gathered with difficulty."[95] The distinction between the two points of view is not clear, unless we remember that Bowles's man is the natural man, a product of the balance of the passions, almost as much a part of nature as a waterfall, and that Byron's is man civilized and purposeful, overcoming and improving his environment with the aid of his intelligence. Perhaps the distinction was not so clear in either mind as stated here, but the trend of the arguments is in that direction. The "artificial," likewise, meant to Byron but the creation of the will and mind of man, of which the Parthenon, a ship, daggers, manners, and tradition, are equally examples. From this angle, the poet is the most artificial, perhaps, of all artists, in his very essence;[96] from this angle also we are justified in speaking of the "exquisitely artificial genius" of the Athenian Greeks.[97] The artifice of art, the selection, ordering, and imprint of the artist's design, are essential to great poetry. "[Buildings and sculptures] are as *poetical* as Mont Blanc or Mount Ætna, perhaps still more so, as they are direct manifestations of mind, and *presuppose* poetry in their very conception; and have, moreover, as being such, a something of actual life, which cannot belong to any part of inanimate nature, . . ."[98]

At the end of the letter, Byron gives expression to a theme that has little enough to do with the rest of the argument but is significant in relation to himself. It arises in the revulsion from the vulgar style of the Cockney School, which we have before treated of, and it leads to a statement of

Byron's critical standards. So great was his good nature that after Keats's death he recommended to Murray that the passage be deleted out of respect to the dead poet, against whom he felt that it was obviously directed. But it must stand as the most eloquent portion of the entire letter:

Far be it from me to presume that there ever was, or can be, such a thing as an *aristocracy* of *poets;* but there *is* a nobility of thought and of style, open to all stations, and derived partly from talent, and partly from education—which is to be found in Shakespeare, and Burns, no less than in Dante and Alfieri. . . . If I were asked to define what their gentlemanliness is, I should say that it is only to be defined by examples. . . . In poetry, as well as writing in general, it will never make entirely a poet or a poem; but neither poet nor poem will ever be good for anything without it. It is the *salt* of society, and the seasoning of composition. Vulgarity . . . does not depend upon low themes, or even low language, for Fielding revels in both;—but is he ever *vulgar?* No. You see the man of education, the gentleman, and the scholar, sporting with his subject,—its master, not its slave.[99]

These two *Letters to* * * * *   * * * * * * [John Murray] *on Bowles's Strictures* are far in mood and background from the *English Bards* and the *Hints from Horace*. Byron, willy-nilly, had one by one discarded many of the theories and most of the mannerisms of that school with which he had first seriously aligned himself. His whole nature, poetical and otherwise, had been tested in the intervening years as by fire. He had lost friends, country, station in life. He had passed into a new environment, was associating with a foreign people, having its own literary history and traditions. It is the more remarkable, therefore, that he retained to the last so much of his earlier attitude. He is still close to the school of Pope in his elevation of man social above man natural and of the mind above the passions, as well as in his recurrent stress upon taste. He was saved by his independence, his greater breadth

THE MAN OF SENSE

of experience, and his susceptibility to the influences of the time, from any slavish mimicry. In fact, so widely had he departed from his earlier models that he is usually set down as a romantic poet. That this is partly due to the greater richness of his admirations, to the admission of Shakespeare, Dante, and Alfieri as well as Pope and Burns, as his models, may be one half of our explanation. The other half, to be treated more at length, will be left for the succeeding chapters.

CHAPTER IV

THE PRACTICAL POET

IN discussing Byron as artist I shall adhere to the general policy, as heretofore, of accepting his words, whether in prose or in verse, at their face value. Byron was so aggressively sincere, and at the same time so fond of confession, that he often flatly contradicted himself. His habit of rapid and summary citation and his dislike of system have made it very difficult to fit all of his thoughts into a coherent outline. But we have, for that reason, a richer field for investigation and a surer record of his poetic pilgrimage, than of those who wrote fewer letters to their friends.

The first public utterance of the poet on his art is to be found in the small volume, *Hours of Idleness*, which attracted the sarcasm of Croker. The preface[1] is prophetic of the later letters. It is the man speaking almost informally to his audience, or, at least, if with the best intention of formality, revealing much more about his own personality than about any theories of composition. The mottoes—"Virginibus puerisque canto" and "He whistled as he went for want of thought"—may be placed beside the preface; they suggest its mood. Many of the statements deserve quotation:

Some few [poems] were written during the disadvantages of illness and depression of spirits.... This consideration ... may at least arrest the arm of censure. A considerable portion of these poems has been privately printed, at the request and for the perusal of my friends... "to do greatly" we must "dare greatly"; and I have hazarded my reputation and feelings in publishing this volume . . . though not without solicitude for the fate of these effusions, my expectations are by no means sanguine. . . . Poetry . . . is not my primary vocation; to divert the dull moments of indisposition, or the monotony of a vacant hour, urged me "to this sin." . . . My wreath, scanty as it must be, is all I shall derive from these productions; and I shall never attempt to replace its fading leaves, or pluck a single additional sprig from groves where I am, at best, an intruder. Though accustomed, in my younger days, to rove a careless mountaineer on the Highlands of Scotland, I have not, of late years, had the benefit of such pure air, or so elevated a residence, as might enable me to enter the lists with genuine bards, who have enjoyed both these advantages. . . . I leave to others "virûm volitare per ora." I look to the few who will hear with patience "dulce est desipere in loco." To the former worthies I resign, without repining, the hope of immortality, and content myself with the not very magnificent prospect of ranking amongst "the mob of gentlemen who write." . . . With slight hopes, and some fears, I publish this first and last attempt. To the dictates of young ambition may be ascribed many actions more criminal and equally absurd. . . . It is highly improbable, from my situation and pursuits hereafter, that I should ever obtrude myself a second time upon the public.

Byron is seldom more attractive than in this modest, apologetic mood. Even here, where he is addressing the general public, he speaks as if to his schoolmates at Cambridge, taking for granted their prejudices, their high spirits, and their capacity for mockery, and betrays what he tries to conceal. He is writing from "young ambition," he wishes to be thought a good or surely a promising young poet, but he is uncertain how well he has succeeded. He is moved by a fever to publish, but he is not certain that he has written well enough; he anticipates the criticism he fears. He desires, in a way, to be taken seriously as a poet but is afraid of ridicule and is himself conscious of being ridiculous. He would, perhaps, like to be a divinely unconscious and prophetic bard, but he is preëminently self-conscious, and so makes fun of what he timidly admires. He leans heavily upon authorities, wherever possible, and revels in quoting, to display his scholarship—but his quotations are always apt. He cannot keep his rank out of his discourse while disclaiming its benefits. His sense of humor, we suspect, is greater than his artistic courage. More than of anything else we are conscious of the group to which the preface is addressed. Classically educated, clever, youthfully cynical, it is his world. If he does not write to please it, he at least does not wish to incur its mockery. Where he does not share its tastes, he accepts its judgment. He is not a cocksure genius, but a shy and sensitive young man, and yet with the aggressiveness necessary to get his poems a publisher and risk them before an audience. He is so timorous, however, of the reception of his poetry that he has already decided that he will not venture again, and he commits himself to that sentiment in his preface. He is already a contradictory and interesting spirit.

The *Hours of Idleness* itself is a polyglot collection. It is imitative in the extreme, with Moore, Burns, Pope, Scott's *Marmion*, and MacPherson's *Ossian* as some of its diverse multitude of models. It is the collective result of much random writing by a young poet who is not yet certain just what he wants to do. Its main weakness, a want of surety and taste, may be attributed to that circumstance, and to a similar weakness in many of its models, particularly in Moore and *Ossian*. More even than for its own sake, the poetry is interesting for the light it throws upon the author. Reading it, we are more than ever convinced of the sincerity of the preface. Here, too, Byron is apologetic toward his friends—a little ashamed and at the same time a little proud of the rôle of poet. But to this note is added the traditional self-confidence and anticritical pique of the poet. No indication, beyond the numbers of imitations of Moore and of Pope, is

THE PRACTICAL POET

given of his artistic ideals. He writes because a style appeals to him or because he enjoys adopting a manner or copying a sentiment. Many of the poems are translations from Greek or Latin—no more than school exercises. The "Fragment Written Shortly after the Marriage of Miss Chaworth," on the other hand, was composed immediately after reading Burns's "Farewell to Ayrshire," because of a liking for the metre, and is the expression of immediate and very personal emotion.[2] There are lines on the independence of the poet, which would be more striking were they not at once reminiscent of Moore, of Pope, and of Burns:

> When Love's delirium haunts the glowing mind,
> Limping Decorum lingers far behind. . . .
> Oh! how I hate the nerveless, frigid song,
> The ceaseless echo of the rhyming throng,
> Whose labour'd lines, in chilling numbers flow,
> To paint a pang the author ne'er can know!
> The artless Helicon I boast is youth;—
> My lyre, the heart; my muse, the simple truth. . . .
> For me, I fain would please the chosen few,
> Whose souls, to feeling and to nature true,
> Will spare the childish verse. . . .
> I seek not glory from the senseless crowd.[3]

In the same poem, Byron shows his usual good-natured acceptance of criticism by friends, even from so obscure a critic as the Rev. Mr. Becher. The two attitudes, in their very antithesis, are included also in another poem, written "To the Earl of Clare," which for being nearer doggerel is more intimate, and on account of its frankness and humor is worth quoting at length:

> 'T is mine to waste on love my time,
> Or vent my reveries in rhyme,
>   Without the aid of reason;
> For sense and reason (critics know it)

> Have quitted every amorous poet,
>   Nor left a thought to seize on. . . .
> Thy [Little's] soothing lays may still be read
> When Persecution's arm is dead,
>   And critics are forgot. . . .
> Still must I yield those worthies merit
> Who chasten, with unsparing spirit,
>   Bad rhymes, and those who write them;
> And though myself may be the next
> By critic sarcasm to be vext,
>   I really will not fight them.
> Perhaps they would do quite as well
> To break the rudely sounding shell
>   Of such a young beginner;
> He who offends at pert nineteen,
> At thirty may become, I ween,
>   A very hardened sinner.[4]

Perhaps he was developing a poetic conscience. There is the same uncomfortable feeling as in the preface, of having done something wrong; but it is not so much at having written poetry as at having written bad poetry. He has indulged in amorous verse, and amorous verse is all very well, but not the voice of reason. There is a hint here of the poetical principles that he later appealed to in his *English Bards and Scotch Reviewers* and in the Bowles letters.

In his correspondence of the time he is likewise apologetic concerning his poetry. He either refers to it nonchalantly, as one of a list of things: "I have been *transporting* a servant . . . ; performing in private theatricals;—publishing a volume of poems (at the request of friends, for their perusal);—making love,—and taking physic."[5] Or he enters guiltily into a defense of it, admitting its failings while defending them; "I need not remind you, how few of the *best poems,* in our language, will stand the test of *minute* or *verbal* criticism: it can, therefore, hardly be expected the

THE PRACTICAL POET 79

effusions of a boy ... can derive much merit either from the subject or composition. ... Johnson has shown us that *no poetry* is perfect; but to correct mine would be an Herculean labour. In fact I never looked beyond the moment of composition, and published merely at the request of my friends ... poetic fame is by no means the 'acme' of my wishes."[6] He refers to the volume as "the offspring of my *poetic mania.*"[7] And he writes a "Farewell to the Muse," forswearing the profession of poet forever.

We are reminded in this insistence on the "request of friends," of that later insistence on the unpresentability of his dramas, when he was clearly sincere. It is only fair to admit that up to a certain point his claim may have been justified. He most likely did write on the spur of the moment, and he was probably advised by friends, or a friend, to publish the result of his labors. But that does not explain sufficiently his many publications at so early an age for an author. He wrote because he liked to, or because impelled by some force which he never thoroughly analyzed; then he desired eagerly that others should see his productions, and searched about for a publisher, impelled by the lust for fame. He was too self-conscious an aristocrat to admit that he cared for the plaudits of the many, and possibly he looked more to the select few, to the critics, the connoisseurs, the élite. It is unreasonable to expect him to have analyzed thoroughly his own motives. However, love of fame, like amorous verse, was to him never entirely within the pale of reason and right. Whatever of it he could he overcame in himself, and what he could not he ignored.

Nevertheless, he was easily flattered by attention. The *Hours of Idleness* volume was well received, considering its merits. It was "praised by *reviewers*, admired by *duchesses*, and sold by every bookseller of the metropolis."[8] The author had ventured the book as a test, with *"sundry palpita-*

tions."⁹ Soon thereafter he had written his "Farewell to the Muse," regretting the departure of his inspiration. Even now he attempted to be calm and to anticipate "the *cooling acids* of forthcoming criticism."¹⁰ But with the spur to his ambition, he turned to writing in earnest. The successive references to his compositions testify that he was composing now, not fitfully, but steadily, and was at last making a bid, definitely, for a permanent reputation: "By the by, I have written at my intervals of leisure, after two in the morning, 380 lines in blank verse, of Bosworth Field."¹¹ "I mean to collect all the Erse traditions, poems, etc., etc., and translate, or expand the subject to fill a volume, which may appear next spring under the denomination of '*The Highland Harp,*' or some title equally *picturesque*. Of Bosworth Field, one book is finished, another just begun. It will be a work of three or four years, and most probably never *conclude*. What would you say to some stanzas on Mount Hecla? they would be written at least with *fire*."¹² "I have written 214 pages of a novel—one poem of 380 lines, to be published . . . in a few weeks, with notes,—560 lines of Bosworth Field, and 250 lines of another poem in rhyme, besides half a dozen smaller pieces."¹³ The final product of his ambition, now thoroughly ablaze, and reaching out in many directions, was *English Bards and Scotch Reviewers,* in which Byron first can be said to have found himself. But it is best, before we continue our story, to indicate, a few salient characteristics, which the remaining chapters will develop.

The apologetic note in Byron's reference to his art did not cease with his first preface, but it underwent a subtle transformation, or rather one half of it was sloughed off, and the other stood out in a symmetric prominence. Whatever had been due to lack of self-assurance or to dissatisfaction with his poetry had disappeared by the time of the publication of the *English Bards and Scotch Reviewers*. It crops up here and there throughout the rest of his work, for the better half of Byron is an essentially modest individual: "I am a mighty scribbler."[14] ". . . the veriest scribbler on earth, . . ."[15] "If I am a poet—Gifford says I am; I doubt it."[16] "I hope that the gods have made [Ada] any thing save *poetical*—it is enough to have one such fool in a family."[17] All such assertions may be ascribed either to self-depreciation or to a sense of humor that saw always in the poet as such someone a little absurd. They are partly a sign of the complexity of Byron's personality, to which E. H. Coleridge bears witness: "Among the 'crowd' which found their place in his complex personality, there was 'the barbarian,' and there was 'the Philistine,' and there was, too, the humorist who took a subtle pleasure in proclaiming himself 'a plain man,' puzzled by subtleties, and unable to catch the drift of spirits finer than his own."[18] There was, in other words, always in Byron a man outside the poet writing, who contemplated his poetic personality almost as if it were that of another, who saw its incongruities from the point of view of a humorist, and who could write of the artist with the eye of the satiric observer. This side of his character never stands out clearly until *Beppo* and *Don Juan*, when the poetic ban on humor was lifted, and he was allowed, by the principles of his art, to laugh at his art. Entangled as this sense of humor is, however, we have always to take it into consideration. And we must recall its tone when we come across Byron's many sarcasms on the function of poets.

It is difficult always to distinguish clearly when Byron is merely being quietly facetious and when he is presuming himself profound. There is fine irony, we are sure, in his assurance to Medwin that when one wishes to be a poet, he should do nothing else than make verses[19]—that is, if Medwin reported correctly. We know that Byron did not tell the whole truth, whether the exact truth or not, when he claimed not to "care one lump of Sugar for my *poetry;* but for my *costume,* and my *correctness* on these points . . . I will combat lustily."[20] Byron, we are assured by Lady Blessington, always became gay when he had an opportunity of ridiculing poets, and ridiculed them, even himself.[21] The attitude cannot be called pose, because there is nothing insincere about it; but it is not to be taken too seriously. His constant sarcasms, however, on the "profane art of poetry,"[22] spring from more than a mere sense of humor. Byron, in various moods, was not attracted by the race of men who write. He and Moore *did* "laugh at *t'others*";[23] he laughed at Moore.[24] But at first sight he detested "Sotheby the scribbler . . . a disagreeable dog, with rhyme written in every feature of his wrinkled physiognomy."[25] He disliked literary men *per se*, except "men of the world, such as Scott, and Moore, etc., or visionaries out of it, such as Shelley . . . your literary every day man and I never went well in company."[26] The last sentence makes the distinction clear. Against the greater writers, or those with whom he was in thorough accord, he had no grounds of complaint. But the "literary" individual, who breathes the air of books and letters and lives, a very chameleon, on the breath of popularity, he detested. Byron had no quarrel with the art or the vocation of poetry; the trade of poet he disliked. He felt uncomfortable in "literary" gatherings, or at least convinced himself so: "They seem to be an irritable set, and I wish myself well out of it. . . . What the devil had I to do with scribbling? It is too late to inquire, and all regret is useless. But, an it were to do again,—I should write again, I suppose."[27] Many men, doubtless, have had the same reaction toward the technical side of their profession.

The explanation of this attitude, besides the obvious one, may be based on several grounds. It must be reëmphasized that much of it was merely quizzical, provocative, a gauntlet thrown down to companions in conversation or correspondence. Byron, furthermore, was by birth and fortune not altogether poet. He was first of all a nobleman, a willing member of a class that imposed its own standards on all, oblivious of idiosyncrasies; and these standards he took only as seriously as the majority of his fellow peers. He shared their prejudice against money-making professions. Like the young bloods of Queen Elizabeth's court, he adopted poetizing as an elegant accomplishment, as a means of self-expression, or the occupation of an idle hour. He handled his pen, as Scott said of him, with the easy negligence of a gentleman. He wrote only as the spirit moved him, but not for money or for fame. When he did meet a demand, with his contribution to the opening of Drury Lane, he condescended. He avoided whatever would class him as "Byron, Poet," at the same time that he was avid to succeed. Above all, he could not risk rivalry with the mass of poets,[28] who were his social —and his intellectual—inferiors; he could allow himself no "literary envy."[29] Whatever his dreams of glory, he was always brought back to the reality that the poet, in the world, was not the equal of the nobleman.

But the influence of his class went deeper than that. He belonged to a group of men who were born to rule and had inherited a tradition of accomplishment which they followed proudly. His ambition, like theirs, was statesmanship: either to uphold the better cause in Parliament or to prove another Washington to a newly rising nation. Into such a tradition, oratory, as an effective instrument in Parliament, fitted better than the practice of poetry, which could have little practical effectiveness. But Byron's ambition to be an orator, fanned by a natural ability, was not equal to the constant discouragement of empty seats and inattentive listeners. His rank, again, was not altogether antithetical to the idealization of freedom, which was a traditional Whig principle; and this ideal, even in the cynical *Don Juan*, often sponsors stirring poetry and takes precedence over his art: "My great comfort is, that the temporary celebrity I have wrung from the world has been in the very teeth of all opinions and prejudices."[30] When fate opened opportunity to him and he sailed for Greece, he turned his back on his art, we can imagine, with a smile of self-content. "Poetry," he told Gamba, "should only occupy the idle. . . . In more serious affairs it would be ridiculous."[31] Of course, Byron went on composing, surreptitiously, when conditions allowed. But that weakness must be attributed to habit and to that other thing over which he had no thorough control—the Poetic Urge.

"It is odd enough," he stated on another occasion to Gamba, "that Stanhope, the soldier, is all for writing down the Turks; and I, the writer, am all for fighting them down."[32] That he was an excellent "fighter down" of the Turks, most historians, among whom Howard Nicholson speaks with greatest authority, are agreed. In fact, Byron is almost more the man of action than the poet. His life in Italy, which might have been a blissful pursuit of art for art's sake, is constantly disrupted by plans to colonize in South America or to help the Carbonari. An exile from his own country, he was in need of some occupation, in addition to that of writing, which should really satisfy his conscience; and therefore he grew tired of his compositions and suspected that his public did likewise.[33] To "all the speculations of those mere dreamers of another existence (I don't mean religiously but fancifully)" he preferred "the talents of action—of war, of the senate, even of science."[34] He feared the literature of sentiment, as injurious to manly and energetic qualities.[35] As we may note everywhere in his correspondence, he was irritated at the literary point of view: "No one should be a rhymer who could be anything better. And this is what annoys one, to see Scott [etc.], who might have all been agents and leaders, now mere spectators."[36] "Windham dwelt much on that regret, that 'he had not entirely devoted himself to literature and science!!!' . . . I cannot comprehend what debility of that mind could suggest such a wish. . . . What! would he have been a plodder? a metaphysician?—perhaps a rhymer? a scribbler?"[37] "I do think the preference of *writers* to *agents* . . . a sign of effeminacy, degeneracy, and weakness. Who would write, who had any thing better to do? . . . 'Actions—actions,' I say, and not writing,—least of all, rhyme . . . what a worthless, idle brood it is!"[38]

Worthless! idle! fanciful dreamers of another existence! that is the poetic brood. Compared to those who really do things in the world, they are singularly ineffective, mere froth on the surface of activity. Fiction is detached from reality, an escape into a universe of dreams by one who has not the courage to face the actual world. Poets are given more to sound than to sense, are not of the highest intellectual calibre. And even their flaunted "ideals" are but useless contradictions to reality: "I have no great esteem for poetical persons, particularly women; they have so much of the 'ideal' in *practice*, as well as *ethics*."[39] Poets give themselves to the portrayal of visions, where it is only the truth that matters: "Poets are said to succeed best in fiction; but this I deny, at least I always write best when the truth inspires me, and my satires, which are founded on truth, have more spirit than all my other productions, for they were written *con amore*."[40]

It is easy here to detect the orthodox neoclassic point of view. In his insistence on truth, his suspicion of the imagination, and his praise of the man of the world above the professional, Byron was following in the broad path blazed by his predecessors. It was easier, in his case, than in that of most of his contemporaries among the poets. He was by circumstance an *honnête homme*, and he associated with a group who were amateurs on principle; to the *souciance* of the artist he opposed the *insouciance* of the gentleman. It was not in the stream of his tradition to take the art of poesy prophetically, or to be bothered about the more technical details of writing. "Great part of the *Siege* is in (I think, what the learned call Anapests, (though I am not sure, being heinously forgetful of my metres and my *Gradus*)."[41] When he wrote, in *Beppo,* "One hates an author that's *all author,* fellows in foolscap uniforms turned up with ink,"[42] he was not only making fun of the Lake School; he was echoing a hundred lines in the poetry of Pope, and could have had in mind the confidential *Epistle to Dr. Arbuthnot:*

> I sought no homage from the race that write;
> I kept, like Asian monarchs, from their sight. . . .
> Heav'ns! was I born for nothing but to write?
> . . . . [Let it] be one poet's praise,
> That, if he pleased, he pleased in manly ways;
> That flattery, ev'n to kings, he held a shame,
> And thought a lie in verse or prose the same;
> That not in Fancy's maze he wandered long,
> But stoop'd to Truth, and moralized his song;
> That not for Fame, but Virtue's better end,
> He stood the curious foe, the timid friend.[43]

However, it is always necessary to modify any general statement regarding Byron. He echoed, but he also believed. While he gave voice to the ethics of a school, he expressed his own reactions. Whether the sentiments would still have been his in another environment, it is impossible to say. These sentiments, at this time, were his own.

An obvious comment on both Pope and Byron is that however much they disclaimed the pursuit of fame, they were keenly alive to their reputations. The creed of each is a gallimaufry of well-meant inconsistencies, of conflicting tendencies and assumptions never thoroughly reconciled.

Pope was at once a rationalist and a sentimentalist; Byron was a gentleman with an inflamed imagination. Whatever the latter's objection to writing, he did write, fortunately for those who enjoy him. The advantages of his prejudice offset the disadvantages. He is saved from an exaggerated emphasis on his importance in the rôle of poet; he is a practiser of the craft of poetry, not a seer, a *vates*. If he does not offer light that never was on sea or land, nor paints for us seductive dwellings for the imagination, he is a refreshing nonconformist among poets. If he is not the perfect poet that he might have been, he is the more a personality, the more a well-rounded figure to write biographies about. True, many other poets were well-rounded men, men of the world and of action, who combined an errant imagination with the prudent handling of affairs. But in none of them, not even in Pope and Dryden, do we feel such a constant emphasis on the immediate reality, such a hatred of humbuggery, such a conscientious and consistent dwelling with the certainty of facts. Byron, we feel, has always an eye on the earth, and his imaginary portraits are but colored reality. That is, at any rate, the man Byron we come to know in his letters and in Mr. Drinkwater's *Pilgrim of Eternity*. The usual contradiction to my own generalization, the extravagant imagination that introduces such a strong antithesis into his artistic nature, I shall reserve for a later discussion.

I have already excused myself from explaining why Byron, in spite of all his theories to the contrary, continued to write. Any explanation, on the ground of any one motive, can be only partial. Even a summary of motives does not seem satisfactory, for I shall still have left out the simple and fundamental fact—*Byron desired to write*. To him, writing, for no external reason, was a necessity, a "temptation too strong for the literary nature, which is not always human."[44] "Not write?" asks Pope,

> But then I think,
> And for my soul I cannot sleep a wink.
> I nod in company, I wake at night—
> Fools rush into my head, and so I write.[45]

Something was always rushing into Byron's head, and demanding that it be put down on paper. He wrote "from ... fullness of mind, from passion, from impulse, from many motives."[46] He composed in a stagecoach, during a thunderstorm, in bed.[47] No man, however, did less to justify his poetizing. He assured Stanhope "that he was so far from being a 'heavenborn poet,' that he was not conscious of possessing any talent in that way when a boy. . . . He also declared, that he had no love or enthusiasm for poetry."[48] If he was quizzing Stanhope, he seems perfectly sincere in a very similar passage in the *Letters and Journals*: "I feel exactly as you do about our 'art,' but it comes over me in a kind of rage every now and then ... and then, if I don't write to empty my mind, I go mad. As to that regular, uninterrupted love of writing. . . . I do not understand it."[49] He is always in the position of one who does something of which he is half proud and half ashamed, and is driven to find excuses to others and to his own conscience. Sometimes he defiantly accepts his rôle, and sometimes he apologizes. Poetry is often with him an instrument, a means of attack, defense, or self-explanation. It is often, too, highly didactic, like his projected newspaper, intended to "give the age some new lights on policy, poesy, biography, criticism, morality, theology, and all other *ism, ality*, and *ology*."[50] In his satires, as Lady Blessington said of him, he looks upon himself as a soldier in action, striking at those within his reach.[51] There are many reasons why he writes. But never is to be found among them the love of beauty for its own sake, or the longing for perfection of form.

The natural result was to accept poetry for what it was to him—a creation of emotion, a thing of momentary passion, a relief without any other ultimate purpose—"the lava of the imagination whose eruption prevents an earthquake."[52] It is, like his travels, an outburst of his general restlessness, no more. Much may be noted in his experience to justify his position. His first dash into poetry, according to his own statement, was the ebullition of a youthful passion for a first cousin, Miss Parker.[53] Whenever he was attacked, he sat down, on the spur of the moment, and wrote "all the *méchanceté* that comes into my head; and, as some of these sallies have merit, they amuse me, and are too good to be torn or burned, and so are kept. . . . All my malice evaporates in the effusions of my pen."[54] His recipe for writing poetry is to be in love, or miserable.[55] He put himself into a passion in order to continue his prose.[56] He believed that it was the air of Greece that made him a poet.[57] He explained poetry as "the expression of *excited passion*,"[58] and defined it as "the feeling of a Former world and Future."[59]

Of course, this is all excellent common sense. Poetry *is* largely a matter of emotion, and being in love is an excellent incentive to composing. Poets are generally men of high-strung and nervous, or exceptionally sensuous natures. Much of the greatest poetry has been written by those who are miserable, partly because they are so. Byron himself was both emotional and frequently miserable. But poets, worked upon by anger, love, fear, or any of a thousand agitations, nevertheless turn for justification to something else, to something external and apart. Furthermore, Byron preached "*excited passion*," not the emotion recollected in tranquillity of Wordsworth. He and the latter, and he unconsciously, were part of the contemporary romantic revolt, which demanded that before one should express one must feel, and the expression must be largely of the feeling. The principle, as he interprets it, is opposed to all deliberate art and to the slow growth of a conception that is necessary to the more extended works of genius. It contradicts the cardinal principle of classicism, that emotion for its own sake is bad, until assured by tradition, bound by form, and purified by taste. It is a contradiction, to a great extent, of those convictions of dilettanteism that we have been tracing. And yet it is largely a result of them. Poetry, in the code of the gentleman, should not become a serious pursuit to him who wished to do well in the world. It was primarily for his leisure moments, and for the weaker side of his personality, to refine his sentiments or to relieve his discontent. If he were of an emotional nature, his poetry was likely to be more emotional than otherwise.

Again I must point out (I fear *ad nauseam*) that this was not a theory in a vacuum, but a fact in the poet's consciousness. When Byron was stirred, he was moved to write, and he wrote best when strongly excited—or at least he then enjoyed his composition and, seeing it against the glow of passion, conceived of it as his best. Even more than this, he could depend, at times, upon his passion to write itself, almost without the conscious help of his will—when he attacked Southey, or composed "She walks in beauty."[60] There is a report, by La Guiccioli, of verses composed during a night of delirium, in their form and texture showing no signs of mental disturbance.[61] Where there was no conscious will or purpose, strong emotion was his muse, and under its impetus alone he wrote.

It was well for his poetical productivity that he was of a highly keyed nature, stirred violently by feelings that could find no sufficient outlet in action. He was worried by the immediate problems of living; he was open to the smallest vexations: his life was a succession of needless quarrels and fits of passion. Especially did certain stimuli settle themselves in his mind, there to create their own irritations: a prejudice, such as his predilection for black eyes; a phrase such as the oft repeated "repair my irreparable affairs"; an unanswered question as to the natures of sin, or death; or more local and individual problems—love, marriage, and infamy—which left him no peace so long as he could not make up his mind about them. These subsisted in and upon his consciousness, feeding on his desires, coloring his mind, stimulating or checking his actions, introducing order into chaos, or disrupting an already disordered universe. Experiences affected him vividly, intensely, and their impression lingered stubbornly with him. Everything about him bore witness to the compressed energy of his nature. "The mind of Lord Byron was like a volcano, full of fire and wealth, sometimes calm, often dazzling and playful, but ever threatening. It ran swift as the lightning from one subject to another, and occasionally burst forth in passionate throes of the intellect, nearly allied to madness. . . . In the dead of night, I was frequently startled from my sleep by the thunders of his Lordship's voice, either raging with anger or roaring with laughter, and rousing . . . all the inmates of the dwelling from their repose."[62] "His conversation resembled a stream, sometimes smooth, sometimes rapid, and sometimes rushing down in cataracts; it was a mixture of philosophy and slang—of everything—like his own *Don Juan*. . . . When he did engage with earnestness in conversation, his ideas succeeded each other with such uncommon rapidity that he could not control them."[63] Energy and irritability together made necessary a constant state of activity that Byron could never thoroughly attain to; and the result was fitfulness, whim, instability, or frenzied exercise. "The irritability of genius," Lady Blessington reports him to have said, "is nothing more or less than a delicacy of organization, which gives a susceptibility to impressions to which coarser minds are never subject, and cultivation and refinement but increase it, until the unhappy victim becomes a prey to mental hypochondriasm."[64] Byron is *"per excellenza . . . une ame qui se tourmente, un esprit violent,"*[65] and only in view of the fever of his disposition may he be judged. He was aware of this quality of mobility or temperament in his nature, as more than one passage in *Don Juan* testifies; and his life is one long battle with it, and triumph over it.

Connected somehow with this superabundant energy, were his frequent fits of deep depression, relieved by hysterical laughter, which have already been spoken of. Their effect was in general the same. They demanded occupation for the mind, release for his spirits, which sought vent most naturally in poetry. "The only relief I find [from my afflictions] springs from the composition of poetry, which necessitates contemplations that lift me above the stormy mist of sensations,"[66] is the avowal of so different a being as Shelley. Byron was, furthermore, pursued throughout life by the fear of madness. His inclination was all the greater, then, toward poetry, which alone, with action, gave his feelings relief. "I have somewhere read . . . that poets *rarely* go mad. I suppose the writer means that their insanity effervesces and evaporates in verse."[67] These fits of melancholy and black bile were the incitements to literary labor, but they did not determine its mood. They drove him to composition, but once embarked, he was open to the suggestion of his subject or to the obsessions of his fancy. The tenor of any of his works is an unsafe indication of the momentary state of the man. He was struck by the fact that much of his best humorous verse was written in his blackest moments,[68] and arrived thereby at the rather commonplace observation that the comic genius is essentially of a melancholy cast. Nevertheless, taken as wholes, his works do reflect, more profoundly than he realized, his inmost nature. Throughout the short period of his creative life, there is the mark of a fluctuating development, or rather an artistic pilgrimage, which is not merely a question of influences or the trial-and-error approach to a literary means of expression, but the gradual growth of a personality. He did not, in *Beppo* and *Don Juan,* find himself, in the sense that he accidentally discovered what had all along been inside him. He had first of all to create himself. Not till the time of his greatest poem, does the man appear in full stature, direct and self-confident.

As influential as any theory of poetry or of the poet, is his theory and practice of composition. Of the external conditions of writing, we have word here and there in the reports of his friends and in occasional assertions in his own conversations and correspondence. He wrote, usually, at night,[69] after returning from the theatre, or from a bout or talk with friends, or at any rate after the cares of the day were over, when he was quiet, alone, and free from the dangers of interruption. He retired, generally, to his study, sometimes locking the door; but at other times, apparently, in a turmoil of friends, stopping to talk with them or to play billiards, or so absorbed in the act of writing that he did not notice their presence. Usually, at his tensest moments, he had to be alone. For the composition of *The Bride of Abydos* he shut himself up in a dark street in London, and refused himself to everyone until he had completed the narrative.[70] Sometimes he drank wine or brandy to support his spirits, but not to excess. He was in the main an opportunist in his methods. He needed no conscious preparation for writing. He wrote when the mood was on him and as the mood directed, tensely or leisurely, and, later in life, by the iron determination of his will. He chose night because it was convenient, and because then he was most thoroughly alive. Maybe he had acquired the habit when at Cambridge, as a relief to anticipated insomnia.

Only in one way did he indulge in eccentricity. He composed at great speed, not merely, we may suspect, by nature, but as a proof of his virtuosity. "I [write] with rapidity and rarely with pains,"[71] is a fair enough statement of his practice. He evidently took pride in his facility. "He told me," writes Dr. Henry Muir, "that he had composed *Beppo* in two days.... Lord B. seemed pleased when telling this."[72] He used his practice of rapid writing as an excuse for poetical lapses in his works,[73] and this excuse was echoed by La Guiccioli: "Who would ever have blamed him for the slight errors which fell from his pen in *Don Juan*—a poem written hastily and with carelessness?"[74] Here was too much, perhaps, of the affectation of the gentleman, who would dash off poetry spontaneously, with a flick of his pen. But here was also the impatience of the man, anxious to put himself on paper and have an end of it. Then, too, Byron was by nature quick. He thought swiftly, he spoke fluently, and his pen had but to keep pace with his thoughts. He is not to be blamed that mentally he was no plodder. Neither are his words to be accepted too rigidly. When he wrote to Murray he nibbled his pen.

Byron, as a matter of fact, had few eccentricities of composition; nor are there to be found in these any notable influences on his work. But in addition to the gentleman, he is, at least in his practice, unconsciously the romantic. Teresa speaks of his appearance when, under the inspiration of genius, his soul was tormented with the desire to expend itself.[75] He depended entirely upon his genius, the immediate desire, not upon careful planning and the slow fruition of the idea. Composition was something removed from common life, a distinct faculty or soul,[76] and could not be called, like Glendower's spirits, from the abyss. "My poesy is one thing, I am another.... My poetry is a separate faculty.... I can only write when the *estro* is upon me; at all other times I am myself."[77] He conceives of writing as a sort of writhing in agony, "a torture which I must get rid of, but never as a pleasure"[78]—the pains of labor to be rid of his poetical offspring, would hardly be a forced simile.

Such an attitude from the first could not but introduce a sharp dichotomy into his works. It is natural and legitimate in the poet to leave much to the unexpected, to the sudden burgeonings or the unplanned shortcuts which no amount of prearrangement can anticipate. Every poet must depend on the inspiration of the moment to write at all; a philosophical treatise or a doctoral dissertation on the Greek verb may be hammered out by the cold reason, but a poem without emotion is unthinkable—or at any rate dull. Short lyrics, furthermore, are often the products of moments of rapture, as several lyrics of Byron's own so thrillingly prove. But the mood unsupported cannot write long epics, or well wrought dramas, or even balanced satire. Byron is just a bit too sincere, when he *must* say what comes uppermost at whatever cost, and can say no more;[79] a seasoning of insincerity is of use to the artist. When the mood passes, Byron turns often upon his own composition; or in a fit of weakness allows it to be published. Thus came to light many poems of which he was not and had no reason to be proud. His development as an artist, if not hampered, is irremediably confused, to the further confusion of the investigator. His productions are marked off distinctly into two classes, those he wrote deliberately at the instigation of his will or intellect and those he fell into. Karl Koenig, in his excellent study of *English Bards*, says of him, "Here unconsciously, within the bounds of a single work, rages the same struggle that was later to lead to a conscious dichotomy in Byron's judgment and creation, the struggle between his intellect, which inclined him to the side of classicism, and his poetic gift, which was wholly romantic."[80] Unfortunately for his ideals, his excuse has a large foundation in fact. He had a mighty *estro* and a smaller poetic will; or rather, the best of his intentions often failed to stir his imagination so much as an accidental longing. He was impelled by the immediate reality, he could not "deal in generals."[81] Much of his poetry in his early years was no more than a reaction, and as a reaction appealed more largely to his public than the cooler product of the will. The result is two series of compositions, the one of the nature of *English Bards and Scotch Reviewers,* and the other culminating in *Childe Harold* and the romances. Of the former series alone Byron was proud, perhaps, as Mr. Coleridge suggests, judging the merit of the work by the difficulty of accomplishment.[82] But the latter established his fame.

If we are to take his words literally, he depended entirely on inspiration for his poetry, wrote once, and never corrected. This is the most convenient explanation of his carelessness, and may have had something to do with his contention, that "no poetry is generally good—only by fits and starts—and you are lucky to get a sparkle here and there,"[83] as an excuse and palliative for his own flagrant offences. This notion of the poet-at-work is very easy to picture, since it has already been worded brilliantly by himself: "I can't *furbish*. I am like the tyger (in poesy), if I miss my first Spring, I go growling back to my Jungle."[84] "There is no second. I can't correct; I can't, and I won't. Nobody ever succeeds in it, great or small. . . . You must take my things as they happen to be. . . . I would rather give them away than hack and hew them. I don't say that you are not right; I merely assert that I cannot better them."[85] Byron, either by his pride or by his petulance, imposed such a view of himself upon his associates and, through them, upon posterity. Medwin writes that he hardly altered a word for whole pages and never corrected a line after publication;[86] and Mary Shelley gives her opinion that in an entire drama he changed no word after he had written it down, that he composed and corrected in his mind.[87] Karl Koenig draws a similar picture: "He confines his labors to the production of the poetry; as soon as he sees his verses before him on paper, he leaves them to their fate. The arrangement of the whole, in short, the entire business of revision is distasteful to him and he surrenders it with joy to obliging friends."[88]

Both Mary Shelley and Herr Koenig are to this extent correct. Byron's impatience led him to write down rapidly what he had to say, and to dislike intensely the (to him) more mechanical business of correcting. Consequently he broke out in wrathful strictures, not only on proofreading, but on mere improvement of the text. It is evident that his joy is in the first step of composition. Thereafter, since he has really expressed perfectly what he had to say, or is content to rest with approximation, he does not return willingly to the poem. He had not Keats's fine sense of a gradually ripening expression, arrived at painstakingly through inadequate attempts. He is like the tiger, not that he does not spring again, but that with him the first spring is the thing, and he returns only reluctantly. He has no joy in building on a mediocre commencement. The slow growth is not on paper, but within him; it is less the maturing of the expression, than the forming of the idea. By the time he is about to spring, his poem is definitely worked out in his head, ready to be stated. Outwardly his dramas develop slowly at first; but meanwhile they are taking shape in his head, and suddenly, with almost incredible speed, he completes three capable acts in a fortnight. Or he worries all the afternoon over humorous rhymes, solves their problems while his horse is at a canter, and composes ten stanzas of *Don Juan* that night in his study.

The simile of the "tyger," however, though a happy

figure and appealing to the imagination, is hardly an exact report of the poet's method. It has been accepted and quoted, we may guess, more because it has been so well expressed, than for the purity of its truth. Byron has suffered too often from his genius for expression, and he has too often been judged by his words, his memorable words, and not by his actions. It is certain here that his actions are not in accord with his theorizings. "You will think there is no end to my villainous emendations,"[89] he wrote on occasion to Lord Holland, and the successive editions of his works or comparisons of manuscripts with the edited writings, bear witness to a frequent if not consistent correction. It is almost impossible to make any general statement about Byron without at once modifying or contradicting it. Dissatisfied with the first draught, he corrected it: "I have never yet been satisfied with any one of my own productions; I cannot read them over without detecting a thousand faults."[90] His earliest poetic production he destroyed scrupulously, in order to give it an *entire new form*.[91] He burnt an early novel and the first scene and sketch of a comedy, and admitted that the pleasure of burning was as great as that of breaking into print.[92] His practice, so he says of himself, was to scrawl rapidly and to smooth as much as he could, though never enough to satisfy him.[93]

Yet, for all the evidence against the tiger simile, there is in it a modicum of truth. His pleasure, as I have remarked before, was in the first composing. Thereafter he corrected, because he was dissatisfied with his work and saw that it must be bettered—conscientiously, as he read proof, and while he corrected, he protested.[94] His improvements are seldom more than emendations. They consist in the removal of obvious flaws or absurdities, or in the substitutions of one word for another for no very clear reason. We do not remember his second thought as we do his first. He does not transform his early attempt, and very often, we feel, he does not improve it. His sympathy is ever with the first child of his imagination, no matter how he may later reclothe it. "In composition I do not think that *second* thoughts are best, though *second* expressions may improve the first ideas."[95] Review of his poetry was to him a rather bleak duty with few compensations, and at times his patience gave way and he balked: "I will let the old couplet stand, with its half rhymes 'sought' and 'wrote'."[96] Partly for this reason and partly because his taste was not always of the surest, he has gained the reputation of being a careless or a clumsy craftsman.

The significance of the textual changes, however, does not cease with the amount of the change. Something in the manner is at once arresting and throws further light on the artist. A great many of the emendations are not Byron's own, but the result of suggestions by others. Byron pays heed to the opinion of many people, far more than we should expect of so impatient and independent a person. His friends seemed surer of the relative merits of his poetry than did he. When Hodgson, for instance, disliked a passage in one of the tales, he informed Byron with great energy; and the latter fretted, but revised.[97] On the advice of Dallas, he altered the verse "Mend thy life and sin no more," to "Mend thy line. . . . ," omitted a passage on Lord Carlisle in the *English Bards and Scotch Reviewers*, and added Crabbe among his list of models for rhyme.[98] He adopted immediately the alteration proposed by so obscure a person as William Bankes.[99] "With bloody beak," in his sketch of Napoleon, he changed to "with bloody talon," because Reinagle, "a better ornithologist than I," had assured him that his trope was untrue to nature.[100] He altered "Bright as the gem of Giamschid" to "Bright as the ruby" when Moore proved "Giamschid" a dissyllable, and re-altered to "Bright as the jewel," when he was further reminded that eyes like a ruby would be bloodshot.[101] He went even further than this. He is continually asking, in his letters, for advice on the fine points of composition. He sends alternate versions of a line, requesting Murray to seek the opinion of others as to which shall be retained. "Which will be best? 'painted trappings,' or 'pictured purple,' or 'pictured trappings,' or 'painted purple'? Perpend, and let me know,"[102] he writes to his publisher, with a semi-humorous shrug. He cannot, on another occasion, decide between "repay" and "reward."[103] Usually it is Gifford who is appealed to as a court of last resort,[104] but sometimes Byron is less specific in his request for authorities,[105] or he appeals to Murray's whole "Utican Senate"—Gifford, Frere, Rose, Hobhouse, and others—for judgment.[106]

There are two obvious comments on such a practice. One is that Byron is good-natured as an artist. Clearly, he is. His scathing satires, written in vexed moments, have overemphasized his occasional fits of wrath. It may be restated as a general maxim that the world has misjudged the poet because of his genius for expression. When he was angry, he wrote well, and we remember and judge him by the fruit of his muse. But outside of his spells of anger, Byron was the most inoffensive of men. He is not given to that deadlier form of satire, the dissection of a character for art's sake. When he attacks, we recognize that he is angry and we take his mood into account; he makes no pretence of being fair, and we do not accept his comments as final appraisals. Once the mood is past, he is ready to admit his bias, and sometimes to destroy his production. He does not hurt for the sake of hurting, but because to take the offensive is the best means of defending himself, and always because he feels that his enemy deserves castigation. When his wit occasionally strikes home where he has not intended to scathe, he is willing to expunge even a witticism from his work.[107]

Our second inference has more to do with the artist. Byron is not so self-assured as we might expect a great artist to be. If he were certain of his productions, he would not turn so consistently to the advice of friends. He is uncertain, ultimately, of his taste. Surrounded as he is by men whose judgment he admires, he nevertheless cannot thoroughly make their judgments his own. Their opinion, and the surviving principle of taste, the tradition inherited from classicism, he accepts as his conscience; but it is never so fixed inside him that he knows just what it is. He is, after all, a barbarian who worships at the shrine of a past civilization. As much as he may, he honors and imitates it; but he remains the barbarian, nevertheless. Of his opinions and his emotions he is sure. He will not change the ideas in his poems to suit the orthodox; "but if there are any alterations in the versification that you would like to be made, I will turn rhymes and tag stanzas as much as you please."[108] He is always conscious of the critic, that bugbear of his classic forerunners. As a poet he feels a little absurd, and as a romantic poet apologetic. Wit he aspires to and succeeds in, but he cannot turn an epigram.[109] He is always conscious of being outside the inner circle. And for that reason he pays exaggerated respect to Gifford, Rogers, and Crabbe, who are among the élite. Partly he is bending to the standards of his group and his caste. But their standards have also become his ideal, an ideal he cannot quite attain to.

And yet, for all his modesty, he is a famous and adored poet. He is received not only by the mob, by foolish romantic women and a lionizing society, but by the very élite, as a great poet. Somewhere, surely, there is incongruity. Either his admirers are grossly mistaken and his poetry is an ephemeral fad, or he has that other quality of the great poet—not polish and perfection, certainly, but force, grandeur, originality. He sometimes feels, giving heed to the demagogue within him, that the final test of his poetry *is* his popularity, and that only in the voice of his public can he discern his right to fame.[110] He is therefore willing at times to seek out its opinion, and to conform to it; he even regards his independence as a weakness, since it mars or prevents his popularity. But always he returns to the small group who know, to the solitary reader,[111] to the few of taste and judgment, who have studied the ancients, who are immersed in the spirit of England's Golden Age, and can determine truly the merits of a poem: "Has any one seen them and judged of them? that is the criterion by which I will abide."[112]

Fame as an abstraction may have lured him on, but he never gave himself whole-heartedly to the pursuit of glory. Posterity he seems to have looked on, humorously, as an unwarranted assumption, or as the consolation of those who cannot secure a more immediate audience. Glory he despised, while enjoying his own, as the pursuit of a demagogue, as a distortion of truth, as "a certain portion of uncertain paper" on which no man can rely. His statement later, that he had been writing from the fullness of his mind and the love of fame,[113] is in need of definition. Lacking Shelley's more vital concern for future generations, he was more at one with the past. His "fame" was partially mere transient popularity; that aspect even his principles could not release him from. But it rested more in the association of his name with the great of old, the being a new figure in the line of a long tradition, not an innovator and not a prophet, but the author of deathless poetry. For such an assumption we have no direct word of his own; but it alone is in line with his instinctive respect for authority, his dislike on principle of those who introduced the new. Here also is complexity, for it is certain that he admired *Christabel* unreservedly and probably modeled the choruses in *Heaven and Earth* upon Southey's *Curse of Kehama.* But in his own practice, he falls back always upon precedent, if not at the moment of composition, at least as an afterthought and an excuse. So he justifies his use of the Spenserian stanza in *Childe Harold* by reference to Thomson and Beattie. And so he censures another innovation, one obviously "upon system": "What does Helga Herbert mean by his *Stanza?* which is octave got drunk or gone mad. He ought to have his ears boxed with Thor's hammer for rhyming so fantastically."[114]

CHAPTER V

ESCAPE

IT was on the whole a hostile world, in 1809, for an author with principles like these. It is true that the critics, in the main, and the great and powerful *Edinburgh Review* would have been on his side, that is to say, as the body of critics is ever on the side of an author—willing to agree with his professions of belief but ready and eager to carp at his failings. The emotional note of the time was for change. And if there was a stronger reaction politically that battled the French Revolution and the new waves of thought, it was confined to the prosaic, the timid, the dull, and the middle-aged, not those who wrote poetry. More powerful than any theories of composition were the stimulations of the time—a world in arms, empires unmade and made overnight, the spectacular passing of an old order and the orgies of a new, the rise to power in England itself of the *nouveau riche*, battening upon the spoils of war, its hypocrisies in pretending to the virtues of the class it was usurping in power, the very fever of the established order in stamping out heresies. Everything tended to stir a young man, impressionable and fiery, to revolt on the principle of revolt. When reaction gained control in politics and patriotism became the order of the day, the older generation of poets turned their attention into other fields, or joined the reaction. Younger spirits vented their daring in artistic innovation or heretical tenets in philosophy or esthetics. Gathering head from the impetus of the last decade of the eighteenth century, from the rise of the ballad and folklore to critical attention, and from the publication of the *Lyrical Ballads,* there sprang to life a new age of metrical experiment—dead and done with since the days of the Elizabethans. The time was not one of authority, but of experimentation; its keynote was not the intellect, but the emotions. For those reasons it is called "romantic."

But stronger than any mere effect of the times was the temperament of the poet. Byron, in appealing to the principles of classicism, was crying out to be saved from himself, or at least from one side of himself. So long as he was in constant command of his creative faculties, he was classic, neoclassic to the bone. But ever his emotion, or his imagination, nourished on the Gothic romancing of the time, intruded, and his principles were forced to the wall.

There is no clearer example of this than in Byron's first significant publication after the *Hours of Idleness,* his *English Bards and Scotch Reviewers.*[1] Two possible interpretations of the work have been mentioned: it was the outpouring of a very angry man, a theory strengthened by several admissions of Byron's own;[2] or it was the deliberate production of a careful artisan, working conscientiously for a purpose and keeping in mind assured models and principles of art. The poem furnishes materials for both points of view, because it is both the one and the other type. In the first draft, the much shorter poem named *British Bards,* it is altogether of the latter type, the conscientious production. But before the work was finally published, something happened to affect the tone of the undertaking. Byron read the scathing anonymous review of his *Hours of Idleness* in the *Edinburgh Review*—not altogether fair but in the main deserved—which he so long and inaccurately attributed to Jeffrey. His first reaction was to accept his fate, and submit in silence.[3] But his anger would not be denied. Within a fortnight he had begun to reply. Poetry leaped from his pen. In a short while he had doubled the length of his poem, but this time in a resentful, bitter mood, that hit for the sake of hitting, in an explosion of wrath. Moore reports in his *Life*, that after the first twenty lines of the reply, Byron, till then in the height of passion, began to feel considerably better.[4] But the critique had already wrought its damage. The satire had ceased to be a deliberate work of art and had become a safety valve. Byron's attitude toward it had changed. For the time he was the belligerent castigator, not only of the enemies or the fools of society, but of his personal enemies in particular. From now on, when he discussed his satire, he kept his hand on an imaginary sword, ready at the least excuse to fight. Even in the midst of the seclusion and the varying interests of his travel-years, the mood persisted: "If any one is savage and wants satisfaction for my satire, write, that I may return and give it."[5] "You refresh me greatly with the tidings of my satire; if there be any of that martial spirit to require trial by combat, . . ."[6] But gradually there is a change. The mood passes, the anger dies away, and, with it, the man begins to feel that he has been unjust and unprincipled. Later, meeting the very men whom he has assaulted, he is the more convinced of his error. The result is that he repudiates not only his mistakes but the whole production, and turns his back on his favorite child: "To the republication of [*English Bards*] will I at no time consent. I would not reprint them on any consideration. I don't think them good for much, even in the point of poetry."[7]

The declaration marks a shift in interests, that is at the culmination of a period. The travels in the Near East are far more deeply important than a mere whim of the poet's put into effect; they had a profounder result than merely to furnish matter for his succeeding poetry. They were entered upon at a time when Byron, more nearly than at any other period, was on the path to being "all author." He had published one fairly successful work, the *Hours of Idleness*, and another, the *English Bards and Scotch Reviewers*, much more popular, which had made his name known and regarded in the best literary circles. After many attempts in many directions, in a fever of writing, he had found himself in satire. He was a willing member of his own class, an admirer of their admirations, an aspirer to their esteem, a would-be member of their society without a markedly different personality of his own. Only in one way was he to be distinguished from the mass—by his eternal restlessness, which led him to writing for a relief and an outlet for his energy. The travels satisfied a similar need for seeing something, taking part in something, leading a colorful and significant existence. But they did more. They carried him, at this impressionable age, away from the influences of his class, plunged him into the midst of strange customs and foreign prejudices, and furnished him the most vivid experiences of his life. Above all, they dammed the main current of his development, turning aside his interests into other channels, weakening his artistic purposes and his ambitions in literature. Once more, when reëmbarked upon his career, he becomes uncertain of his intentions; once more he questions his desire to be an author: "I keep no journal, nor have I any intention of scribbling my travels. I have done with authorship, and if, in my last production, I have convinced the critics or the world that I was something more than they took me for, I am satisfied; nor will I hazard *that reputation* by a future effort. It is true I have some others in manuscript, but I leave them for those who come after me; and, if deemed worth publishing, they may serve to prolong my memory when I myself shall cease to remember. I have a famous Bavarian artist taking some views of Athens, etc., etc., for me. This will be better than scribbling, a disease I hope myself cured of."⁸ The habit of scribbling was too strong in him to overcome, but he was no longer proud of it. Or maybe the old doubts of himself and his purposes had once more intruded. At any rate, he was no longer the self-confident and arrogant author, sure of what he wanted to do and doing it.

His purposes retained somewhat of their former impetus, but mainly they were a spent wave. In the month of March, 1811, he composed two satires in the heroic couplet, one, *Hints from Horace*, even more Popean and self-renunciatory than the *English Bards*, in its faithful adaptation of Horace "to our new school of poetry."⁹ After his return he composed a third, distinctly inferior satire, *The Waltz*, from which the spirit of satire seemed to have departed and left only the corpse behind. Too much, here, must not be attributed to the effect of his travels. The truth is that in *English Bards and Scotch Reviewers* and in *Hints from Horace* he had said all that he had to say in conventional satire. Any repetition of his success would have been repetition merely; he had no spur to prick his intent. His new experiences, even his reading, were not the most appropriate matter for the older satire; he needed a newer, more elastic form, which would admit the enthusiasms and the raptures he was experiencing. This form he happened upon in *Childe Harold*.

Any analysis of *Childe Harold* must commence with a description of its nature. Since the preface was written long after the poetry, as an apologetic introduction to a possibly hostile audience, it is not thoroughly to be trusted. It is better to look at the poem itself. This has, as Mr. Drinkwater claims for it, "vigour, rapidity of movement, and sharpness of impact. . . . [But] of design there is little or none, nor is there any evidence that Byron knew what selection meant. We can discover no controlling impulse that subdues the brilliant material to its own purpose."¹⁰ The poem is noticeably a medley, from many sources, without conscious aim or conscious selection, having more unity in its derivation than in its destination. It derives artistically from the traditional Spenserian stanza, through Thomson, Shenstone, and above all Beattie, with that stanza's characteristic rhythms and its pseudo-archaic diction. Into its composition enter the many strains of influence from Byron's reading, more notably from those modern productions against which he had fulminated in the *English Bards*. The songs of Moore, the immorality of Strangford, the narrative style of Scott, verbal tricks and turns of the ballad, and the weaker more fantastic neoclassic diction sometimes reminiscent of Pope's *Iliad*, but more often of lesser poetasters, intrude upon the original tone of the Spenserian stanza. There is little choice, almost no effort at arrangement. The poem is "on Ariosto's plan, that is to say, no plan at all."[11] The strength is in the conception of the hero and the spirit and fire of the poetry. The unity is entirely one of tone, not of artistic structure.

The poem, briefly, is not a conscious work of art at all, in its broader outlines. It is essentially a travelogue, a poetical diary of Byron's journey, a series of poetical impressions of scenery and peoples, with notes attached for accuracy and for additional information. Evidently, though it absorbed Byron's attention for the while, he did not look upon it as a great effort of the imagination. The clearest hint we have of it from any source other than Byron during its composition, is a statement of Hobhouse, on October 22, 1809, that "Byron is all this time engaged in writing a long poem in the Spenserian stanza."[12] The poem is written with a minimum of artistic will. It is a travelogue not because Byron admired travelogues and was particularly anxious to compose one, but because while he was traveling it was the easiest and most natural thing to write. He was giving way to the poetic impulse to express his emotions, without any very assured intention of ever publishing the result. "[His] creative power," to quote again from Mr. Drinkwater, "is almost uniformly at the command of external suggestion. . . . Like some altogether smaller poets, he needed occasion upon which to work, but unlike them he did not have to wait for occasion; not only would any occasion serve, but almost any occasion had to serve."[18] Be that as it may, the occasion, or occasions, was with him, and he acted upon it blindly. He stumbled upon destiny by following his old weakness, of giving way to the emotion of the moment.

The genesis of the poem, finally, may be traced back to Byron's old motive and excuse for writing—escape from the moment and relief of his feelings. Ticknor records a reference by Byron to the impressions of extreme discontent, under the spell of which he composed *Childe Harold*.[14] Byron broke out into poetry as into a rash, from fever, and wrote, not because he had any ultimate end in view, but merely because poetry, the more personal and emotional the better, was for the moment necessary. He had no reason either from his motives or, in his judgment, from his accomplishment, to be proud of the composition. He kept the manuscript packed away half-forgotten in his trunk, and showed it to Dallas alone, almost by accident, on his return.

The consequent story is too well known to repeat. Dallas probably took on himself greater credit for the publication than was his due. But it is clear that Byron was indisposed to risk his poem before the public, that he yielded only reluctantly to Dallas's insistence, and that he preferred to it his *Hints from Horace*. Even Hobhouse in a contradictory mood admitted the influence of Dallas.[15] Byron slowly set about preparing the volume for the press, altered passages in the proof, composed additional stanzas, modified the extreme skepticism of some of its observations, submitted the manuscript to the inspection of Campbell and Gifford,[16] and, if we may accept Dallas's word for it, followed docilely the good advice showered on him by his cousin.[17] Even thus emended, the poem still called for an apologetic preface, in which the weaknesses, uneasily sensed, were explained sophistically or admitted.

With the immediate popularity and fame of the poem, Byron's appreciation of its virtues was naturally enhanced. He looked back on it, during his London sojourn, as his unquestioned masterpiece: "If ever I did any thing original," he wrote in 1814, "it was in *Childe Harold*, which *I* prefer to the other things always, after the first week."[18] He vaguely promised Dallas to complete the work,[19] though his indecision prevented him, at least as he had originally intended; partly, as he told Ticknor, because he had not the opportunity to devote all his thoughts to it,[20] but mainly because the original stimulus of travel was lacking. The completion was left until another and severer stimulus had been suffered. Byron's fondness for the poem was apparently that for a first very successful work. To his appreciation, there is later added a note of humorous half-disparagement suggesting that he did not, at least then, take the first two cantos as seriously as did his public: "The two first cantos of C^e H^d were completed at twenty-two, and they are written as if by a man older than I shall probably ever be."[21]

One phase of his popularity was not an unalloyed satisfaction. He had attempted, with the publication of the poem, to forestall any identification of himself with his hero. For this reason he objected to the appearance of his name on the title-page,[22] and added a warning in the preface, that the Childe was a fictitious character introduced to give some connection to the piece. But in spite of his protests, the public accepted him as that dark and sinister person whom he had described. He could never quite escape from this creature of his imagination. Wherever he went women were startled and intrigued by what they imagined to be behind his pained shyness and reserve. Dowagers condemned and foolish younger women, notable among them Caroline Lamb, fell violently in love. Byron, no matter what his protests, bore about with him an aura of hidden sins and secret griefs, an abysmal melancholy and misanthropy, not altogether at one with his nature.

And yet, his protests must not be heeded too rigorously. Childe Harold was, in a way, Byron. His original name had been "Childe Burun," borrowed from the older form of "Byron," and he had developed as a sort of perverse phantasm of the poet's imagination. Unsubstantial creation that he is, it is impossible to explain him in the poem except as a personality whom his creator imagined himself to be. He is not intruded on the poem for the sake of regularity. He is with the poet from the beginning, almost the *raison d'être* of the poem, and takes on so readily the characteristics of the man Byron that the two cannot be fundamentally opposed. Had they been thoroughly differentiated in the mind of the poet, he would not have been forced to protest so violently. The difficulty was that Byron was near enough by nature to the Childe to be confused with him readily. Too easily he could be suspected of the wickedness and satiety that he had depicted, and it was to save himself from being interpreted altogether as the other, that his protests were made, unavailingly.

The impression effected by the poem was far-reaching in its influence upon the character and career of the man. He was received everywhere less as a poet than as a striking, romantic, and mysterious figure. Such a reception could not but react, finally, on his idea of himself. For the next four years his life is the disastrous result of playing up to the popular conception of him. He was caught in the stream which he had unintentionally let loose, and swept by the current off his feet, poetically and otherwise. After spasmodic attempts to recover himself, he gave in fully. His imagination itself was made captive. His heroes in successive romances are but slight modifications of the Childe, undergoing adventures Byron liked to imagine for himself, and eternally the victims of brooding misanthropy and lawless desire.

That Childe Harold is not a very original figure, in his combination of characteristics, is generally recognized. He is another phase of an already fashionable type, of which Moore's Zeluco, Mrs. Radcliffe's Schedoni, Lewis's Ambrosio, and Scott's Marmion were outstanding examples. He is the ideal hero of the Gothic novels with which the young imagination of Byron had been fed. But to name the sources or the predecessors of the character is merely to explain why the material was ready to his hand. The Byronic hero is not a mere compendium of inherited vices and virtues, nor is he a pale reflection of someone else's idea, but a striking personality, very much alive. The description of Lara is unforgettable:

> There was in him a vital scorn of all. . . .
> He stood a stranger in this breathing world,
> An erring spirit from another hurled;
> A thing of dark imaginings. . . .
> His early dreams of good outstript the truth,
> And troubled manhood followed baffled youth, . . .
> And wasted powers for better purpose lent;
> And fiery passions that had poured their wrath
> In hurried desolation o'er his path,
> And left the better feelings all at strife
> In wild reflection o'er his stormy life; . . .
> He called on Nature's self to share the shame,
> And charged all faults upon the fleshly form
> She gave to clog the soul, and feast the worm;
> Till he at last confounded good and ill,
> And half mistook for fate the acts of will:
> Too high for common selfishness, he could

> At times resign his own for others' good,
> But not in pity—not because he ought,
> But in some strange perversity of thought,
> That swayed him onward with a secret pride
> To do what few or none would do beside.[23]

The description, keenly analytic, introspective, is telling; and it is the more suggestive for what it does not explain. Lara is not a clothier's model to drape fine phrases over, but somehow, across the abyss of time, he appeals to the imagination. He is a strong character, an apotheosis of mind caught and betrayed in a recalcitrant body, just the kind of man to appeal to a young man's fancy,—a great one fallen, a mighty wreck, an impressive ruin. And ever his sin is of too mysterious a caste to alienate our sympathy; we may take a pleasure in his transgressions, since he has clearly been the very devil of a fellow. Mr. Mallock, in his incomparable recipe for making a Satanic poem, has expressed the matter far better than I may hope to: "Take a couple of fine deadly sins; and let them hang before your eyes until they become racy. Then take them down, dissect them, and stew them for some time in a solution of weak remorse; after which they are to be devilled with mock-despair."[24]

The figure is not a difficult one for the average man to imagine himself, or at least to want to imagine himself, and Byron, at this time, in both his strength and his weakness, was closer to his creation than perhaps he realized. Great powers rusted in him unused; meant for better things, he was given to drifting, to secret meaningless amours; above all needing to seize control of himself, it was easier for him to imagine himself another and forceful character. It is all a question of the imagination. Here was one who could withdraw his creator from an intolerable present to a brilliant dream, from impotence to the possibility of action, though that action was to be crime, from existing as a mere man of society to being the wandering outlaw of his own dark mind, who could renew the memories of Byron's most vivid experiences and live through more vivid experiences still. He is enough like Byron for the latter to enter easily under his skin, but unlike him he is free, even from the shackles of a conscience. He is a weakness and an indulgence of the poet's imagination; but the poet contracted a fondness for the rôle. Byron was accused by the artist, W. A. West, of assuming a Childe-Harold expression when sitting for his portrait.[25] At another time he flew into a fit of half-humorous rage when he discovered that his hero had been satirized in Moore's *Fudge Family in Paris*, as a "fine, sallow, sublime sort of Werther-faced man."[26]

In practically all the romances written in England, the hero dominates the story. Not only is he the center of the action, not only is the story told from his point of view alone, but all developments seem an outgrowth of his character. The story is secondary to the character so completely that at least in one case Byron had not decided on his catastrophe when the narrative was already well under way.[27] The construction of the plot seems as if undetermined beforehand, or only vaguely conceived. Passages are added to *The Giaour*, after the type is being set up,[28] and the poem is expanded from an original four hundred to fourteen hundred lines.[29] The opening lines of *The Curse of Minerva* are transferred bodily to *The Corsair*, for no better reason than that they are good and ought to be published somewhere.[30] Byron, in the romances, was not so much telling a story as talking about somebody or allowing somebody to talk. *Parisina*, the sole exception to the prevailing carelessness of form, is made up almost entirely of dialogue, we might almost say of monologue, since the tone is hardly one of repartee.

Neither is there, in the romances, any clear evolution of

Byron's art that points to a gradually arrived at ideal. Admittedly, there are the inevitable improvements in technique. Neither *The Bride of Abydos* nor any of the following tales is so episodic as the early *Giaour;* but in the latter Byron had in mind a model, Rogers's *Voyage of Columbus,* which was itself careless of structure, and sudden in its transitions. There is a return, in *Lara,* to the heroic couplet, and somewhat to the tone of Pope's *Iliad* and of the narratives of Ariosto and Tasso. *Parisina,* the last of the group, is incomparably the finest. But *The Siege of Corinth,* immediately preceding it, is the most slovenly in workmanship of all, and is close to the very irregular *Christabel* in its versification; so much the offspring of the latter, indeed, that twelve of its lines are an unintentional borrowing.[31] In this Byron but allowed himself to be influenced; he had not sought out a model, for he was unaware of the plagiarism. The virtues of the romances are the virtues of genius alone, not of design. There was a strong reason why, later, he should have been ashamed of this period of his authorship.

The explanation, again, must be sought in the man and his manner of life. He was, for the time being, cut adrift from any purpose either of authorship or of statesmanship. His popularity was an open sesame to the society of the time, but it was too unexpected, too unprepared for, and too much the result of a work for which he had originally no great esteem, to spur him on to further effort. During all this period he was not entirely the social butterfly, fluttering from one group to another. His independence saved him from being ever at the beck of society. But it was not enough to save him from himself. He was too preponderantly a personality, that fictitious personality of his tales, to be once more the author. As frequently as he was away from London, he was too much of the world, if not too much in it. And, as he complained to Lady Blessington, his genius faded, "like snow before the sun. . . . My ideas became dispersed and vague, I lost the power of concentrating my thoughts, and became another being."[32] His genius, if I may correct him, was still at hand, but his will was in abeyance. He was attempting a compromise which, sensible as it is to the majority of mortals, did not call forth his supreme powers. His plea, that "he who would make his way in the world, must let the world believe that it was made for him, and accommodate himself to the minutest of its regulations,"[33] is not the spirit of his greatest poetry.

Composition, into such a scheme, fitted as an intense recreation. His depression, unrelieved by any steady employment of his faculties, continued. After the unsuccessful termination of a love affair, it became unbearable, and he turned for relief to verse: "For the last three days I have been quite shut up; my mind has been from *late* and *later* events in such a state of fermentation, that as usual I have been obliged to empty it in rhyme, . . . This is my usual resource; if it were not for some such occupation to dispel reflection during *inaction*, I verily believe I should very often go mad."[34] "All convulsions end for me in rhyme; and to solace my midnights, I have scribbled another Turkish story."[35] "It is a relief to the fever of my mind to *write*."[36] At such times he wrote only from one point of view, to escape the thoughts of an intolerable present by occupying his mind and by turning his attention to what most readily intrigued his imagination, the old figure of the Byronic hero in the romantic setting of the East. Such, then, was his sole principle, to give his imagination full control on a pleasing theme, with only one restriction, that it should not touch on "reality"—his immediate circumstances, which were driving him to desperation, unmentionable things, which might be connected with actions of the author. "[*The Giaour*] was written in a state of mind . . . that made it necessary for me to apply my mind to something, anything but reality."[37] "I have written this, and published it, for the sake of *employment*—to wring my thoughts from reality, and take refuge in 'imaginings', however 'horrible'."[38] "These two last would not have done. I ran into realities more than ever; and some would have been recognized, and some guessed at."[39] "I am much more indebted to *The Bride of Abydos* than I could ever be to the most partial reader; as it wrung my thoughts from reality to imagination, from selfish regrets to vivid recollections."[40] "To withdraw *myself* from *myself* . . . has ever been my sole, my entire, my sincere motive in scribbling at all; and publishing is also the continuance of the same object, by the action it affords to the mind, which else recoils upon itself."[41] Here is much of his old acceptance of writing as a relief to emotion. Only in this case the emotion is deeper and more insistent, and the material he draws upon is mainly his own experience.

One other effect of such a method is inevitable. Obviously such extreme attacks of depression were not continuous; neither did they occur often. Writing under such circumstances was fitful and rapid. Byron shut himself away from the world in a dark room at a bare desk and plunged into his story until it was completed. His speed of composition was extraordinary. *The Corsair* he wrote in ten days, or eleven, *The Bride of Abydos* in four. At so great a rate the unity of mood could be kept throughout. Written at a breath, each tale has a complete singleness of tone. But on the other hand there was no time for planning or for the gradual growth of a conception and the infiltration of new ideas, and the execution must be either bare or careless. Hence the style of the romances, hasty and bold, yet swift, direct, vivid—excellent narrative style, if the narrative had been strictly adhered to. The tales are still quite readable if we sympathize with their subject matter; in their weakness lies much of their strength.

In the chorus of praise that greeted Byron's successive publications, there were minor discords, to which he may have given heed. Gifford was evidently not satisfied with Byron's use of his powers, as he mentioned in a letter to Murray, regretting that a great mind was running to seed and wasting itself in rank growth.[42] His corrections of *The Siege of Corinth* were sufficient though indirect reproof to that poem's slovenliness of style. Even Murray, usually respectful, on occasion twitted Byron about the "big Tear" of Parisina "which is very fine—much larger, by the way, than Shakespeare's."[43] However, compared to the idolization of Byron by the people at large and the infatuation which even the critics showed for his poetry, these flies in the ointment were few and small indeed. There was enough adulation to have satisfied a poet much more praise-hungry than Byron allowed himself to think that he was.

But Byron was not satisfied. His later disparagement of his tales was not a sudden change of front, to accord with a temporary mood of Pope-worship. There are hints throughout his correspondence, in the five years of his life about London, that all was not well in the Byronic conscience. He may have felt that his reputation was based on his romantic figure, more on the man than on the poet. It is difficult to determine his final reaction to each of his works, since he judges mainly out of a mood and is likely to change his mind next day, and since he is likely to be apologetic about what he is really proud of, to forestall criticism, or to be in accord with criticism already expressed. It is clear, from assertions in several letters of the time, that he was ashamed of *The Giaour*;[44] but when it was well received, his apologies ceased.

The dissatisfaction must be sought in subtler places than in direct references to his works. It is evident mainly in the tone of the whole period—discontent with himself, and a slowly increasing indifference to all good intentions. He forsook oratory in Parliament, not having made a sufficient impression on his colleagues, and disgusted, doubtless, with the real unimportance of parliamentary debate.[45] Everything tired him, himself more than anything else. He was bored in society, and yet too lethargic or too good-natured to escape.[46] The resolutions to forsake poetry continued; and if they were no more frequent than ordinary it was because he composed seldom—it was after a spree of composition that he resolved never to indulge again. His heroes, who might have been judged by purely literary standards, he felt it necessary to apologize for and to present as moral examples; and he expended much energy and several footnotes in proving Conrad a natural character.[47] Sophistry in Byron is so often a form of his humor that it is unwise always to take it as the symptom of an uneasy conscience. But in this case he did not seem to have his tongue in his cheek. He was unwilling to let his poetry speak for itself—true, an old state of mind with him—and he resorted to proving it what it was not.

Less ambiguous than this indirect evidence are two excerpts of some length, one from Hobhouse's *Journal* on March 28, 1814, strikingly like a passage already quoted in our discussion of the Bowles controversy:

This evening, after dinner, I [Hobhouse] read aloud the *Rape of the Lock*, and the "Elegy on the Death of an Unfortunate Lady," also the "Characters of Women." Nothing will do after Pope. I am convinced that even my friend's poetry would have been thought monstrous and affected in an age still ringing with the melody and sense of that greater writer. Indeed, the great success of *Childe Harold* is due chiefly to Byron's having dared to give utterance to certain feelings which everyone must have encouraged in the melancholy and therefore morbid hours of his existence, and also by the intimate knowledge which he has shown of the turns taken by the passions of women. He says himself that his poems are of that sort, which will, like everything of the kind in these days, pass away, and give place to the ancient reading, but that he considers himself fortunate in getting all that can now be got by such a passing reputation.[48]

The second quotation is from a letter of Byron to Moore, written on the eve of his own final departure from England:

I agree with you . . . that I have written too much. . . . I know not why I have dwelt so much on the same scenes, except that I find them fading, or *confusing* . . . in my memory, in the midst of the present turbulence and pressure, and I felt anxious to stamp before the die was worn out. I now break it. With those countries, all my really poetic feelings begin and end. Were I to try, I could make nothing of any other subject, and that I have apparently exhausted.[49]

The passages suggest two reactions of Byron toward the poetry of this his middle period: he was pleased and he was displeased with it. There had been in his life one truly poetic experience, one period of which the recollection itself was an emotion, and the scenes and atmosphere of which were poetry. To this he loved to return in his imagination; it was a sure retreat from a too actual existence. At times when the writing mood was on, and he had to say something, he turned back instinctively to these scenes and "vivid recollections." These he expressed when he wrote his tales, though the tales themselves were hardly more than excuses, to his public and to his reason. One other thing only appealed to his imagination, the melancholy figure of the Childe, which he at times had dreamed of being himself, as he wandered on his travels. So the two were combined as he wrote, escaping reality. He lived again, in the unsubstantial body of his hero, the youthful experience of his journeyings, with the added zest of being a character in a drama. From this character the plot evolved; around this character others grouped themselves and in contact or conflict with him were stirred to life. Byron for the time was at one with his hero, but only for the time. When he laid aside his pen and returned from fiction to reality, he became himself again, and was consequently irritated when identified with his creation. Hence he could plead, though with a strain of sophistry, that the Giaour, or Selin, or Conrad, was merely an imaginary creature. He could be, in his imagination, both Dr. Jekyll and Mr. Hyde, but he did not wish to be held responsible as the latter.

This, it must be admitted, is only a suggestion, though strongly pressed. What is certain is that he was pleased with his poems as conveying to his audience much of the poetry that he had lived, as exploiting his surest "poetic" vein. But beyond this he had no intention and no expectation. His scruples did not make further demands of him, except to hint his doing the same thing better. He was acquiring the notoriety of a moment, but if he did at times cheat himself with the hope of a permanent fame, always the insistent doubts returned: What have you accomplished? What canon have you satisfied? In what way are you like the great ones of the past? Are you any more than a freak who, popular for the moment, will be forgotten the next generation? In some such moment as this, he may have felt the need of taking himself in hand, directing his energies into paths worthy of him, and making his bid for fame. But he was drifting, drifting. Only a cataclysm could save him. It was well for him that the cataclysm came.

CHAPTER VI

REBIRTH

GOETHE remarks somewhere that Byron's is preëminently the genius of pain, from which bitter source he has imbibed his surest inspiration. Scandal, separation, exile, were obviously painful experiences to one of his sensitive disposition. But it is a mistake to accept the catastrophe as mere tragedy, even to the man Byron. It was more on the order of a cold morning plunge which some doctors prescribe for their patients—too much of a shock if one cannot stand it, but invigorating if one can. It is true that Byron was precipitated from a high and moderately comfortable situation to a much lower place in the world; he was damned by the godly and leered at by the multitude; he lost, or found wanting, many whom he had considered friends, and he was separated from the rest; like Dante he was driven out of a city he loved, out of a country he was attached to, to abide a restless exile in a strange land; he suddenly lost his place in the community, his social right to be. But all this leaves out the fact that for once he had a good fight on his hands. Now for once, much more than ever his Lara or Conrad, he was pitted against society. His attacks on Lady Byron's maid, his sarcasms in *Don Juan*, may have been unwise—though it is hard to see how a man of Byron's power could have avoided an occasional outburst—but they were essential to the circumstance. Once more existence had ceased to be drab, monotonous, colorless; for the first time he had a worthy opponent. He could once more take life as a saga and live it heroically in his imagination. Overwhelming misfortune of such a kind was but an added urge to be alive. Maybe, as Goethe remarked, it was the genius of pain that impelled the subsequent greatest of his works, but it was pain controlled by a superior will. For a while, as he bore his bleeding heart through Europe, there was within him the chaos of frustrated ambitions and the torture of despair. But with the turn of the year came a rebound: "My run of luck . . . seems to have taken a turn every way; but never mind, I will bring myself through in the end—if not, I can but be where I began."[1] "If I live ten years longer, you will see . . . that it is not over with me."[2] He was at least no longer bored.

If the exile from England had been of benefit in no other way, it would have helped him by being exile. As he said of himself, he was stifled in the crowd. He was too good-natured, too much under the domination of friend or mistress, to stand apart and go unhindered after his own intents—he could not make up his mind. One fruit of the loneliness is the great body of his letters, diaries, and journals, the first full picture of the man. Also, he was thrown, as in his early travels, into the midst of an alien social system, foreign manners and foreign prejudices. Two of his old mannerisms were gradually rubbed from him—he was no longer the Byronic hero, nor was he altogether the English gentleman. His greatest about-face was in the matter of money. Once he had refused to handle it, and had had Murray turn it immediately over to friends, Dallas or Godwin; now he haggled, drove hard bargains with his publisher, was so very sensible and businesslike about his affairs that he gained a reputation for avarice. That he was not avaricious, but merely sane and matter-of-fact where his brothers in rhyme were romantic, Mr. Drinkwater has pointed out; he had never pretended to be merely the poet, and now he was also the business man. But in England the pursuit of gain would have been impossible; he would have been surrounded by those who, however much they might have liked the earning of money, would have resented its implication. In Italy he was no longer forced to be the dilettante in his serious affairs. He could honestly make money, and his thoughts could turn unashamed to the pursuit of fame. The transformation in his attitude toward his work had begun while he was still in England, after domesticity, if not domestic peace, had given him leisure to examine and control his genius. Just before the unexpected separation, he had written, "I do not like to risk any fame . . . which I have been favoured with, upon compositions which I do not feel to be at all equal to my own notions of what they should be."[3] Italy but gave the mood opportunity to develop.

Of a greater practical consequence, perhaps, than any change in his point of view, was another circumstance with which his attitude may have had something to do; he had more time to himself. He was carried away from the distractions of society—or of domesticity—to be once more fundamentally alone, and his life sank, or rose, into a more definite routine, more monotonous, externally, but more productive of thought and work. Moore, who was certainly in touch with his manner of living, from contact both with the author and with his associates, emphasizes the characteristic again and again in his *Life*: "He appears, indeed, to have, even thus early [at Southwell] shown a decided taste for that regular routine of life—bringing round the same occupations at the same stated periods—which formed so much the system of his existence during the greater part of his residence abroad."[4] "At Diodati, his life was passed in the same regular round of habits and occupations into which, when left to himself, he always fell."[5] "His habits of life, while at Pisa, had but very little differed . . . from the usual monotonous routine into which, so singularly for one of his desultory disposition, the daily course of his existence had now, for some years, flowed."[6] Of the schedule at Diodati, we have a hint in the diary of William Polidori: "Up at 9; went to Geneva on horseback, and then to Diodati to see Shelley; back; dined; into the new boat—Shelley's—and talked, till the ladies' brains whizzed with giddiness, about idealism. Back; rain; puffs of wind."[7] Trelawny, too, gives a digest and summary of Byron's habits at Pisa, which are probably closer to the norm of his Italian sojourn: He remained in bed, generally, till noon. After an afternoon ride on horseback, he returned to a frugal dinner. At nine he visited Count Gamba and his family. On his return home he sat reading or composing until two or three in the morning, after which he went to bed.[8] His old servitor at Ravenna complained to Lady Blessington during her later progress through Italy that his lord had been too abstemious and too incessantly at work, for one so rich.[9] The sole exception to this regularity was possibly at Venice; but here, too, we have only doubts, no proofs, and we do know that in the composition of *Beppo* he set himself the task of completing two octaves a day.

Assuming for the moment that the censures of Byron's friends are conclusive proof of his profligacy, it has usually been a subject for astonishment that one living so profligately should write so much and so well. But we have long since learned to discount criticisms of the man and to make independent search for the fact. The objections of his friends were not directed against the extent of his aberrations, but against the aberrations themselves—not that he took up so frequently with women, but that these were the lowest women of the street procured by gondoliers and common panders. Much, apparently, of what was reported, came from hearsay and scandal, of a piece with the gossip about the "league of incest," or any number of tales that attached themselves like lurid halos to the popular portraits of Byron and Shelley. Much of the public horror concerning both was excited by reports of practices superficially taboo in London but openly legitimate in Italy. But even if it all were true, it tells us little of significance concerning the life of the poet. It is with the regularity of his habits as affecting literary production that we are concerned, and this need not have been impaired by his amours. Brigham Young complained once—or perhaps a great many times—that while he was chiefly interested in affairs of state, monogamists could discuss nothing but his wives. Byron could have made a similar complaint in regard to his mistresses.

Some of the old habits of composing, it is true, remained. When the *estro* was upon him, he sat up all night and into the day, with a seeming obliviousness to the dawn:[10] "In this room . . . Lord Byron slept. Often has the light been seen burning in it till long after day had appeared."[11] "He told [Shelley] he had been writing all night, and had had no food but biscuits for three days, but had taken strong stimulants."[12] But these were only variations in a fairly steady mode of life, temperamental deviations from an established routine. Less and less Byron was taking composition as a fever, a momentary relief to an overwhelming emotion. It was no longer a thing of fits and starts, an expenditure of energy completed in a fortnight. It was the constant business of his life, an activity daily—or nightly—returned to. He could fix his mind upon a long and exacting task, brooding over a portion of it for the day, and jotting down the result of his cogitations when alone at night. Occasional hints in the letters point to a preoccupation with his work that had been impossible in London. Often, according to Polidori, he would compose a hundred verses in the morning, and after his return from the theatre in the evening, still under the spell of remembered music, reduce the number to five-and-twenty.[13] The careless workman, the scrupulous dilettante, was lost or submerged, and a businesslike author had taken his place. Much, also, may be inferred from a comment of Medwin in his *Conversations*: "Sometimes, as I call, I find him at his desk; but he either talks as he writes, or lays down his pen to play at billiards till it is time to take his airing. . . . Such talent is that of an *improvisatore*."[14] There still remain somewhat of the dilettante, or rather the gentleman who does not make too much of his art. But the poet is far from the Byron of the middle years writing feverishly and intensely to relieve an overburdened heart. By now he is the author of *Don Juan*.

The growing earnestness in his attitude toward his art is not, however, everywhere obvious in his conversation and correspondence. He was too much the scoffer, the humorist, the good fellow, to put on a serious artistic air in the presence of company. Romantic persons like Lady Blessington were piqued and disappointed at his frivolous comments upon poetry; they seem to have believed that he should speak of it with bated breath or at least spare it the raillery which he visited upon everything else. Byron, furthermore, was saved from too high a seriousness by that old neoclassic strain within him; always there was the reaction against those fools and pedants who would make of an author a semi-divine and prophetic presence, because they themselves were given to literature. His attitude, nevertheless, had perceptibly altered. The change is too gradual to trace step by step; it must often be sensed rather than discovered outright. But there is a presumption throughout the rest of his life that he turns to writing no longer as a recreation, but as the sole thing which makes life meaningful to him, that he twines his "hopes of being remembered in my line with my land's language."[15] At a late date we have his word for it: "To keep my mind *free and unbiassed* by all paltry and personal irritabilities of praise or censure;—to let my Genius take its natural direction, while my feelings are like the dead, who know nothing and feel nothing of all or aught that is said or done in their regard."[16]

To some extent Byron adopted the romantic idealization of the poet. Passages in *Childe Harold, The Lament of Tasso*, and *The Prophecy of Dante* picture the true poet as prophet or seer; the last poem mentioned is based upon that conception. One passage in *The Prophecy* might have been written by an idealistic Shelleyan-Hugoistic enthusiast, such as Byron certainly was not:

> What is poesy but to create
> From overfeeling good or ill; and aim
> At an external life beyond our fate
> And be the new Prometheus of new men,
> Bestowing fire from heaven . . .
> . . . all they
> Whose Intellect is an o'ermastering Power
> Which still recoils from its encumbering clay
> Or lightens it to spirit, whatsoe'er
> The form which their creations may essay
> Are bards. . . .[17]

In the same poem there is almost a restatement of the conception, with the added and still romantic principle that he who feels is a poet, although he express nothing—that confusion of emotion with art which played havoc many times with his own poetry:

> Many are poets who have never penn'd
> Their inspiration, and perchance the best:
> They felt, and loved, and died, but would not lend
> Their thoughts to meaner beings; they compressed
> The god within them.[18]

Further grounds for the attribution of such a belief to Byron may be gained in other passages of his poetry. But it is notable that only in his poetry does he give expression to the thought, and only at those times when he is strongly under the influence of Shelley. The idea, if not foreign to one side of his nature, could hardly become a moving principle of the whole man. It is a stimulus, not a belief, an intoxication, not a fixed idea which he would affirm in his calmer moments. He is in a more characteristic mood when he writes, three years later, "I shall . . . continue to publish, till I have run my vein dry . . . I shall do so for nothing; till, indeed, it becomes actually a loss; and this, because it is an occupation of mind, like play, or any other stimulus";[19] or again, "I know only *one* motive for publishing *anything* with a sensible man, and I think Johnson has already quoted that."[20] It is because he is at once a sensible man and a genius that he is sometimes hard to understand, and often contradictory.

Byron's manner of applying his ideal was more practical than to announce the poet divine. His primary difficulty was with his own nature. He lacked artistic independence. He was too readily discouraged by adverse criticism, or plunged by it into petty outbursts of temper. Under encouragement from Shelley, without parade of his resolution, the whole of his later life was an effort to find himself, as a poet and as a man. His old hobbies, the reviews, he began to avoid, because of possible references to himself in their columns. He forsook his old style, renounced any intention of writing for women,[21] and begged Murray to send him no more criticisms of his poetry: "I have also [requested] him to send me no more reviews either of *praise* or censure, or opinions of any sort from him, nor from his friends. The fact is, that they irritate and take off one's attention, which may be better employed than in listening to either libels or flattery."[22] He desired to turn his attention to "greater objects,"[23] to avoid soiling the current of his mind,[24] to follow the bias of his disposition, "without considering whether women or men are or are not to be pleased."[25] With the resolve, there was a growing actual independence of the opinion of others, occasionally almost truculent: "As to *Beppo*, I will not alter or suppress a syllable for any man's pleasure but my own."[26] Once he even defied his literary prophet and master: "*Restore 'the'* for 'some,' which I had altered against my creed, to please G[ifford]."[27] Only in the light of this independence may his reactions to the criticisms of *Don Juan* be interpreted. He was by that time determined to satisfy no one's conscience but his own. He had earned his right to freedom. The defense of *Don Juan* is largely due to the combative bent of his nature, aided and abetted by his newly acquired conscience in deciding his problems for himself.

Further reverberations of his conscience are in the direction of self-discipline and will be traced later in the treatment of the successive works. But a new spirit is now manifest in his poetry, separating it from the body of the romances. There is no longer any escape from reality, nor is there any flinching before the hardest facts. There is growing emphasis on the world as it is, preferably on its seamy side, an increasing effort to make his poetry accord with the literal. At times his imagination, working on a fact, transforms it unconsciously or fuses it into a deeper truth; at times, in *Don Juan*, his imagination escapes from the fetters that bind it, and takes a short swallow-flight into the ideal; but always he knocks it back to earth, usually with humor and biting sarcasm. Especially is this habit noticeable in *Mazeppa*, and *The Prisoner of Chillon*, when we compare them with his preceding narratives. Romantic as they may be, they do not, like the earlier, subsist in the wilderness of the imagination, where there is no law. They happen in an actual world of credible people, as indeed their foundation is historical. A single sentence in the preface to the *Prisoner*—"When this poem was composed, I was not aware of the history of Bonnivard, or I should have attempted to dignify the subject by an attempt to celebrate his courage and his virtues"—sufficiently indicates the contrast. From now on Byron's creative energy, however diverse its form, was bent to a single task—the celebration of unadorned reality. It is difficult to conceive of Keats working happily with like fetters on his imagination, or of Shelley dwelling contentedly with the low and the sordid. But to Byron the principle was not merely congenial—it was the center and core of his genius. From this point even his failures gain a power they have never shown before—the power of a deeply felt sincerity.

To treat of the successive stages in this later period is to dwell again upon ideals. Always there is the drive of a critical idea, which advances like a wave upon a beach and spends itself. Byron is testing, testing—unconsciously, perhaps, and moved by the persuasion of a hearty belief, but feeling his way toward his individuality even while working on a borrowed theory. It is in this period that his former classic conscience returns—more in accord with his final mood than was the spiritual solace of Shelley.

It is difficult and hazardous to demarcate exactly the reciprocal reactions of Byron and his fellow poet. That both came to have like views on some subjects is obvious. It is also true that there are echoes of the odes to the Skylark or the West Wind in the latter half of *Childe Harold,* or that the former lyrics echo the latter, and that certain unusual words, like "immedicable," spring up in both poets at about the same time. But whether the one affects the other or the other the one, or they both draw from the same source similar material, or arrive by like trains of thought or through similar reading at the same result, is in the separate case indeterminable. It is generally said that Shelley was the better scholar, but he could not have been a wider reader; though he had some success in impressing on Byron Wordsworth and his pantheism, the extent of his influence even here is uncertain. The relation, after all, was rather between the men than between the poets. The reaction is that of two noble and yet utterly unlike natures and two antagonistic points of view, in close contact—not that of literary association. It is to the credit of each that he could go so far toward recognizing the greatness of the other. Shelley worshiped Byron the poet, and was his close friend until the dispute over Allegra— even then they were not finally estranged. Byron, while he did not adopt the tone of schoolboyish adoration attributed to him by Trelawny,[28] profoundly admired the other as an individual. It is one modern trend, indulged in by Amy Lowell in her life of Keats, to condescend toward Shelley as a freak. Freak unquestionably Byron considered him; but like all others who knew him intimately, he fell in love with the man, regarding him as the noblest nature he had ever known. "I do not at all mean to defend his sentiments," he told Kennedy (less pompously, it is probable, than he is reported) "nor to approve of the mode in which he published them; but Shelley possessed many virtues, and many excellent qualities."[29]

The superficial difference between the two is so great that it is difficult, at first glance, to see how one could have affected the other, except negatively. Morally and intellectually they appear to have been at exactly opposite poles. Shelley's sentiments toward Byron are, of course, well known from his poem *Julian and Maddalo*. Comments in his letters upon Byron are a medley of praise and expostulation: "Lord Byron [is] the spirit of an angel in the mortal paradise of a decaying body."[30] "The spirit in which [*Childe*

Harold] is written, is, if insane, the most wicked and mischievous insanity that was ever given forth. It is a kind of obstinate and self-willed folly, in which he hardens himself. . . . Nothing can be less sublime than the true source of these expressions of contempt and desperation. . . . But that he is a great poet, I think the address to ocean proves."[31] Neither could the two agree on the purposes of art; Byron, the conservative and the insister on fact, is the opposite of Shelley, the logical radical and idealist. Shelley had no sympathy with Byron's admiration for Pope and the classicists and did his best to discourage it: "We talked a great deal about poetry . . . and as usual differed. . . . He affects to patronize a school of criticism fit for the production of mediocrity, and although all his fine poems and passages have been produced in defiance of this system, yet I recognize the pernicious effects of it in the *Doge of Venice;* and it will cramp and limit his future efforts, however great they may be, unless he gets rid of it."[32] "I certainly do not think Pope, or *any* writer, a fit model for any succeeding writer. . . . true genius vindicates to itself an exemption from all regard to whatever has gone before."[33] The contrast is evident. Byron, with no well schematized principles of his own, writes in accord with a blended instinct and conscience, a gallimaufry of precepts and practices never thoroughly in harmony with one another—seeking justification, when in need of it, not in reason but in authority. Shelley, trained logician, rationalist, descendant also from the eighteenth century, but following another lead of its thought, arrives at his own principles on hypothetical premises but with masterly deduction, despises authority, proclaims the ideal, can neither understand nor sympathize with the ordinary man's haphazard methods of arriving at conclusions—which are also Byron's methods. Only the splinters of his philosophy could stick in Byron. The latter was impervious to its inner spirit—

that certain general ideas are true. His habit of mockery made it impossible for him to accept any theory as undeniable. His final appeal was to the outer world of the senses, whereas Shelley's was to the inner world of the spirit and the reason. And yet—

There was another Byron, with whom Shelley had much more in common. He is the Byron of *Childe Harold, The Lament of Tasso, The Prophecy of Dante,* and, to a lesser extent, of *Heaven and Earth.* He is the religious Byron, the scorner of compromise, the champion of freedom, the idealist whose sense of humor would not quite let him go. It was to this inner man that Shelley appealed. He came at a time when Byron's world was in ruins, and he helped him to believe. He gave him self-confidence by trusting in him. He held up to him "energy, and simplicity, and unity of idea,"[34] as the true tests of greatness in writing. And he inspired him with the courage to follow his own instincts, to stand alone. Even while he was discouraging the dramas, he was as greatly encouraging *Don Juan*: "[Byron's determination to write a series of plays] seems to me the wrong road. . . . He will shake off his shackles as he finds they cramp him. I believe he will produce something very great."[35] So far he saw into Byron.

It was one of those rare tricks of Fate, so exactly timed as to seem intentional on her part, that the friendship of the two should have commenced at so opportune a moment. Before or after, Byron might have seen in Shelley only the eccentric or the somewhat misty idealist with impossible dreams. But just now the latter furnished him with the food which his whole nature craved. It was a time when his own world was breaking up around him, and he was reaching out desperately for something to cling to. The mood, almost of desperation within, though on the outside reflected only in the fighter, is expressed in *Manfred* and the last two cantos of *Childe Harold*, the two poems with which his greatest period may be said to begin.

It is a commonplace to say that Byron, in these years, was casting about for that form which should express his complete personality and that all experiments failed until, on the suggestion of *The Monks and the Giants*, he produced *Beppo*; some similar assertion has been made before and will again be made within these pages. It is near enough so to be a half-truth, but it is a dangerous half-truth and needs qualification. We are badly mistaken when we assume that Byron was ever in difficulty about expressing himself. His artistic life is one long exercise of that unhappy faculty. What introduces the diversity among the works of his different periods, is that he had so many selves to express, that sometimes one of them is uppermost and sometimes another, and that different theories of poetry and caprices of poetic faith led him to pour into poetry now one stream of his energy, now another. Byron's many-sidedness as a man was long his weakness as an artist. Seldom could he throw himself into one mood without another mood breaking in; humor had a way of cropping up in the midst of passion, and when he excerpted it he gave the impression of having omitted something. The limited, compact, objective form was foreign to the necessity within him of talking about himself. When he denied himself he deprived his compositions of their greatest impetus, and yet to intrude his personality was to mar the whole. This acute and apparently insoluble problem he never met consciously. It is doubtful that he was at all aware of it. Either he wrote blindly, with no particular thesis, or he wrote in accord with a particular thesis, and could not understand why he could not apply it whole-heartedly. It is this difficulty that makes the *English Bards and Scotch Reviewers* a more imperfect work of art than the *Baviad*, and nevertheless a greater poem. It is the denial of himself that made *Hints from Horace* a dull poem, and his rendition of *Morgante Maggiore*, so faithful and so painstaking, nevertheless so monotonous a translation. Every creed of his own, in these early years, is a conscious effort to draw him out of himself. And yet all his labors on the *Drury Lane Address* did not prevent its being a mediocre poem, while his *Parisina* is a beautiful, if a minor, romance. Nor can we, in retrospect, hold a brief that he should have disregarded his conscience and written only on the spur of the impulse. *The Giaour, The Siege of Corinth,* and *Werner* are the fruits of unprepared inspiration. The difficulty, a very practical one, is unanswerable in the terms of ordinary logic. It was a knot for time to unravel, or to cut.

The problem, as a problem, largely ceased to exist after the time of the exile. Desperation, from the débâcle of his fortunes, was a reënforcement of strength. The mood from now on was a surge that caught and bore along with it the contradictions of his personality. It is finally possible for him to express both sides of his personality, the emotional and the willed, without artistic incongruity. Humor no longer mars passion, but enriches it. Form ceases to be a meaningless diagram and attains of itself a potency to express the idea or the mood. By the time that the flood has again subsided, he has gained supreme control over his genius. His dramas display the spirit of imperious artistic will. And *Don Juan*, though free, is intentionally free—free only by permission.

The works of this period, though they cannot be taken up in too great detail, have a clearer significance than those that have preceded. From this point Byron lives his poetry, and is reflected even more intimately in it than in his incomparable letters. Through it he dares to paint the inner man, whereas in the letters he covers thought with wit. There he is the social man, but here he is communing and confessing in the privacy of his cloister.

The poetry of these concluding years may be placed artistically into three groups, the first to include *Childe Harold, Manfred, The Lament of Tasso,* and *The Prophecy of Dante,* the second the dramas, and the third the ottava-rima poems, *Beppo, Don Juan,* and *The Vision of Judgment.* It is a tribute to his genius that this arrangement produces strange bedfellows and that many poems are not touched by it at all, as being unclassifiable or without fundamental artistic import. Of the latter type are the personal poems, several fine lyrics, and the humorous occasional verse included in letters. We are not dealing with the single inspired moments but with the major artist. We cannot include all of this life abundant, but must rather, by seizing on the greatest work, attempt to dig to its roots.

The resemblance between *Manfred* and the second wave of *Childe Harold* is one of circumstance and impulse, not of form. It is difficult to know which poem to take up first, since *Manfred,* both in time and in inspiration, is surrounded by the other and involved with it. Neither were the two cantos of *Childe Harold* intentionally a consecutive poem. But they may better be treated as a unit, and their relation to *Manfred* left to the intelligence of the reader. The two poems are alike, furthermore, in being not what they appear. *Childe Harold* is not a mere travel poem on scenery, and it is less and less a biography of the Childe, while *Manfred,* though in dramatic form, divided into acts and scenes and given settings and dramatis personae, "is not a drama properly . . . but a dialogue."[36] Both poems are dialogue, or rather, *Childe Harold* is monologue and *Manfred* almost so, with Byron always for protagonist. Nor is Byron, in either poem, the undiluted Byron of the letters. In the drama he speaks through the mouth of Manfred, the resurrected hero of the romances, the greatest hero of them all. "Manfred is the consummation of the Byronic hero-type. A philosophical meaning, a depth of thought is given to the melancholy which in the poems of his youth had been merely fashionable."[37] In *Childe Harold* Byron returns to the Childe, but here, more notably than in the drama, he is unable always to speak in character. Each work, indeed, is but a convenience and an excuse. Byron is impatient to speak for himself, and these are but the artistic moulds into which he pours his thought. The freedom of poetry is the freedom of the novel: it is at once personal and impersonal, and the poet may utter his own moods while claiming to express the emotions of another. In poetry was a freedom which no one thing else offered: Byron could cry out and reason aloud without being held accountable personally. He had not anticipated *Astarte*.

There is a further problem in *Manfred*, which fortunately suggests its own solution. The third act is distinctly in two drafts, the second, far superior to the first, added after an interval of months. This makes it necessary to interpret the first draft of the play, before we turn to the interpretation of the newer third act. The matter is a fairly simple one, since we have the aid of the author. Byron, as well he might have been, was dissatisfied with the drama he sent to Murray in March, 1819. He was uncertain exactly what the poem was; the phrases "a sort of metaphysical poem,"[38] "a sort of drama,"[39] were his most rigorous attempts to define it, and he admitted that he had no notion what it was good for.[40] In its primeval state, *Manfred* bears no marks of being good for anything. It is not a drama. It has fine poetic touches, and some of its scenes are imaginatively conceived, but it falters as a poem. In so far as it is metaphysical—and from this angle mainly Byron spoke of it—it asks a question, vaguely, and does not answer it. Perfectly, it mirrors a storm-tossed mind, but the mind gets nowhere—it flounders about in a morass and sputters out, at the end, like a snuffed candle. The poem could mean nothing except as the cry of a hurt soul, and as such Byron had reason to be ashamed of it.

Artistically, the work is still more conglomerate. Parallels[41] have been noted in *Faust, René, Werther,* Shelley's *St. Irvyne,* and Walpole's *Mysterious Mother,* in Coleridge's *Remorse,* Maturin's *Bertram,* Lewis's *Monk,* Beckford's *Vathek,* and Shelley's *Queen Mab* and *Alastor.* Manfred himself is the Byronic hero, but intenser, and denied the chance for action; he can only probe his soul and find nothing in particular to do about it. The most noticeable characteristic of the drama is the extreme richness of the matter upon which it draws, without conscious artistic selection. And yet, as Mr. Chew has pointed out, Byron admits its derivation from no preceding work.[42] The keen mind of Thomas Love Peacock, among his contemporaries, was not slow to recognize this quality in the drama, and to turn it into ridicule:

According to Mr. Toobad, the present period would be the reign of Ahrimanes. Lord Byron seems to be of the same opinion, from the use he has made of Ahrimanes in *Manfred;* where the great Alastor, or Κακὲς Δαίμων of Persia, is hailed king of the world by the Nemesis of Greece, in concert with three of the Scandinavian Valkyrae, under the name of the Destinies; the astrological spirits of the alchemists of the middle ages; an elemental witch, translated from Denmark to the Alps; and a chorus of Dr. Faustus's devils, who come in the last act for a soul. It is difficult to conceive where this heterogeneous mythological company could have originally met, except at the *table d'hote,* like the six kings in *Candide.*[43]

There is nothing really objectionable in such an eclecticism. Byron was not writing historical drama. The witches, fates, and devils are not exact portraits, but the creatures of Byron's imagination. The work can be interpreted only as "an attempt to give objective expression to intensely subjective emotion."[44] The wealth of images that are brought together in it, from such romance as Shelley's *St. Irvyne*, the resurrection of the old Childe-Harold mood, the choruses, which have half a hundred possible sources, and the reflection of Shakespeare in the style—are but the indications of a glowing imagination. *Manfred*, like *The Dream*, is an "expression of remorse."[45] It is a natural outcropping of the period when Byron was "half mad between metaphysics, mountains, lakes, love inextinguishable, thoughts unutterable, and the nightmare of my own delinquencies."[46] It is written without a very clear artistic aim. It is the eruption of a feverish desire for relief and self-expression. Herein lies its weakness. It is not a perfect expression of remorse, for it is in form a drama, and, furthermore, it seems to propound a problem, which it does not succeed in answering. After the first two acts, when the agony has been voiced and the question broached, there is no need for the third, which can but express more remorse, and as first executed does so weakly. Yet without the third act, the first two break up into an incoherent succession of scenes.

Byron was quite conscious that something was wrong, as his references to the poem at this time attest: "I have no great opinion of this piece of phantasy."[47] "A drama as bad at Nat. Lee's Bedlam tragedy."[48] "The thing could never be attempted or thought of for the stage; I much doubt it for publication even. It is too much in my old style."[49] "A sort of mad drama, for the sake of the Alpine scenery. . . . You may suppose what a Bedlam tragedy it must be."[50] His criticism of it is justified; it is a *mad* drama, an opium dream or a nightmare, nothing to be proud of. He senses, also, that the third act is the weakness: "The first two acts are the best; the third so so: but I was blown with the first and second heats."[51] "The third act is certainly damned bad. . . . It must on *no account* be published in its present state. I will try and reform it . . . but the impulse is gone."⁵² His accusations and promises point to one thing further, that the impulse was in the first two acts; they had expressed what he had to say; the third was but a tag; and the impulse, it is evident, is that of suffering and doubt. A new third act was necessary; and so, when the mood came upon him, he rewrote the old act almost entire.

The poem, in its unsatisfactory draft, is metaphysical. It is the cry of a doubting intellect and an unsatisfied imagination. It asks the question, What is one to do when there is no consolation, in the world, in God, in one's conscience? Manfred has curiosity, but desperate curiosity. His is not the intellectual longing of Faust, to know all things for the sake of knowing; he must know to still the serpent in his own breast. The question is not met squarely in the drama. The one strong answer, in the third act, "Old man, 'tis not so difficult to die," is drowned by the succeeding exclamations of the servants, and is not prepared for. It is hard to see why it is not difficult for Manfred to die, except insofar as it is more difficult for him to live. The treatment of the Abbot is neither clever nor convincing; the satire on his cloth is petulant. The impression left by Manfred is that of a half-mad despairing spirit trying vainly to deceive himself into self-respect.

But with the revised third act, the whole effect is transformed. Cheap sarcasm at the expense of the clergy disappears; but the Abbot remains ineffectual. Manfred is still the Manfred of Acts One and Two. But he is the ripened Manfred, finally at peace with himself, and confident against the world of spirits. His great speech near the end of the act is a complete answer to his former vain questionings:

> Back to thy hell!
> Thou hast no power upon me, *that* I feel;
> Thou never shalt possess me, *that* I know;

REBIRTH

> What I have done is done; I bear within
> A torture which could nothing gain from thine;
> The mind which is immortal makes itself
> Requital for its good or evil thoughts,
> Is its own origin of ill and end
> And its own place and time: its innate sense
> When stripped of this mortality, derives
> No color from the fleeting things without,
> But is absorbed in sufferance or in joy,
> Born from the knowledge of its own desert.

The drama is given a significance which it lacked before. The first two acts point toward the third, and the third is now the greatest and the strongest of all. The complaint of Byron to Murray—"You have destroyed the whole effect and moral of the poem by omitting the last line of Manfred's speaking"[53]—is justified.

It remains to be noted that Byron was at the same time solving two problems, one artistic and the other personal. The artistic problem has already been portrayed, but the personal one is equally important. Manfred was at bottom Byron. His sufferings, his regrets, his doubts, and his questionings are those, in the main, of his creator, though their poetical expression may be the work of his creator's imagination. The conundrum put by the first two acts is at this time the conundrum which Byron himself has to solve. He fails to meet it at first, because he has no solution; his third act is therefore lame and unconvincing. But after he has sent the manuscript to Murray, while still dissatisfied with it and with himself, the solution comes upon him, suggested by an old faint memory from Milton. It answers for both him and the needs of his drama; it creates a new third act, and it voices to him a reason for living. The man is no longer a dilettante, and his art is no longer the expression of idle moments or unsatisfied desires. There is no more question of the conscience of art apart from the conscience of the man.

No comparable artistic problem is to be found in *Childe Harold*. The poem does not pretend to unity; the last canto is not meant to be a continuation of the preceding; though the title of the poem is retained, the Childe is dropped and the reason for the title is lost. Canto III is but a travelogue, in the order of the earlier cantos. So loose is the structure of Canto IV that passages are added almost at random, without any appreciable damage to the total effect. Byron for a time continues to speak through the mouth of Harold, but, tiring of the pseudonymity, in the last canto he speaks in his own person. The second half of the poem shows no advance in structure over the first, written seven years previously. Its greatness is in its poetry, its force, the splendor of its diction, and its perfect sincerity.

Byron had left it uncertain, with the publication of the first two cantos, whether he would continue the poem. In his preface, he had announced the work as "merely experimental." The nature of its reception, according to his statement, would determine whether or not he should further conduct his readers to Constantinople, through Ionia and Phrygia. The reception was certainly enough to please his most fastidious anticipations. But the stimulus of travel was removed, and he left his masterpiece alone, content to rest upon its reputation. In an addition to the preface, he affirmed that, had he continued the poem, the character of the Childe would have deepened into the full figure "of a modern Timon, perhaps a poetical Zeluco." The assertion may be taken for what it is worth—a half formed dream or idea, with no sufficient impetus to make of it reality. Dallas, when visiting him, exacted from him the renewal of a promise to continue the poem, but this is as far as his lethargy allowed him to go.

As a matter of fact, the nature of *Childe Harold* did not call loudly for a completion. The work is by its nature formless, a succession of fragments rather than a single truncated fragment, bound together only by the character of the Childe, who is now present, now hidden by the scenery. The only way of continuing the poem was to let the Childe go on traveling, as the only way to complete it was by allowing him to finish his journey. Byron intended originally, it may be inferred, to approximate the itinerary closely to his own and to bring it full circle, after a Turkish tour and a sojourn in Constantinople—relieved probably by a swim across the Hellespont—with his return to England; that is to say, insofar as Byron had an intention of completing the poem. The intention has already been doubted. The poem is not a premeditated work of art, but a result of impulse, a reaction in verse to the stimulus of travel. With this stimulus removed, its author had no further reason for continuing the composition, except as it might add to his reputation—a hard and risky experiment, and better conducted by new original works, in *The Giaour* and *The Corsair*. It was wise from a practical point of view to let very well alone. The only motive that could recall Byron to his production was a new stimulation, a renewed enrichment of his poetic nature with impressions and emotions. This he found in the exile from England, the high tension following the break-up of his domestic affairs, and the resumption of his travels. *Childe Harold*, with *Don Juan*, is the most sensitive register of its author's opinions and reactions, and as much so as the later poem, for whereas it is limited by its prevailingly serious tone, the other is limited by its constant effort at humor. Each, again, accurately reflects its background, for at the time of the one, Byron was serious to the verge of despair, and of the other, he had regained his aplomb.

Neither with the completion of Canto IV did the poem

come definitely to an end. There are three suggestions much later that Byron had still an intention of returning to his former favorite: "I have some thoughts of taking a run down to Naples . . . this spring, and writing, when I have studied the country, a fifth and sixth Canto of *Ch^e Harold;* but this is merely an idea for the present."[54] "But for this Greek business I should have been at Naples writing a fifth Canto of *Childe Harold,* expressly to give vent to my detestation of the Austrian tyranny in Italy."[55] "If I live another year, you will see this scene [night time off Strombouli] in a fifth canto of *Childe Harold.*"[56] The poem is always associated in his mind with scenery. And since it is his opinion of what he looks upon, and apropos his opinion of everything else, he is at perfect liberty to say what he wishes, so long as he does not depart from his style.

Byron takes advantage of this liberty by talking in the first person, about himself, his enemies, his hates, his ideals, and his conceptions of life and art, with a growing disregard of the now preëmpted Childe. At the same time that he writes poetry, he indicates why he is writing, and his comments in the poem give excellent information, supplementary to the letters, about his present attitude towards his art.

It is possible to take the two cantos as a whole, but as in the case of *Manfred,* they assume meaning only when studied in the order of their composition. Each is unified and set off from the other, by a single philosophy and mood—philosophy and mood which harmonize and are one. Canto III is "metaphysical"; its theme is the sympathetic investigation of madness, or of those souls who make men mad by their contagion —Napoleon and Rousseau; as Hobhouse said of it dubiously, "there is an air of mystery and metaphysics about it."[57] It stresses continually, though in an undertone, the duality of spirit and clay, painting the soul as struggling to break through clay-cold clouds around it. Its poetry lies mainly in

REBIRTH

its intensity and in the realization of a great abiding presence, transcending and dwarfing ordinary reality: "The feeling with which all around Clarens, and the opposite rocks of Meillerie, is invested, is of a still higher and more comprehensive order than the mere sympathy with individual passion . . . it is the great principle of the universe . . . of which, though knowing ourselves a part, we lose our individuality, and mingle in the beauty of the whole."[58] This presence is felt sometimes as Nature, the pantheistic spirit of Wordsworth, and sometimes as the creation of the mind, the ideal. The latter conception is suspiciously unlike Byron and yet not exactly Wordsworthian. Its parallels are to be found in the letters of Shelley: "The imagination surely could not forbear to breathe into the most inanimate forms, some likeness of its own visions."[59] "Meillerie . . . Chillon, Clarens . . . were created indeed by one mind, but a mind so powerfully bright as to cast a shade of falsehood on the records that are called reality."[60] "The contemplation of [Rousseau's] imperishable creations had left no vacancy in my heart for mortal things."[61] Not only is the idea the same with the two poets, but it springs from the contemplation of the same sights and centers in the same figure that they had discussed together—the Swiss country and Rousseau. Evidently, it was the subject of their conversations upon idealism, on the Lake of Geneva, and in the study at night till the brains of the auditors swam. And since it is the essence of Shelley's philosophy of composition, whereas it is in stark contrast to anything that had appeared in Byron's mind before, it is clearly the suggestion of the former. But let us be content to call it "suggestion," and postulate no master-and-pupil relation. Byron, in despair over his life and fortunes, was open to any hint of a solution. The aim of this third canto, as stated in its motto—"A fin que cette application vous forçât de penser à autre chose; il n'y a en vérité de remède que celui-là et le temps"—is escape from an intolerable present reality. The creations of the mind[62] are such an escape, and though they are not the less convincing for that reason, they must disappear with the return of Byron to normality, and they were present in his poetry long before his acquaintanceship with Shelley. They answered always the need of a part of Byron's nature, but it required his mental agony and the suggestion of his brother poet, to fashion them into a philosophy. Shelley furnished the form alone; *Manfred*, which meets the same crisis and has much of the same spirit, owes but little to him.

Canto IV is written in a very different vein from the preceding canto. It comes at the end of a period, when Byron was again in thorough control of himself and his thoughts and the fires of torment were dying down. In the preface, he takes leave finally of Harold. His work, he asserts, is to stand on its own merits, and the passages in the first person must be understood as the author speaking himself; no longer is the conception of the Byronic hero a permitted portion of his poetry. He intentionally avoids metaphysics.[63] He mentions the ideal creation again, only to renounce it:

> The beings of the Mind are not of clay;
>   Essentially immortal, they create
> And multiply in us a brighter ray
>   And more beloved existence. . . .
>
> Such is the refuge of our youth and age,
>   The first from Hope, the last from Vacancy;
> And this wan feeling peoples many a page—
>   And, may be, that which grows beneath mine eye;
>   Yet there are things whose strong reality
> Outshines our fairy-land; in shape and hues
>   More beautiful than our fantastic sky
> And the strange constellations which the Muse
> O'er her wild universe is skilful to diffuse.

> I saw or dreamed of such,—but let them go,—
> They came like truth, and disappeared like
> dreams. . . .
>
> I could replace them if I would. . . .
> Let these too go—for waking Reason deems
> Such overweening phantasies unsound.[64]

The fourth canto is Byron's final, complete break with the past. The Childe, the fevered dream of something beyond reality, "metaphysics," all that marks him as the romantic and visionary poet, he casts aside. He is from now on committed to truth and reason. Always he keeps himself close to those credible things which he has been able to perceive for himself or learn from others. No longer does he live in a universe of dreams, attempting to escape from himself. The dreams persist, and write for him most of the third canto of *Don Juan*. But he has no more faith in them. From now on he ridicules them, or turns from them to history or to experience. From now on he is careful in the investigation of his sources and relentlessly conscientious in pulling his imagination down to earth. Even the divine poems, *Cain* and *The Vision of Judgment*, are no exceptions to his scrupulosity; they are but the application of reason to the sublime. *Werner* is a partial exception, and to that extent is weak; but its core is a moral truth. *The Island* is a near return to the spirit of the romances; its loss of their verve is sufficient indication of a change. Byron even here, however, bases his story upon the account of an actual mutiny. His principles apply even in the case of a pot-boiler: "I have two things to avoid—the first that of running foul of my own *Corsair* and style, so as to produce repetition and monotony—and the other not to run counter to the reigning stupidity altogether. . . . I am trying to write a poem a little above the run of periodical poesy."[65]

Byron was well pleased with the last canto. In regard to the preceding, he became uncertain a little and ashamed of the metaphysics, which he looked upon as a product of semi-madness. And yet even of this he was quite proud when the glow was still strong upon him: "I care not much about opinions at this time of day, and I am certain in my mind that this canto is the *best* which I have ever written; there is a depth of thought in it throughout and a strength of repressed passion which you must feel before you find; but it requires reading more than once, because it is in part *metaphysical,* and of a kind of metaphysics which everybody will not understand. I never thought that it would be *popular* . . . but those for whom it was intended will like it."[66]

Byron might well have been proud of both of the latter cantos. Whatever their inspiration and models, they are intrinsically his own. The feeling for nature may have been affected by Wordsworth, and the idealism by Shelley, but they are essentially Byron. There is not, in the total effect, the loss of individuality in the pantheistic contemplation of nature that is characteristic of the older poet. Rather, in the words of Lord Morley, "Nature, in her most dazzling aspects and stupendous parts, is but the background and theatre of the tragedy of man."[67] Byron was justified in claiming that he had written a human poem, that he had resorted to no outworn machinery, and that the thoughts contained might have been the basis for twenty tragedies.[68]

The two cantos are in another sense at the meeting of the waters. They bring to a head tendencies long formulating in the poet's mind, reflecting frequently in their diction earlier poems and anticipating in their ideas what is to come. Much in them has been said before, but never so well. It is now spoken with such vigor and sincerity that it is as if uttered for the first time. In "this force, this powerful rhythm, in this irresistible and mounting movement,"[69] Shelley might well have recognized a superb genius. There is no padding in this poetry; it is clean, concentrated, superbly free from excess. However close to the romantics it is at times in its subject matter, in its manner it belongs to the age before. The splendid generalities of the neoclassicists Byron applies to nature; his description has not the wealth nor the encumbrance of detail that was coming into fashion. He paints in broad strokes, clearly; and always, as he looks out upon nature, he remains a man. We see through his eyes and senses, not as if nature herself were speaking: "In the poetry of lucid and unaffected sense, Byron now proclaimed himself a great master. *Childe Harold* . . . had a romantic warmth that marked him clearly enough as of the new spirit, and in combining this with . . . forthright sagacity . . . it came more nearly perhaps than any other masterpiece of the time to reconciling the great manner of the eighteenth century with that of the early nineteenth."[70] The poetry is supreme because of this one thing, its "grand manner"; which must again be traced back to the artist. It is free from affectation and over-adornment not merely because he was a follower of Johnson, nor because he imitated Pope in his youth, though these have had their effect. But the verse is magnificent because Byron was living magnificently; it is the voice of a great spirit speaking out in intense sincerity.

CHAPTER VII

DRAMA AND PROPAGANDA

IT is well to read the dramas immediately after *Childe Harold*.[1] *Don Juan* is so informed, so overlaid and so incrusted with the comic that its style seems at times the work of another craftsman; only when we understand the difference in approach can we perceive an underlying kinship between the two poems. But the dramas continue the tone of *Childe Harold*. They, too, are written in broad strokes of character as of diction. In them the same voice speaks, without prejudice, without rant, nobly, sincerely. Their style is so nearly that of *Childe Harold* that the one peculiarity—the influence of Shakespeare on the phraseology—is all the more noticeable. It is as a type that we must study them, in order to discover their individuality. And with this in view, we must recollect their background before we explain them fully.

Byron was both inexperienced and experienced in the theatre. He had never acted professionally, and his few amateurish attempts could have taught him little about the practical side of playwriting. He had never composed a play for production, to have the benefit of correction and advice by an experienced manager. And yet, very early, his interest had been aroused in the drama; and his relationship with the theatre, in another sense, was close.

This relationship had been the result partly of accident and partly of his fame; it strengthened an instinct in the poet which, had it not been encouraged, might have led him nowhere. There are several references in the early letters, in the *Hours of Idleness,* and in later comments on his youth, to plays in which the future poet took part. One poem in particular, "On a Distant View ... of Harrow on the Hill." recounts his playing Zanga and Lear, and imagining himself a great actor reviving Garrick and outshining the rest. With this and with some private theatricals after his return to England, his histrionic ambitions largely ended—though Medwin relates in his conversations a projected performance of *Othello,* prevented by the timely intervention of La Guiccioli. There is also an "Occasional Prologue" written for a private performance of *The Wheel of Fortune,* and in a few ways anticipating the "Drury Lane Address." In the *English Bards* Byron attacked the contemporary theatre, and called for a return of the golden days of the past, but the mood was too much an application of the prevailing theme of the satire to be of deep significance. Much more spontaneous was a diatribe on the immorality of the opera. In *Hints from Horace* there was a similar attack on the theatre, largely in imitation of his original. During this period, at any rate, he was familiar with the stage and interested in it critically. Beyond that it is not safe to generalize.

English Bards and Scotch Reviewers may have had something to do with the request of the committee for Byron to write an address for the opening of the newly rebuilt Drury Lane Theatre; but the main factor must have been the recent success of *Childe Harold* and his reputation as the greatest poet of the day. The effect on Byron was to make him work feverishly on what he was not especially fitted or inspired to do, with the result that the *Address* is among the mediocre, though the most conscientious, of his writings. The incident, however, prepared the way for his being placed on the Drury Lane sub-committee toward the end of 1814 as one of a group of three who were to experiment with and actively manage the business of the Theatre. As indicated above, the appointment does not mark the sudden introduction of Byron to the theatre. His interest therein had been constant since his return from his travels. He had a passion for the theatre which made it impossible for him to "resist the first night of anything."[2] The number of quotations from Colman alone attest how keenly he felt the appeal of the stage; they indicate also, with the body of quotations from other plays, that he enjoyed comedy much more than tragedy, Shakespeare's masterpieces being the sole exceptions. As sure a proof of his interest in the theatre is the cropping up of dramatic terms in unexpected places in his correspondence. Like Shakespeare he enjoyed looking on his life as a play, though he did not put the conception into a memorable figure: "How you will laugh at all this! So should I were I not one of the Dram. Pers."[3] "As I am one of the principal performers in this unfortunate drama, I should be glad to know what my part requires next."[4] The more technical association with Drury Lane brought him closer to the theatre; it did not arouse nor did it altogether determine his interest. But it did introduce him to another side of the drama and help to crystallize an already critical attitude. He was obliged to read the first drafts of plays submitted to the theatre, in the effort to choose the best from among them. The effect was largely the same as that of the constant and enforced perusal of a body of efforts in composition on anyone of a literary turn of mind. His ideals of what ought to be were heightened, while he grew more and more disgusted with what was. Particularly was he irritated with the audience, which seemed perversely to prefer the worst in drama. To offset a bad condition, he negotiated with the greater authors of the time, among them Coleridge, to secure better plays. "As it is fitting there should be good plays, now and then, besides Shakespeare's," he wrote Moore, "I wish you or Campbell would write one:—The rest of 'us youth' have not heart enough."[5] He looked first to Maturin and then to Sotheby to reform the English stage, lending them his good will and assistance. But in spite of the best intentions, "all such efforts failed." Not only were the better plays not well received—Sheridan, he complained, was their worst drawing card—but he lost confidence one by one in his protégés, Coleridge, Maturin, and Sotheby.

His main inspiration, in these dark days, was the excellence of the acting. Constantly in his letters he refers to Kemble, Mrs. Siddons, Kean. The last must have affected greatly his conception of many Shakespearean characters, especially that of Richard III, while Mrs. Siddons's interpretation of Lady Macbeth he praised warmly. His attitude toward the theatre was partly that of an amateur actor. Ticknor speaks of his imitating perfectly the manner of Munden, Braham, Cooke, and Kemble, while affirming his enthusiasm for the theatre.[6] Byron's capacities as orator and as reciter have been confirmed by numerous acquaintances—his soft, well modulated voice, his musical ear, and his instinct for the right dramatic key. The two threads of interest unite in the tragedies, where he can be both imaginary actor and declaimer. The interest in the individual actor dominates all his plays, with the sole exception of *Heaven and Earth;* one character possesses the attention of the audience, if not throughout the play, at least for the duration of a scene. The multiplication of important characters, in *Werner*, is the indication of a later period, when he is beginning to depart from his original conception of the dramatic art.

The severance of his connection with the theatre left him with mingled feelings. His hostility toward the English public as a whole he vented on the English audience. But his revulsion from the stage and the practical side of playwriting does not spring from so immediate a cause. It was a result of his dislike of writing down to the crowd, of his inexperience, of his uncertainty as to "how to make people go on and off in the scenes,"[7] and above all of his contempt for an audience that had so bad a taste in plays. His dislike of production is evident in his efforts to prevent the staging of *Manfred*, and he states his opinions on the question frequently and convincingly: "I did not, and do not write for the stage; and would not alter a line, to draw down the upper gallery into the pit in thunder . . . the past experience shows that in the present state of the English stage, no production of mine can be adapted to an audience."[8] "I have at last rendered [*Manfred*] *quite impossible* for the stage, for which my intercourse with D[rury] Lane has given me the greatest contempt."[9] "I composed it actually with a *horror* of the stage, and with a view to render even the thought of it impracticable [for] that for which I have an invincible repugnance, viz. a representation."[10] "The more I see of the stage, the less I would wish to have any thing to do with it."[11] He even objected, now, to putting himself at the mercy of the actor, did not wish to "cringe to some favorite of the public, neither give him too many nor too few lines to spout, think how he would mouth such and such a sentence, look such and such a passion, strut such and such a scene. Who, I say, would submit to all this?"[12] His repugnance to the performance of his plays takes extreme and sometimes absurd forms, but it is none the less genuine on that account. His reaction threw him, necessarily, into the arms of the other public, the solitary reader interested in the drama as a form of composition. It is at such an audience that the plays are directed: "Of course I write for the reader, and not for the stage."[13] "I want neither the impertinence of their [the audience's] hisses nor the insolence of their applause. I write only for the *reader*, and care for nothing but the *silent* approbation of those who close one's book with good humor and quiet contentment."[14]

The wisdom of the choice must be determined according to one's opinion of closet drama as a permissible artistic form. To Byron, the advantages must have seemed immediate and striking. He was freed for once from the necessity of pleasing anybody, and could write with his eye, not on a possible audience, but on his ideals, and on the play itself. He was saved experiment and revision to meet exactions which had aroused his angry contempt. He could appeal, not to the mob, but to those of taste and judgment who read plays at home. For his authority he had *Samson Agonistes*, "a tragedy written in imitation of the Ancients and never designed by the author for the stage,"[15] and all the contemporary serious poetic plays, which, however great their good intention to please, had every characteristic of closet drama.

In another way, he was stimulated to dramatic composition. His strictures on the drama were, unavoidably, a self-invitation to carry out his theories. His artistic conscience was encouraged by his objections, to write plays against which those objections could not be made. Any crusade in letters would lead him inevitably to the drama, since here his criticisms were the more concrete and consequently his aims could be the more clearly defined. Crusade or no, he was early making experiments with dramatic composition. Once he speaks of having burned a comedy which had dissatisfied him, and his first draft of *Werner*, written at this period, is still in existence. Something of his aims must have entered his conversation, for George Ticknor surmises, in June, 1815, that Byron next may turn his thoughts to the stage.[16]

At the time of his departure from England, therefore, we have reason to believe that he had his poetical eye on the theatre with a view to reforming it and furnishing plays which might serve as models for the future serious drama of England. With the contemporary popular plays he was out of patience, and he was disgusted with the audience and its tastes. Though in presentation he seems to have preferred comedy, his ambitions led him instead to an attempt in the more esteemed form of tragedy. Here the greatest absurdities were perpetrated, in the name of romanticism, by Kotzebue and the Gothic school, and here was the prime need for improvement. In tragedy, furthermore, though England had already a great literature in the plays of Shakespeare, yet these were irregular, the products of a bad school triumphed in only by the genius of the dramatist. The stage was crying for reform, and when Byron's conscience became strong enough to lead him, he must turn to its correction. *Manfred* testifies first to this desire to dramatize, and also to the old aversion to any possibility of an audience. But it was written under too great perturbation to be other than what it has been already called—the objectification of a mood and an idea. The reform could come only as a result of a definite *ars dramatica*, which had not so far formed itself in his mind.

The formation of such a body of principles was as much the result of chance as it was of instinct; but chance and instinct in conjunction effected the series of plays from *Marino Faliero* to *Cain*. It was chance that removed Byron from England, drew him into close personal contact with at least one branch of the Continental drama, the Italian, and with Alfieri's theory and practice of dramatic composition, and plunged him into a heated controversy with Bowles on the very theme, classicism, that was at the basis of his revolt against the contemporary stage. Everything threw him back upon the classic drama, both the ancient Greek with Aristotle as its prophet, and the more modern French and Italian, particularly the latter. Much about his tragedies may be explained by reference to his own experiences in the theatre.

But the close similarity between his surest plays and those of Alfieri, stronger because in some ways intangible, can be the result only of direct suggestion.

His purpose, wherever it touched on the Bowles controversy, led him into extreme statements that have caused much misunderstanding as to his sincerity. He had been gradually weaned away from the English drama. He saw its weaknesses as perhaps more vivid than they were. To his Continentalized eye, the Elizabethans were both a quite admirable and a rather barbarous people. Their plays were good theatre, full of action and of striking situations, adorned with fine tremendous lyrical outbursts, but essentially crude. They were uneven in their sudden descent from high poetry to utter bathos; their beauties were marred by rant, bad puns, and manifest absurdities. They were all against "nature" and common sense—that compound personality which remained so alive in the neoclassic substratum of his consciousness. Above all, in structure the plays were incoherent and disjointed, victims of their very richness. There were too many characters, too many incidents, too many plots and subplots, for the average auditor to follow the story easily. The lapses in time between acts or even scenes put a tax upon the credulity of slightly unwilling spectators. The result was a greater emphasis upon the incident, the character, or the passage of lyric rapture in verse, than upon the single organic play. Only the supreme genius of Shakespeare had been able to mould his plays into recognizable wholes, and even he, in *Henry V*, had to resort to an unsatisfactory chorus to supplement the action and apologize to the audience.

The French and Italians, on the other hand, and behind them the Latins and the Greeks, used a dramatic form unified, coherent, and sane. If they indulged in rhetoric, they avoided rant. They presented one story, and presented it well, so that they could be followed easily by an audience;

they escaped the subplot, or the minor eccentric character with no direct relation to the action. Their simplicity was to their advantage on the modern stage, in the technical business of representation. And it threw emphasis upon the idea or the theme, the one supreme thing that the author desired to convey. Whereas the Elizabethan drama had been the product of practical playwrights working in a narrow local medium, the Continental had developed more as a form of art, with definite ideals of composition. The contrast was not altogether superficial. The classical drama, in the hands of any but a supreme dramatist, was a more convenient, utilizable form of art than its chaotic cousin in England. The trend of modern playwriting, partially because of the demands of staging, is away from the Elizabethans.

Such an attitude was a normal development in a mind like Byron's, situated as he was. It led him afoul, to his great glee, of his more provincial contemporaries in England, who would hear nothing ill of the Elizabethans. His comments on Shakespeare, even in the first Bowles letter, take upon them the tone of banter; he is resorting to his hobby of baiting his acquaintances. His assertion, "I deny that the English have hitherto had a drama at all,"[17] was a striking thing to say, particularly when it brought red to the face of many a worthy gentleman. There may have been in the mood some irritation, too, at the undiscriminating worship of Shakespeare, and a very little jealousy of his predecessor's preëminence. But irritation and jealousy were but skin-deep. Whatever was in the foreground, Byron's background was the English drama, the drama of Shakespeare and of Sheridan. It was part of the fibre of his dramatic experience; and his purpose, as expressed in his more serious moments, was not so much to contradict as to supplement and improve it: "To be sure," he said, of his own plays, "they are as opposite to the English drama as one thing can be to another; but I have a notion that, if understood, they will, in time, find favour . . . with the reader."[18] "No reform ever succeeded at first. I admire the old English dramatists; but this is quite another field. . . . I want to make a *regular* English drama."[19]

There is a similarity here to Pope's resolve to become a correct poet; the parallel is in one respect close. Both appealed to a foreign and an ancient tradition, neither really denied in his heart the greatness of his country's literature, but each wished to institute something new, a classical tradition *within* English, and to project his own works as models for succeeding poets. Pope, when he adapted the heroic couplet as his main instrument of expression, was not breaking with England's past, but perfecting a distinctly national metre. Byron, likewise, derived dramatically from the English in his technique and his mannerisms. He borrowed from Alfieri and the Greeks only a conception and an ideal in accord with the latent classicism within him.

His kinship with Alfieri is both spiritual and cultural. Both derived ultimately from the rationalism and traditionalism of the eighteenth century. They had each a deep instinct for authority and the habit of justifying themselves before a cultivated audience, whose judgments were based upon antiquity, on the one hand, and the demands of reason, on the other. There was in each the combination of violent passion and imperious intellect. Each, with an effort at classic restraint and impersonality, depicted primarily himself and appealed to his generation almost as much because of his character as of his art. In the dramas of both is a striking similarity of effects—tempests of passions, lengthy declamations, noble but somewhat unconvincing women, dynamic men, a stress and intensity that seem not so much the result of effort to be effective as of powerful natures held in leash, a feeling, to requote Mr. Drinkwater, for the saliences not the subtleties of character, a definiteness of outline and simplicity of plot. Both sets of plays seem to project, if the figure is allowable, as bas-relief; they stand out clean-cut from their flat background. Whatever their weaknesses, those weaknesses are not in mediocrity, nor are they in the lack of power or of conscious purpose.

The difference lies in the significance of the plays in the lives of their authors. Alfieri, after a wasteful youth, devoted himself whole-heartedly to the drama, with a steadiness of purpose that bespoke the power of his will. Byron's plays (exclusive of *Manfred*) were the product of less than two years of labor, and were deserted for a return to the startlingly dissimilar *Don Juan*. Alfieri derived primarily from the French and corrected them by an admiration for the Greeks. Byron derived primarily from Alfieri. The instinct and aims of the two were the same, but the conditions they met were different. Whereas Alfieri rode on the crest of the classic wave and was still at one with the temper of his time, Byron was consciously battling his audience. The latter poet had come after the deluge, when the old standards had already been swept away. Besides, as an expatriate, he was out of touch with the more national impulses of his race. Alfieri's spirit, whatever its extraction, is nevertheless markedly Italian. Byron's dramas, while copying the English in style, are essentially alien. This is true not only of the type of their classicism. The motivation of Faliero, as Byron complained, so obvious to a Venetian, seemed insufficient to the English playgoer. This play, and *Sardanapalus*, and *The Two Foscari*, failed to establish an English classic tradition mainly because they came in the heat of the romantic revival, but also because they were Italianate, if not Italian. The neglect of the three, even with the modern reader, in spite of a certain splendor that suffuses them, attests their unpopularity, over and above the universal injustice that has been visited upon the fame of Byron until the last few years. *Manfred* and *Cain* are, and will most likely continue to be, more suitable pabulum to the public taste.

To criticize the results, however, is but to admit the obvious. It is in no way to impugn the motives or the capacities of the dramatist. Byron is surely among the most intelligent if not the most profoundly intellectual of English poets, and, in this instance, he knew very clearly what he was about. Even his addiction to the Unities does not deserve the condescension it aroused in the breast of the good Goethe. He adopted the Unities not blindly, not in a mere perverse mood. They meant to him, for one thing, the approbation of authority and tradition, that twofold standard which was always, in poetry, the ultimate basis of approval. But they were also convenient means to an end—an end which for the time being had almost ceased to exist in the creative consciousness. They added to the plays an impersonality of touch that is lacking in the earlier poems. Byron, if he was not carried away from himself by virtue of his theories, transformed himself by working upon them. He is never so serious as when discussing his purposes in the drama; for once in his life he did not joke or grow cynical. And it is only fair to allow him, for a little space, to speak in his own behalf:

"I think him [Barry Cornwall] very likely to produce a good tragedy, if he keep to a natural style, and not play tricks to form Harlequinades for an audience. . . . I am, however, persuaded, that this [to produce a great tragedy] is not to be done by following the old dramatists, who are full of gross faults, pardoned only for the beauty of their language; but by writing naturally and *regularly*, and producing *regular* tragedies, like the *Greeks*; but not in *imitation*,—merely the outline of their conduct, adapted to our times and circumstances, and of course no chorus."[20]

"It appears to me that there is room for a different style of the drama; neither a servile following of the old drama, which is a grossly erroneous one, nor yet *too French,* like those who succeeded the older writers. It appears to me, that good English, and a severer approach to the rules, might combine something not dishonorable to our literature. I have also attempted to make a play without love. And there are neither rings, nor mistakes, nor starts, nor outrageous ranting villains, nor melodrama, in it. . . . Whatever faults it has will arise from deficiency in the conduct, rather than in the conception, which is simple and severe."[21]

"My dramatic simplicity is *studiously* Greek, and must continue so; *no* reform ever succeeded at first. . . . I want to make a *regular* English drama, no matter whether for the Stage or not."[22]

"The Simplicity of plot is intentional, and the avoidance of *rant* also."[23]

Several facts are clear from these statements. Byron was not repeating an achieved success, for classic tragedy had never existed effectually in English. Classic comedy, or neo-classic, had succeeded in the plays of Jonson, Congreve, and Sheridan. But in tragedy it was necessary to introduce the ancient spirit, in contrast to the popular theatre on the one hand and the romantic on the other. Like Alfieri, Byron went back for his inspiration to the Greeks. But also like Alfieri and like the school of Pope in other fields of literature, he did not transfer bodily an entire technique, as Milton had attempted to do in *Samson Agonistes,* to be criticized therefor by Johnson. He rather tried to catch the spirit of the Greeks, and by adapting it to the English stage to create a form at once national and universal. There is always some discrepancy between aims and accomplishments. Alfieri, in copying the Greeks, had produced a form much closer to the drama of France, and a spirit more profoundly Italian and personal than Greek. Byron, with a similar purpose, is closest in technique to Alfieri, altering his form mainly by lengthening it, and yet is always distinctively Byron.

DRAMA AND PROPAGANDA

In the plans of both men the Unities played an emphatic and significant part. Not only were they the standard and the battle-cry of an older tradition. They were instruments of clarity and common sense in the drama, watchdogs over the spirit of restraint, counteractants against looseness of thinking and of construction, safeguards from the absurdities of imaginative license. "The French," claimed Byron, "very properly ridicule our bringing in *'enfant au premier acte, barbon au dernier.'* "[24] Johnson's rebuttal, by reference to what was better worded, in another connection, by Coleridge, as a "willing suspension of disbelief . . . which constitutes poetic faith," and gives the creative artist right to carry the auditor's imagination as far as it will go, is profound but unconvincing. The principle can be applied only in the case of the ideal audience, which does not exist either in actuality or purely in the artist's mind. The average spectator cannot for more than a very short period of time completely surrender his imagination to the creative artist without a conscious exertion of the will, and this conscious exertion no true artist wishes to demand. Art must carry its own illusion and must follow its own laws of probability. At a symphony the average music lover may devote himself to enjoyment of tone, rhythm, and contour, since music is purely artificial, in the highest sense of that term, and makes no pretence to reality. But in the drama, which treats "of human things and acts," the suspension of disbelief is only partly willing. There is the distinction between poetic faith and poetic credulity, of which every spectator is more or less conscious. A play, accepted as a mere evening's entertainment, may indulge in the most impossible flights of the imagination without awakening resentment. But regarded as an argument about life, it is the less convincing for any departure from reality. The structure of *Henry V* or of *The Winter's Tale* makes greater demands on the imagination than the average theatregoer can supply, and the result is a stress in most productions on the comic portions or on the poetry of the prologues, and not on the single and complete action. The Unities, at a time of imaginative skepticism and hard common sense, like the eighteenth century in England, were not slavish mimicry of the past, but an actual aid to the audience in its enjoyment of the play. The fact that no tragic playwright sufficiently reconciled them to imaginative freedom is a comment upon the times and upon Englishmen.

The Unities, finally, make for a better reading drama, of a kind, than the more lawless tradition. While they deny the liberty of the playwright absolutely to determine his form, and discourage the purple patches of poetry which were so popular in early nineteenth-century selections, they have their eye turned ultimately toward the critic, in appeal for his approval. They make for a simplicity of structure and of language which is at least of negative value to the student. Above all they stress the plot and the conception, the singleness of design, as was nowhere else encouraged in the drama until the newer and freer ideal of organic unity that developed in the nineteenth century. They were a school for Byron's instincts, educating them to the capacity for planning ahead and following an approximately wrought-out scheme, without too great an allowance for momentary whim. Their sureness is not only a deftness of touch, a singleness of mood, and a complete mastery of instruments that make *Beppo* a unified work of art, for all its digressions. The latter poem seems to spring and burgeon from a single root, and has more the oneness of a plant than of an edifice. The dramas are wholes because they have been planned. Even *The Deformed Transformed*, which does not fall within the main group in allegiance to any unity, is like them in its deliberation of design. "I do not know how he meant to finish it," reported Mary

Shelley of the drama; "but he said himself that the whole conduct of the story was already conceived."[25]

It is easier, therefore, to trace in the dramas their original design, which was, as Byron said of it, "simple and severe."[26] The basis of each tragedy is passion: in *Marino Faliero* the passion of outraged pride, in *Sardanapalus* the passion of softness and voluptuosity with military ardor breaking through, in *The Two Foscari* "suppressed passion,"[27] and in *Cain* the passion for knowledge. The passion, "*furious, criminal,* and *hapless,*" not "melting and maudlin,"[28] is placed in the character of a single and exalted individual, who is brought thereby to an impressive catastrophe. Byron, in his treatment of his heroes, considered that he was following Aristotle and Rymer, at least as interpreted by Johnson: "I must remark from *Aristotle* and *Rymer,* that the *hero* of tragedy and (I add *meo periculo*) a tragic poem must *be guilty,* to excite '*terror and pity,*' the end of tragic poetry. But hear not *me,* but my betters.[29] 'The pity which the poet is to labour for is *for* the criminal. The terror is likewise in the punishment of the said criminal.' "[30] But he was prevented by his disposition from absolutely attaining his end. The dramas do not awaken pity and terror in just the manner he intended. We are conscious in them more often of the sweep and power of the passion than of any grim relentlessness of an incomprehensible fate. Hard as it is, sometimes, to enter thoroughly into the spirit of a Faliero or a Foscari, our sympathies, if we accept the Italian background, are as much with the crime as with the criminal. Byron does not justify the gods; in fact, the gods hardly enter into his cosmos. The elder Foscari is not a criminal, and the other protagonists are essentially noble characters, thrown into sharp relief against a debased society. Not fate, but social forces determine the course of the action. The conflict is that of the individual against the whole, and our interest is centred on his point of view. The theme is continuous at least until the production of *Cain*, where it is most thorough and convincing. Thereafter, there is a letdown in the force and assurance of its expression, as if the author were suddenly tired of his position, or disillusioned as to its efficacy. A still better explanation is, perhaps, that after it had reached a nearly perfect expression, there was no longer the same urge, in the artistic nature, toward its utterance.

The devotion to the Unities was confused, in Byron's mind, with his hostility to dramatic representation. They had come to him as a literary, not an histrionic tradition, and it seems to have been his habit mentally to oppose them to practical stagecraft. "It is not intended for the stage," he asserted of *Marino Faliero*. "It is too regular—the time, twenty-four hours—the change of place not frequent—nothing *melo*-dramatic—no surprises, no starts, nor trap-doors— . . . and no *love*—the grand ingredient of a modern play."[31] Some of this may be explained as an outgrowth of the common habit of the times just gone, of accepting the classics as absolutes without relation to the immediate causes of their production—a position that was to be gradually demolished during the long quarrel over the authorship of the *Iliad*, and by the researches of modern scholarship. There is some excuse for Byron's plea, "I cannot conceive how Harris or Elliston should be so insane as to think of acting *Marino Faliero*; they might as well act the *Prometheus* of Aeschylus."[32] But there is none whatsoever for his statement concerning the same play, that it is "constructed on the French model, and therefore more properly to be styled a poem than a play."[33] The assumption is but a combination of his dislike of the stage and his admiration for the past, assisted by an uneasy feeling that he was appealing to a foreign rather than a local tradition and could not meet the demands of a concrete contemporary audience. "It was written," to quote another gloss on *Faliero*, "solely for the reader. It is too regular, too simple, and of too remote an interest, for the Stage."[34]

How he expected to found a tradition of the theatre by the means of unactable plays he never made clear. Perhaps he had some sort of sublime trust in the taste of succeeding generations, who should overlook mere questions of technique in the enjoyment of critical excellences. The criticism of his purpose, however, has little reference to the drama of posterity. Whatever his moving impulse, he wrote his plays in a spirit of close kinship with the past, and attempted to meet, not the immediate requirements of a popular stage, but those ideal requirements, laid down by the great of the past, which he felt to be for all time and for all peoples. He laid plans for the future; but he corrected the present by restoring the spirit of the past, he replaced "the miserable trash which, from Milman to Barry Cornwall, has been intruded on"[35] the English stage, by dramas based on the practices of his predecessors. His watchword was not succeeding generations, but what he felt to be the steadier opinion of mankind, not posterity but permanence: "My object is not *immediate* popularity in my present productions, which are written in a different system from the rage of the day. But, *mark what I say*, that the time will come when these will be preferred to any I have before written."[36] "I am determined to make a struggle for the more regular drama."[37] The instruments of that struggle were the plays which, with *Manfred*, he wished put together in his works, *Sardanapalus*, *The Two Foscari*, and *Faliero*,[38] and to a lesser extent, because of a subsiding enthusiasm, *Cain*, *Heaven and Earth*, *Werner*, and *The Deformed Transformed*.

As the initial step in the process, *Faliero* is of the greatest importance in any judgment of his methods. The multitude of references to it in the letters indicates that Byron gave more thought to its artistic structure, both in promulgation and retrospect, than to that of any of the other plays. The play, written during the bustle of Teresa's divorce suit,[39] was admittedly not so perfect as Byron would have wished. Its major theme, public wrong and private grievances, "the head conspiring against the body for refusal of redress for a real injury,"[40] is evident in lightning flashes rather than in the steady light of the whole. The idea of writing a poem on the subject of Marino had come to Byron while gazing on the black veil over the Doge's picture in Venice. "The black veil, which is painted over the place of Mar. Faliero among the Doges, and the Giant's Staircase, where he was crowned, and discrowned, and decapitated, struck forcibly upon my imagination; as did his fiery character and strange story."[41] "My object [in publishing *Marino*] was to record one of the most remarkable incidents of the Venetian Republic, embodying it in what I considered the most interesting form—dialogue, and giving my work the accompaniments of scenery and manners studied on the spot. . . . I painted the men as I found them, as they were, not as the critics would have them."[42] The play had for Byron a personal interest, in some ways as great, though not so intimate, as *Manfred's*. In genesis it has little enough to do with any intention of reforming the theatre; but its theme was particularly fitted to Byron's purpose, and with this double view of the matter it was composed.

The preface is less in line with his other prefaces, than with the "Pareri" of Alfieri. The author is immediately at home with his listeners, speaks in the first person, and reviews frankly the successive stages of composition. No humor creeps in, nor any apologies. Indeed, when Byron turned to the drama, he seems to have lost his sense of humor, as that very bad effort at humor, Idenstein in *Werner*, testifies. For that reason Byron was never absolutely at home in his adopted medium. He was ever in need of a flow of passion to feed the verse, without the possibility of descending to the "pedestrian Muse" of *Don Juan*. His plays have the force and compactness of sincerity and of a consciously adhered-to intent, but they lack the greater human richness that is characteristic even of the later narrative poems.

The preface, nevertheless, is a very thorough explanation of the spirit and methods of the author in writing the play. Nothing could be more circumstantial than its statements:

> It is now four years that I have meditated this work; and before I had sufficiently examined the records, I was rather disposed to have made it turn on a jealousy in Faliero. But, perceiving no foundation for this in historical truth, and aware that jealousy is an exhausted passion in the drama, I have given it a more historical form. . . . I have had no view to the stage . . . the desire of preserving, though still too remote, a nearer approach to unity than the irregularity, which is the reproach of the English theatrical compositions, permits, has induced me to represent the conspiracy as already formed, and the Doge acceding to it; whereas, in fact, it was his own preparation and that of Israel Bertuccio. The other characters (except that of the Duchess), incidents, and almost the time . . . are strictly historical, except that all the consultations took place in the palace. Had I followed this, the unity would have been better preserved; but I wished to produce the Doge in the full assembly of the Conspirators, instead of monotonously placing him in dialogue with the same individuals.

This, in a nutshell, is a fair enough summary of the play. *Marino Faliero* is the combined product of two impelling desires—for regularity and for historical truth—and is welded together with a practical eye to effect. Byron's classicism, if not derivative, is largely the same as that of Alfieri. His interest in historical justification is his own. Alfieri had also turned to history, but his main interest was in the passion.

The mood is not a mood, as Coleridge would have it, but a principle shared equally by all the later products of his genius. It is but a part of that constant effort to enslave his imagination, that we have spoken of earlier in this paper. Here, as elsewhere, the effort did not totally succeed, but between the dramas and the narrative poems *Beppo* and *Don Juan* there is a marked distinction. In those others he gives licentious rein to his imagination, only to bring it violently back to earth. Here the imagination and the sense of fact are one—the play, in its main outlines, is historical, but its matter is worked upon and transformed by the creative will. It differs from history as we should expect poetry to do—it lacks the historian's proper skepticism, while it breathes the fervor of its author. It takes advantage of the opportunities of history, but is not ultimately concerned with depicting the past. To speak in Aristotelian terms, it is imitative, but imitative of a higher reality. Byron did not think in such terms; but his predecessor, Alfieri, while discussing a play of his own, had prepared for Byron full justification: "This historic fact has been, through the ill-nature of some, denied or minimized. But that matters very little to the poet, who on a possible and plausible basis, related and believed by many, builds the story and conducts it according to his own discretion. . . . Every theatrical invention, out of which is to grow some grand and sudden effect, is sufficiently justified when it does not seem untrue to life and when it produces its effect."[43] Nowhere as in *Faliero, Sardanapalus*, and the *Foscari* did Byron come so close to the spirit of the Greeks. The underlying differences, like those of Goethe's classic dramas, are the results of epoch and personality; it was impossible for a nineteenth-century Englishman to be an Aeschylus. *Marino Faliero* bears upon it the stamp of its creating environment; and yet, in contrast with the body of his works, it is a commendable approach to the classic spirit.

A natural foil to it, among the other dramas, and unlike it in nearly all its virtues, is the immediately antecedent *Manfred*. The latter is not based on history, it has no regard for facts, it pays no respect to the Unities, and it is so careless of plot that the whole design of the third act is an afterthought. *Manfred* is the projection of a mood on a screen, is the poetical threshing out of a vital personal problem, is of its nature preëminently subjective. *Faliero* is, at least in its best intentions, the objective analysis of conditions and beings foreign to the poet's self. *Manfred* is important, aside from its excellences, as indicating Byron's first completed approach to dramatic composition. It is like the other drama only in the personality behind the whole, in the nature of its blank verse, and in the influence of Shakespeare everywhere apparent. It serves to break a path and prepare a way, but it hardly anticipates the dramas which are to follow. It is absolutely original, to the extent that it has no model, and transforms its multitudinous sources into harmony with its atmosphere. *Marino Faliero* has as forerunners both Alfieri and *Venice Preserved*.

Of the two other dramas of our persistent group of three, we need say but little, except that, even more than *Faliero*, they obey the rules. The preface to *Sardanapalus* says nothing new; it is of interest, however, in reflecting the coldness which met the zealous efforts of the author. Byron, in it, reaffirms his devotion to the truth of history, whereas *Sardanapalus* is really the least historical of the three. He restates his aims at length, and accepts the challenge of the romanticists by a defense of the Unities: "The author . . . is aware of the unpopularity of such a notion in present English literature; but it is not a system of his own, being merely an opinion which, not very long ago, was the law of literature throughout the world, and is still so in the more civilized parts of it." The curtness of the rejoinder is modified by an admission of the insufficiency of his attempts; the Unities are pictured as a goal to which the dramatist has not quite been able to attain.

The preface is practically the swan song of Byron's narrower purpose. Thereafter, though he continued to write plays, there was a sudden loosening in structure and a departure, not only from the Unities but from the spirit of classical tragedy, which seems at first sight complete capitulation to the enemy. And yet, especially in *Cain*, there is the mark of a divergent purpose and stronger will than in *Manfred*. The later drama, though "in my gay metaphysical style, and in the Manfred line,"[44] and magnificently as it departs from the unity of place, has a compactness and sureness of treatment, an impersonality of touch that are lacking in the earlier. Where Manfred and the Abbot are primarily emotional, Cain and Lucifer are intellectuals, puzzling out or arguing over a cosmic problem. The sudden explosion of wrath which results in the death of Abel and the expulsion of Cain, is in some ways as incongruous as similar explosions in the works of that other intellectual playwright, Shaw. Cain's universe, also, is far different from Manfred's. It is presided over by God and the angels, not by a horde of miscellaneous devils and spirits. In this aspect, indeed, is much that may explain it. *Cain* is a Biblical play, copies the language of the Bible, and therefore turns, for its traditions, not to classic drama but to the mystery plays of the Middle Ages. Byron in all likelihood had but a vague idea of what a mystery was like, beyond the notion that it treated heavenly subjects, made use of Biblical material, and was addressed to the religious feelings of its audience. His notion of the form, according to Schaffner's suggestion, was probably borrowed from Warton's *History of English Poetry*.[45] The structure is hardly more than the splendid adaptation of an idea to a medium. The result, if it is not classic, has certainly little of the atmosphere of contemporary drama. It is, as has been stated, mainly Biblical in tone; but the "scriptural foundation of the mystery is hardly more than a *cadre*, furnishing in broad outline the general situation, the climax, and the catastrophe. The action of the first and second acts has no basis at all in scripture."[46] It is not counter to the medieval spirit to invent and to improve upon the original account. The Middle Ages, when they used the Bible, expressed the Middle Ages; Byron, likewise, expressed Byron. In *Cain* he is a compound of the intellectual rebel, the rationalist cynic of the Age of Reason, and the profoundly religious nature. As an artist, he is more open-minded but not otherwise different from the author of *Marino Faliero*. He appeals to another tradition of the theatre, but, as he claims in his preface, he does not allow himself the liberties of broad humor, horseplay, and scenes unnecessary to the plot, to be found in earlier mysteries. *Cain* is a regularized mystery, treating its medieval origins with an artistic restraint almost entirely lacking in *Manfred*. Not for nothing had Byron planned earlier to make it one of a group of "four tragedies to be written, . . . *Sardanapalus, Francesca of Rimini . . . Cain . . .* and . . . *Tiberius*."[47]

For all his *ex post facto* plea of not having foreseen "this war of 'Church and State'" in writing "a speculative, but still a harmless, production,"[48] he seems to have realized, to some extent, his iconoclasm in *Cain*. He displays an uncomfortable feeling in the preface that the drama is daring and needs vigorous defense. But of course he did not anticipate the violence of the storm, nor did he foresee the desertion of his best friends to the opposition. After an adverse article in the *Edinburgh Review* and the criticism of his friend Hobhouse that the poem was irreligious, and as bad as "the worst bombast of Dryden's"[49]—a statement which, according to Hobhouse, "had made him nearly mad"[50]—Byron was too taken up with its defense on moral grounds to recollect previous artistic theories. His contention that "Cain is . . . a drama, not a piece of argument,"[51] is merely a reminder that every person in it speaks in character, as part of the development of the whole, and is not a mere mouthpiece of the author.[52] The plea is both sincere and misleading. No one can deny that the ideas of any artist may run away with him and that Byron is but defining the attitude of the dramatist toward his work when he states, "like all imaginative men, I, of course, embody myself with the character while I *draw* it; but not a moment after my pen is off the paper."[53] But though consciously he may have applied a strict, judicial impartiality in the upbuilding of the whole, unconsciously he furnished Satan with some compelling and poetic arguments. The closest parallel, as he himself noted, is *Paradise Lost*, which to the imagination of modern man does anything but justify the ways of God to man. The play breathes a spirit of iconoclasm and revolt. Before the great figures of Lucifer and Cain, Adam and his cortège are puny and tame. As Manfred and Marino had been pieces of self-portraiture of the poet's emotional nature, so Cain portrays his religious intellect.

Cain is the last of the great dramas. *Heaven and Earth* is such a falling off that Goethe declared it might have been written by a bishop—though it still, for all its loss in verve, contains glimpses of *Cain's* immensities. Of *Werner* little of good may be said, beyond admitting that the conception is powerful—and this was borrowed. *The Deformed Transformed* is a fragment, and in all probability fortunately so. It betrays, on the part of the author, a loss of interest in the drama, that was more profound than any mere desertion of the Unities.

The truth is that Byron's faith in his artistic principles was constitutionally too weak to weather the neglect that had been visited on the dramas. The poet had received encouragement from nobody. "Murray and his synod"[54] threw cold water on the attempt. Gifford had not taken to the dramas.[55] The *Edinburgh Review* had attacked them.[56] Shelley, who was often Byron's sole strong supporter for his forlorn hopes, thought this the wrong road,[57] and considered it affectation to write plays not destined for the stage.[58] Worst of all, the public reception had been a cold one. He had expected this but was not used to nor prepared for neglect. He did not court popularity, he detested the public to which his verse appealed, yet he wrote to be read.

His independence remained with him as long as the fervor of the crusader lasted. But as ever, the fire died down. His weakening was evident even at the time when he was outwardly most defiant, in the tone of petulance he exhibited toward his public: "You see what it is to throw pearls to swine. As long as I write the exaggerated nonsense which has corrupted the public taste, they applauded to the very echo, and, now that I have really composed, within these three or four years, some things which [they] should 'not willingly let die,' the whole herd snort and grumble."[59] His "general unpopularity, and the universal run of the period against my productions,"[60] was becoming an obsession with him, to an extent unwarranted by facts, until he exclaimed in rueful despair, "Every publication of mine has latterly failed." His reaction to this largely imaginary unpopularity remained twofold: a feverish effort to encourage himself and to retain his independence—"I am not discouraged by this, because writing and composition are habits of my mind, with which Success and Publication are objects of remoter reference—*not causes* but *effects*"[61]—and a gradual relinquishment of his "fruitless experiment."[62] Sometimes, in Byron, and always when in action, there was true and steady courage, but in literature he was never more than fitfully persistent. After a while, in any contention, his boldest statements became but bravado. He lacked the patience necessary for final accomplishment, the fixity of purpose of a Shelley or an Ibsen. He was at heart too good-natured, too mercurial. His fits of remonstrance were but outbursts of energy, to be followed always by a sharp reaction. But if in literature he was the creature of mood and impulse, it was not because he was incapable of a steady purpose—the Greek expedition disproves that hypothesis. His trouble was that he was never absolutely sure of what he wanted to do, for longer than a brief time. In poetry, as in religion, he lacked capacity for faith.

The relinquishment of his intention was preparing even while he was conducting a pamphlet—or preface—war with the world. During the composition of *Sardanapalus*, his will was already wavering: "I am in the *third* act of a *third* drama; and if I have nothing to expect but coldness from the public and hesitation from yourself, it were better to break off in time. I had proposed to myself to go on, as far as my Mind would carry me, and I have thought of plenty of subjects. But if I am trying an impracticable experiment, it is better to say so at once."[63] After the battle over *Cain*, he more and more gave ground. He allowed whole passages to be omitted in *Heaven and Earth*,[64] changed the name of Michael to Raphael,[65] and softened down disturbing portions to satisfy the godly. His disillusionment with the dramas was complete, as one of his talks with Leigh Hunt at least suggests.[66] His last references to them, in the conversations with Kennedy, give no indication that he wished to return to the form: "I am tired of tragedies, having so completely failed in them, as they say."[67]

And yet Byron did not need to be ashamed of his dramas. Their public reception was colder than they deserved; partly, the times were at fault, partly the foreignness of their air. Not their weaknesses—except, perhaps, an inadaptability to the stage—were against them, but their lack of English idiom. They were composed, in the prophetic words of Alfieri, "simply . . . plausibly . . . warmly."[68] Their theme, the protest of the individual against the static and retarding power of society, was behind the defiant romantic literature of the time. But though their spirit was defiant, their rationale was the discouragement of revolt—the individual always failed. "In all the plays the force of the individual will is shown succumbing to the power of the norm."[69] The contrast between the reason and the instinctive emotional sympathies of the author, however, did not make against the power of the plays. It is the appeal of great tragedy that the strong man whom we love goes down before stronger circumstances. Neither did the desire for the tragedies "to be as near truth as the drama can be,"[70] really stand in the author's way. He paints upon reality, he gives the appearance of life, but at least in his major characters he transcends ordinary existence with the transfused glow of his passion. Marino, like Alfieri's Raimondo, is "a character possible rather than realistic."[71] The very excess of his pride and his anger might be made telling on the stage, in the hands of a great actor. His speech on the decadence of Venice is as compelling as anything in *Childe Harold*.

Indeed, if the dramas have an outstanding virtue beside their construction, it is in this convincing depiction of overwhelming passion. The compactness and clarity of their form, with its background of Alfieri and the French classics, allowed a treatment of the one theme, a turning over and over in the hands of the artist to show all facets. But Byron, though his plays are twice the length of Alfieri's, has no interest in the subtleties of passion. His plays are long because of the abundance of his language. He uses them as opportunities for invective; "almost always the interest of the poet is obviously in the sentiments more than in the plot."[72]

Except in Sardanapalus, there is hardly a hint of dramatic conflict within any character. In fact, we do not have to look long at the dramas, in order to see that Byron is living in them the life that he cannot live in actuality, that his own agonies, thinly coated with circumstance, are the real themes. His soul, as he said, is in *Marino Faliero*.[73] "The play may be good or bad, but I flatter myself that it is original as a picture of *that* kind of passion, which to my mind is so natural, that I am convinced that I should have done precisely what the Doge did on those provocations."[74] The cry of Byron's nature was for action and expression. There may have been much of the Hamlet in him, but his instinct was toward Richard III and Napoleon. The plays reflect, in their very rhetoric and lack of activity, this need for action. They have therefore a strength of their own, the strength of a great force guided.

Not in the plays themselves is to be found the reason for the bitterness of his disillusionment. That is to be attributed rather to the reception, or lack of reception, by the public, the hostility of friends, and the discouragement of misunderstood ideals. Moreover, the poetic will was tired, and when it sprang again into life, it returned, not to the dramas, but to a former and deeper love—*Don Juan*.

CHAPTER VIII

ACHIEVEMENT

THE history of the dramas is in a way a judgment on Byron as an artist. They are a result of an enthusiasm for the right, not altogether the result of a deep-seated instinct seeking expression. Their intensity attests their sincerity. But their form is too limited to accommodate a variety of impulses. At the time, they satisfied an artistic need in the poet, for giving certain ideas a classic, or apparently classic, form. Although into each of them Byron poured himself, it was, after all, not his whole self, but only one aspect of his complex personality. *Manfred,* if I may include it for the moment with the other tragedies, expressed his despair and its solution; *Marino,* his detestation of society; *Sardanapalus,* less successfully because more consciously, his weakness and mercuriality; and *Cain,* his religious skepticism. But drama of this nature demanded, in addition to formal perfection, a sustained high seriousness lacking in the man. It excluded afterthought or humorous byplay. As long as the immediate inspiration continued, the tragedies kept to a fairly high level, but when it began to die down, there was no other stimulus to replace it. Not Byron's passion, in this case, stood in the way. The neoclassic drama, in the hands of Alfieri, had been a competent instrument for the expression of passion. But it demanded that the inspiration should blow always in one direction, and Byron, being of a variable temperament, was hampered by its purity of form. Impure art (to accept that word in its aesthetic connotations) was necessary to a heterogeneous poetic nature. *Don Juan*, in its tradition of the Italian burlesque and the Italian heroic epics, allowed for both emotion and mockery, and much besides.

It is this tradition of *Don Juan* that was in its favor, not theories behind its composition. Where the dramas drew upon a fairly well defined type, the epic harked back to the whole field of Italian epic in ottava rima, and through it to all related poetry. The type had never become fixed even in Italian, for where there was a Boiardo to write seriously, there was a Berni to burlesque him. In its inclusiveness, the liberty of its license, lay its appeal to Byron. And yet to leave the matter here, as if the poem were wholly whimsical narrative, is to give but one facet of the whole. Byron, in *Don Juan*, was not merely disporting himself in print, though he may have been having a very good time. Here and there in the poem are hints of an *ars poetica* as interesting of definition as that behind the dramas.

Don Juan as it now stands is a gigantic torso. It breaks off in the midst of a canto as if Byron had been suddenly called from writing it to transact business. Hence no absolutely final word may be passed on its structure, in the absence of an absolutely final word by its author. The spirit of the poem, however, is obvious. It is a humorous epic, in an atmosphere of rather serious fun—of the nature, sometimes, of those practical jokes its author resorted to in order to distract his attention from unpleasantnesses.[1] In the style and manner of *Beppo*, it is "meant to be a little quietly facetious on everything."[2] It seeks out the humor in every situation, and when to this it adds pathos or ecstasy, it is applying its license, not its law. Byron's purpose may best be seen where he came nearest failing—in Cantos VII and VIII, where he indulges in such a bad pun as "bulletin—bullet in," and garners glee from the strangeness of Russian names. His aim was to scoff, to "laugh at all things, great and small things,"³ in particular those small things that ought to be laughed at. It is true that the laughter has often a metallic ring, but it is going too far to say, with Herr Koenig, that "untrammeled good humor is so seldom, properly speaking, never, to be found in his works that in reading him we never feel cheerful and at ease."⁴ Byron, it must be admitted, is seldom "content to have his laugh and to set others chuckling;"⁵ he espouses theories and attacks creeds. If he follows Pulci, he is more embittered and denunciatory than his master. But mingled with more violent elements are full-blooded fun, which at times becomes boisterous, and, in the later cantos, a broad if cynical tolerance, which has in it something "cheerful and at ease." The laugh exists often for the laugh's sake. There is no malice directed against Don José in the couplet,

> A better cavalier ne'er mounted horse,
> Or, being mounted, e'er got down again,⁶

and none against the ship in the tag to the shipwreck,

> She gave a heel, and then a lurch to port,
> And, going down headforemost—sunk, in short.⁷

Sometimes the humor is unconvincing, as has been noted in respect to Cantos VII and VIII; the puns are forced, or the incongruence does not ring true. Such failure, however, is the exception, not the rule; it is but the weather vane to show which way the poet's mood blows. In general, the humorous afterthought comes pat. The illusion is shattered, sometimes by a maul and sometimes by a gimlet, and the laugh rises spontaneously.

Don Juan is too great and too varied a work to confine within a formula. It is now pathetic, now gay, now vitriolic. But at bottom it is a humorous poem, with these other qualities as mere adornments. It is impossible, therefore, to know, in many instances, how to take Byron. Maybe he did not, as

Chesterton gave him credit for having done, teach the British author how not to take himself seriously. But if he is not the mainspring, he is in the great tradition of English humor. It is the habit of humor to laugh at itself, even at many things it counts important and assured. Humor is but soft merriment applied to all things, and may have, but more often does not have, malice behind its laughter. The bitterness in *Don Juan* is confined mainly to the first half; satire runs through the entire poem; but satire of the nature of Dryden's, Pope's, or Churchill's is not its keynote. It is in the broader, more tolerant tradition of the Italians; its basis is not so much indignation as cynicism. The attacks on Southey and Castlereagh in the dedication are but momentary exhibitions of spleen; they might be removed entire without marring the poem. The description of Donna Inez, if it is meant to satirize Lady Byron,[8] has enough of the broad, impersonality of humor to make it, at least, more telling than Byron's customary direct frontal attacks. If it is the most circumstantial character sketch in the poem, it is so because Byron was more familiar with the model than with the originals of the other portraits. Don José, who is for the moment obviously Byron, is not a flattering likeness. The satire of persons in Canto I is not so much intentional as it is the normal result of a strong sense of humor working on experiences through which Byron had passed, and gazing at them from Byron's point of view. It was natural, under the circumstances, for him to sympathize most with himself and to see his wife in a not very favorable light.

The satire in *Don Juan*, on the whole, is less personal than that in any other great satire by a disciple of Pope. Where it is serious, it is at one with that "liberal extension of morality"[9] which Byron claimed as his purpose; it is truly "a *satire* on the *abuses* of the present states of society,"[10] less on individuals than on groups. In the words of Mr. Chew, "If

Byron laughs at much upon which his contemporaries set store, it is in order that he may destroy abuses by ridicule."[11] But ridicule is not the life of the poem. The epic is made up now of narrative, now of apostrophe, now of conversational asides and long confessions by the author to the reader. Into this, ridicule enters only as one ingredient. Cantos VII and VIII are weak largely because they are a philosophical attack on soldiery and tyrants,[12] unrelieved, as is the rest of the poem, by the personality of the man. The greater portions are a compound of many elements; but the seriousness of their purpose is relieved by the sentiment, *"What, after all, are all things but a show?"*[13]

But *Don Juan* had its sting. That accounts both for its great popularity, in part, and for the storm of protests it aroused even among the poet's friends. The objections to *Don Juan* did not spring entirely from outraged morality. Byron claimed rightly that he was no more licentious than many accepted classics that his critics admired. His defense has much of the truth in it, on both this and another ground: "I take a vicious and unprincipled character and lead him through those ranks of society, whose high external accomplishments cover and cloak internal and secret vices, and I paint the natural effects of such characters. . . . It [is] time to unmask the specious hypocrisy [in high and noble life], and shew it in its native colors."[14] That is the excuse of all satire. It is misapplied only so far as Juan is hardly very vicious or altogether unprincipled, and manages with all his vices to attract. The satire is directed not at him but at society itself, which is to blame for transforming an ingenuous, charming, idealizing youth into a hardened, though not a hard, man of the world. The successive disillusionments of the hero are the real subject of the narrative. The epic is less episodic simply because each separate adventure is a step in the training, if not the growth, of a soul.

And yet not even society is uniformly damned. Juan's first seducer, Donna Julia, is herself not altogether to blame. Byron, in tracing vice to its source in passion, uncovers some of its seductiveness, and to that extent offers its apology. But the apology is not an ordinary one. The poetry is fired by a hatred of hypocrisy, but not of that usual object of satire, the unctuous profession of a faith in which the pretender to virtue does not believe, and which he does not practice. The odium here is visited on the euphemism of sentiment, the false faith in which the pretender actually thinks he believes. The morality of *Don Juan* is to correct those people who, "while . . . looking after the shadow, ... lose the substance of goodness."[15] It assails the "cant of sentiment" which his own *Childe Harold* had encouraged.[16] It is a counterblast to the cult of sentimentalism, which had matured in the last century and was still clinging to the fringes of British intellectual life. Byron supposed his poem most objectionable to women, the arch sentimentalists; "it is TOO TRUE, and the women hate everything that strips off the tinsel of *Sentiment*; and they are right, as it would rob them of their weapons."[17] Women, nevertheless, proved a ready audience for *Don Juan*; perhaps they were not so sentimentally inclined as the worldly-wise Byron believed. But the apology in one phase is unanswerable. *Don Juan* is neither incentive nor palliative for vice. "No Girl will ever be seduced by reading *D. J.* . . . Little's poems and Rousseau's *romans* . . . will encourage her, and not the Don, who laughs at that, and—and—most other things."[18] "The sentimental anatomy of Rousseau and Mad^e. de S[taël] are far more formidable than any quantity of verse. They are so, because they sap the principles, by *reasoning* upon the *passions*."[19]

The morality is stringent but hardly dainty. Hence many delicate and gentle persons, or aesthetes like Mr. Powys, are revolted as much as they are attracted by the poem. The attack on sentiment is impelled, if not by a gross cynicism, by an imperious way of seeing life broadly without distinction between the subtle shadings of passion. The poem may best be judged in antithesis to the third and fourth cantos of *Childe Harold*. The old conflict of flesh and soul, or of clay and spirit, is continued, only here flesh has its way. Byron's lingering fondness for the ideal is for something which has become unreal and unattainable, existent only in dreams. His world, in the interim, has turned to clay; reality denies the spark. As he comments in *The Vision of Judgment*, he borrows his very comparisons from clay, "being clay myself."[20] There is no attempt to reconcile imagination with reality. This is this and that is that, and never the twain shall meet, he seems to tell himself. The poem, while it ridicules sentiment, ridicules also all the finer sensibilities and ideals, sometimes regretfully. Don Juan on deck, forsaking love for seasickness, would prove an illuminating figurehead for the poem.

Byron characteristically confuses his mood with the desire to express the whole, simple, and unvarnished truth, where he is really but expressing his personal criticism of the world. It is not only that his muse is "the most sincere that ever dealt in fiction."[21] It does not entirely "sketch your world exactly as it goes."[22] It is too much bounded by the personality and interests of its possessor to state the whole truth about life. Byron is not a universal genius. But for that reason perhaps he is more striking and keen than might be expected of catholicity. His personality pervades and warms the poetry, carrying the narrative over rough places, or interrupting it with the interpolation of extraneous but illuminating matter. Even his hostility to fiction[23] is part of his individuality. He shows us with a grand gesture, this is how things really are. And if things are not exactly as he tells us, the gesture is none the less impressive and sincere.

The effort to arrive at exact verisimilitude engaged a major share of his conscious preparation for writing. The poem is not an altogether mad poem because there is madness in it. Behind the narrative is such research as a scholar would expend on preparing a linguistic monograph—perhaps not so thorough or so accurate as the ultimate ideal of the scholar, but, for the poet, exacting. Don Juan is drawn from real life, either that of the author or of people he knew;[24] when Byron's experience failed, he resorted to research for exactness. He first gathered "a repertory of facts, of course with some reserve and slight restriction,"[25] and let his imagination work creatively upon them. At some times he followed his source more slavishly than at others, and the result is a varying degree of prosiness from canto to canto. When he utilizes his own experience he is less hampered, but he makes effective use of borrowed materials. The description of the furniture, in Canto III, is taken from Tully's *Tripoli*.[26] The siege of Ismail is based mainly on the account of Castelnau in his *Essai sur l'histoire de la nouvelle Russie*.[27] And the shipwreck, as E. H. Coleridge has amply demonstrated, has a dozen sources. The poem loses and gains by its scrupulosity. Sometimes the emphasis on "statistics, tactics, politics, and geography"[28] palls. The parts that depend on Byron's own experience are handled more easily and more gracefully. But when his imagination works upon and conquers its raw material, it produces the superb spectacle of the shipwreck, the most convincing of all the episodes. The gain is in that quality which composed one of the fundamental instincts of his nature—the appeal to authority, the authority of facts: "You may rely on my using no nautical word not founded on authority, and no circumstances not grounded in reality."[29]

The insistence on fact, furthermore, was not an added characteristic, but the very nature and guiding principle of his humor. If he observed that the chief wit of the Italians seemed to be in telling home truths,[30] he illustrated the applicability of the observation as well as any of his predecessors. There is more truth in his humorous sallies than in the serious confessions of others. He wandered "on pedestrian muses," and like Sancho Panza, he could laugh at those who traveled "on the wingèd steed."[31] In holding up his mirror to Nature, to show her all her warts and callouses, he was but following the dictates of his genius. He was not following Aristotle, in letter or in spirit. "It is not the function of the poet," had declared that critic whom the neoclassics worshiped this side idolatry, "to relate what has happened, but what may happen—what is possible according to the law of probability or necessity."[32] Byron cared less, on the surface, for probability or necessity than he did for actuality. But the two, in his greatest work, are combined.

The poem lacks a tone of stark morality, however, because it is, after all, fundamentally a humorous production. The moral is to be found for the looking, and sometimes it is thrust upon us; but what Byron seems to be interested in, is primarily himself. *Don Juan* is the greatest of informal epics. There is no attempt at sustaining a grand style; and when the author does lapse into it, he hastens to cover it over with puerilities or whimsicalities, as a man might do in conversation. On just this side *Don Juan,* like *Beppo,* is the glorification of chitchat, what a whimsical man would write to a woman with whom he is alternately sarcastic, in love, angry, and tenderly playful. The style, possessing a directness and power of passionate utterance, and a complexity, nay inconsistency of thoughts, depends, for its effectiveness, upon the carelessness, the slovenliness of ordinary speech. If for the instant it rises above itself, it does so but for a time. "A nondescript and ever varying rhyme,"[33] it has the inconsequence and the wit, the glow, and the lucidity that are to be found in the correspondence. Byron, for the first time in poetry, as formerly in his letters and his conversation, had the right to utter whatever came into his head, without thought of consequences, to

> rattle on exactly as I'd talk
> With anybody in a ride or walk.[34]

He might speak seriously, or with tongue in cheek, but at any moment he could fall back upon the plea of humor, when taken to task for an assertion. The result of the method—or mood, for it is the most unmethodical of methods—which would have been fatal in the hands of a lesser man, is a "wonderful fertility of thought and expression," that moved even Croker to enthusiasm. "The 'Protean' style of 'Don Juan,' instead of checking (as the fetters of rhythm generally do) his natural ability, not only gives him wider limits to range in, but even generates a more roving disposition. I dare swear . . . that his digressions and repetitions generate one another, and that the happy jingle of some of his comical rhymes has led him on to episodes of which he never originally thought."[35]

The digressions, however, are but part of the business. Byron had never been thoroughly at home when pursuing a rigid scheme, and his bent had been always to break away from the fetters of design. For long his muse had "admired digression,"[36] particularly at genial moments. In the plan of the whole, digressions are the humor of it. "He digresses because he has much to say; because his poem is a criticism of life."[37] But he also digresses to relieve a situation, to show that things are not so serious as they seem, or that there are other things worth talking about, or that the real subject of the poem is Byron and what Byron thinks, not the miscellaneous adventures of Juan. In bulk the digressions have "an analogy with the general system of his character, and the wit and poetry which surround . . . hide the darkness of the thing itself."[38] They do not intrude upon the narrative. They are but a stage, or an ever recurring background, against which Juan's travels pass in strong relief.

Into the cauldron go many things, wit, poetry, passion, imagination, philosophy, epigram, irony, idealism, sarcasm, sentiment. The style is indeed "Protean." Sometimes the elements are fused one with another; but usually they contrast strikingly. The gravity serves to heighten the fun,[39] and light sentiment to deepen the succeeding impression of gloom. Nothing is forbidden in this frolic of the fancy. Remarks on the technique of writing intrude into the text, as they had in Cervantes, Pulci, Casti, and occasionally Ariosto. The author admits us behind the scenes as he writes, and points out to us how the show is manipulated. There are comments on the form,

> Also, our Hero's lot, howe'er unpleasant
> (Because this Canto has become too long)
> Must be postponed discreetly for the present.[40]

And there are good-natured admissions of the straits to which an author is carried by "the wicked necessity of rhyming":

> (The rhyme obliges me to this; sometimes
> Monarchs are less imperative than rhymes) . . .
>
> The 'tu's' too much—but let it stand—the verse
> Requires it.[41]

Yet there is a unity of tone, gained, if not by uniformity, by a consistent return to the note of humor. When the author grows too metaphysical, quite forgets "this poem's merely quizzical, and deviates into matters rather dry,"[42] he brings himself back to earth with a single stroke of his pen, and resumes his gaiety. Even those recollections of his former work which occur again and again are transformed either in their expression or by the turn of the final couplet. The following passage, for instance, though distinctly reminiscent of the *Prophecy of Dante*, and *The Lament of Tasso*, is nevertheless neither, but unmistakably *Don Juan*:

> Men who partake all passions as they pass
>   Acquire the deep and bitter power to give
> Their images again as in a glass,
>   And in such colors that they seem to live;
> You may do right forbidding them to show 'em
> But spoil (I think) a very pretty poem.[43]

The ottava rima allowed and encouraged this final humorous sally, by its couplet at the end of each stanza. But it is important for more than its flexibility in the hands of its user. It carried with it memories of great Italian literature that had gone before. Authority, for the first time, Byron does not seem to have worried about. But the stimulation of example worked strongly upon him. He always showed the tendency to adopt a style suggested by the works of another. In *English Bards*, it had been the style of Gifford and Churchill, rather than of Pope; in *Childe Harold*, that of the Spenserian stanza, in many hands; and in the early tragedies, Shakespeare's. It may be said that he was inspired rather than that he copied. But he was open to the stimulus of diction or of a lilt, which carried him as decidedly as the flow of his thought. Whatever came into his head from a contrasting style, if it worked its way into the composition, was felt to be foreign matter, and set off by quotation marks. In the case of *Don Juan*, the background is that of the Italian romance and burlesque epic. *Whistlecraft*, though it may have suggested to Byron a similar effort to translate the manner of the Italians into English, was not the inspiration of his poem; the answer to the contrary is that the two are essentially unlike. Neither is Pulci, nor Berni, nor Casti, nor the three of them, enough to explain the "tradition" of *Don Juan*. There are echoes of *Jerusalem Delivered*, and of *Orlando Furioso*, both great epics removed by a nobility of treatment from burlesque, as definite as echoes of closer models. Even Spenser, from his connection with Ariosto in critical parlance, is sometimes mirrored, though grotesquely, in the style.

This is not to say that Byron slavishly copied, or even imitated. Good evidence may be adduced to show that he did not. But in writing *Don Juan* he had the earlier epics constantly in mind. He had the advantage of observing and testing the methods of others before trying them himself. He fell heir to suggestions in technique that are lacking to the pioneer in a form of art. He shaped and stamped the whole with his personality; but without the example of a long tradition, he could hardly have produced *Don Juan*.

All this has been made clear by Mr. Fuess, in *Lord Byron as a Satirist in Verse*, and by Mr. Waller, in his preface to Frere's *The Monks and the Giants*. What they have not considered necessary to point out is another and modifying influence—the Rules, or the background of the neoclassic tradition. Our epic, as I have been at pains to assert, is an essentially humorous composition. It laughs at all things, or attempts to. And for that reason it is impossible, as in a more responsible work, to say, "Lo here!" and "Lo there!" and let quotation end the argument. It is necessary, for understanding, to enter into the spirit of raillery, and this the present study, as a serious investigation, cannot pretend to do. Byron's irony, at its best, like Swift's, succeeds in meaning and not meaning eactly what it says, at one and the same moment. It seems to remark that the present is a very serious matter, but that it must not be taken seriously. It at once ridicules its subject and ridicules its own ridicule, until the reader is at a loss to determine what the author believes.

The latter remains aloof from the question, turns it over and over in his hand, looks at it, and says something quizzical about it. It is not always safe to say that he is sarcastic. He is having intellectual fun. His mind is fermenting.

Of such a nature is Byron's real preface to *Don Juan*, placed by him near the end of the first canto.[44] It can only be recognized for what it is, a humorous discussion of the standards of literary composition, as they had been accepted in the age of Pope. It is not, because it is humorous, necessarily sarcastic, any more than the preface of Martinus Scriblerus to the *Dunciad* is an attack on neoclassic canons. It merely shows, as did that other preface, that the canons are in the author's mind and that his sense of humor is working on them. The announcement of purposes cannot be taken literally, because we know that they were not, and were not likely to be, followed.

These thirteen stanzas, which I have been pleased to call a preface, are even more of a burlesque than the notice of Scriblerus. They are a hodge-podge of neoclassical ethics and reminiscences, thrown together into an unbelievable though plausible statement of good intentions. The poem, it is asserted, is an epic. Therefore there are to be twelve books, and three episodes. Each book is to contain, "with love and war, a heavy gale at sea, a list of ships, and captains, and kings reigning"—a catalogue of ships, in the manner of the *Iliad*. There will be a panoramic view of Hell, after the style of Virgil and Homer, new mythological machinery, and "very handsome supernatural scenery." All is to be written "with strict regard to Aristotle's rules," except that there will be less embellishment, a greater care for the truth —"This story's actually true." There is to be a moral, which nevertheless may be hard for some people to find. If in time the author should descend to prose, he will write new poetical commandments, to supersede all those just now accepted, with others much severer, to be entitled "Longinus o'er a Bottle, or Every Poet his *own* Aristotle." Now he says nothing; but if he were to speak, he would command reverence for Milton, Dryden, Pope, and Crabbe, and scorn of the Lake School:

> Thou shalt not write, in short, but what I choose;
>   This is true criticism, and you may kiss—
> Exactly as you please, or not—the rod;
> But if you don't, I'll lay it on, by G-d.

The passage might very well be judged alone, in the spirit of the whole poem. Here is Byron disporting himself with what in other moods he reverences. He is committing sacrilege against poetry and religion by burlesquing both the Rules and the Ten Commandments. But it is all in fun. He means no harm to either the Ten Commandments or the Rules, though they have their funny side, and one may point it out, in such a poem as this. Incidentally, he has arrived at a truth, that his standards are his own because they are his, and when he preaches them he is imposing himself upon others. But that is no admission that he does not believe in them, and will not uphold them stoutly.

The passage might very well be judged alone, but it is better to check it up with other portions of the satire. The occasional references to Horace[45] and Pope[46] are not reverential, but neither are they carping. Homer is referred to humorously as a model,[47] when Byron is obviously not in an Homeric vein. There is a recollection that even Homer nods,[48] and a serious echo of Homer in the description of the army at night.[49] Aristotle is dealt with as irreverently, but more respectfully. For while the appeal to "the opinion of the critic . . . from Aristotle *passim*"[50] is ironical, another passage,

> As I have a high sense
> Of Aristotle and the Rules, 't is fit
> To beg his pardon when I err a bit,[51]

is not clearly so. There is, indeed, a constant resort to "the ancient epic laws,"[52] with a tendency to quote them and then disobey them, or to bring them in wherever they are most incongruous. *In medias res* is cited, only as "the usual method, but not mine—my way is to begin with the beginning."[53] Aristotle's principle of the beginning, middle, and end, is echoed in "the riddle of epic Love's beginning—end—and middle"[54] and in an extended precept consciously quite as obvious as Aristotle's analysis:

> Firstly, begin with the beginning—(though
>   That clause is hard); and secondly, proceed;
> Thirdly, commence not with the end.[55]

Byron, in his own way, was declaring his independence as conclusively as any of his contemporaries were doing. But there is a difference in the point of view. He is, in the last analysis, not revolting against the past, but adapting the past to the present, though less rigidly than he has done in his tragedies. As the poem proceeds, citations and comments prove that the great critics and established writers of the past are in his thoughts, if he does not obey their injunctions to the letter. He has precept and standard in mind; but here he must to a great extent adapt precept to his own situation. Aristotle had laid down no rule for the burlesque epic. As it had been claimed in the age before, that his pronouncements in the *Poetics* would have been modified by a perusal of the *Aeneid*, so much the more would they have been affected by the newer and far different epics. After all, the laws of poetic composition had been distilled from the usages of great writers. Every additional great writer was like past great ones, but he differed from them insofar as his purposes and the nature of his task demanded. It was no disloyalty to one's predecessors to work out one's own practices. If Byron was in need of a "lofty wing plumed by Longinus or the Stagyrite," he after all sang "Knights and Dames . . . such as the times may furnish."[56] There is no advantage in taking Aristotle too literally. *Don Juan* "shall have twenty-four books, the legitimate number. Episodes it has, and will have, out of number; and my spirits, good or bad, must serve for the machinery. If that be not an epic, if it be not strictly according to Aristotle, I don't know what an epic means."[57] Of course that is not strictly according to Aristotle, any more than Byron was sure of writing only twenty-four cantos; but it was what Aristotle might have approved of, if he had faced Byron's problem in Byron's time. *Don Juan* is an epic, but a modern epic, that cannot be judged completely in terms of an inherited critical jargon. "If you must have an epic, there's *Don Juan* for you; it is an epic as much in the spirit of our day as the *Iliad* was in Homer's. Love, religion, and politics form the argument. . . . There is no want of Parises and Menelauses, and of *Crim-cons* into the bargain. In the very first canto you have a Helen. Then, I shall make my hero a perfect Achilles for fighting . . . and, depend upon it, my moral will be a good one; not even Dr. Johnson should be able to find a flaw in it."[58] The proposition is advanced jocularly, as was fitting in any serious discussion of *Don Juan*. And in just the proper manner, the truth is neatly summed up.

Byron's chief concern, in his adherence to the classics, was one of form. There is some talk about morality, and a mention of coloring

> With Nature manners which are artificial,
> And rend'ring general that which is especial.[59]

In the incongruity of the application of the Rules to modern circumstances lies much of the fun. But Byron was not really concerned with the spirit of Aristotle. His classical spirit is more subconscious than conscious, a disinclination to let himself go completely, a reaction from excess, or the correction of a momentary extravagance; it is derived from his immediate forbears, Pope and Johnson, rather than from the dictates of Aristotle. When he quoted or paraphrased the critics, it was the more obvious precepts that impressed him. As in the dramas his chief concern had been the Unities, so here it was matters of where to begin and how to continue, not, for instance, the doctrine of imitation. One of the most classical of all maxims is, perhaps, that "men should know why they write, and for what end";[60] and it is in complete and conscious command of his powers that much of his classical quality consisted. To speak approximately, Byron knew what he was going to do and went deliberately about doing it.

We have, unfortunately, Byron's word for the opposite: "You ask me for the plan of Donny Johnny: I *have* no plan—I *had* no plan; but I had or have materials. . . . You might as well make Hamlet (or Diggory) 'act mad' in a strait waistcoat as trammel my buffoonery. . . . My thoughts would only be pitiably absurd and ludicrously constrained. Why, Man, the Soul of such writing is in its licence; at least, the *Liberty* of that *licence*, if one likes—*not* that one should abuse it."[61] The facts of the case, however, if they do not contradict his assertion, define it curiously. *Don Juan* from the first has a plan and continues to have a plan, if a developing one. There is not necessarily a rigid scheme, with headings and subheadings. Rather, the conception grew with the execution; but the poem had first to be conceived and then to develop.

In Canto I, to repeat, he had promised love, war, a heavy gale at sea, and a panoramic view of Hell—a visit to Hell, after the manner of the trips of Odysseus and Aeneas to

Hades, probably, not "Juan's last elopement with the devil."⁶² He had also promised a "list of ships, and captains, and kings reigning," which he may or may not have intended ironically. Juan, obviously, was to have been the hero, or the victim, of the adventures. There would be a chance to paint the modern world and to follow the character through illuminating experiences. The predicted events Byron does not say will be all; there may be others that do not fit into the stanza. There are enough, however, to connect the poem with earlier epics. It is to survey the modern world through the eyes of the hero, to report its weaknesses and absurdities and to laugh at them, as Homer and Virgil had reported, though in a serious vein, their own worlds.

If Byron was right in a later recollection, he meant to have made Juan "a *Cavalier Servente* in Italy, and a cause for a divorce in England, and a Sentimental 'Werther-faced man' in Germany, so as to show the different ridicules of the society in those countries."⁶³ The parallelism with his own career, even to the "Werther-faced man," is obvious, and, to Byron, inevitable. "The tour of Europe," which Byron also speaks of having intended, is suggestive of *Childe Harold*. But the "proper mixture of siege, battle, and adventure" is added, and has more to do with his stated intentions in Canto I. Here the emphasis again is on war, love, and satire, as the three guiding stars of the epic. Satire is its undertone, war and love are to be the subjects, and humor the instrument.

Even at this late date, Byron had fixed upon no one certain conclusion for his epic. On one page of the letters, he mentions three or maybe two possible endings for the career of Juan: to finish as Anacharsis Cloots in the French Revolution, to "end in Hell, or in an unhappy marriage, not knowing which would be the severest."⁶⁴ The unhappy marriage was probably apropos of Hell and his own experiences. A guillotining in the French Revolution had most likely been decided on, for it was also mentioned to Medwin.[65] In the latter instance, there was additional talk of taking Juan from Constantinople to Russia—as "man-mistress to Catherine the Great"—and to England, where there should be a case of unrequited affection on the side of a rescued girl, and the chance for depicting town and country life at home, with "room for life, manners, scenery, etc." This, indeed, is exactly what he did. And since there seems little reason to doubt Medwin's good faith, though his memory and his judgment are often at fault, it is probable that by this time the plan was fairly well matured in Byron's head.

It was not a plan hit upon instantly—nothing so hasty as that. Byron had enough of an idea, at the start, to launch him on the composition of several cantos, while the design was as yet "simply in concoction."[66] But the long intermission between the writing of the fifth and sixth cantos was due to causes utterly different from any uncertainty about planning. Byron was turned away from his intention, for the time, by discouragement and by the writing of his tragedies. His conception of the poem, meanwhile, must have expanded vastly, for he could say, during the intermission, that "the fifth is so far from being the last of *Don Juan*, that it is hardly the beginning."[67] His promise of the first canto was completed with the eighth, with "sketches of love—tempest—travel—war—all very accurate."[68] But already, having schemed new adventures for "the hero of this grand poetic riddle,"[69] he had no thought of concluding. By the end of Canto XII, he was speaking of the precedent part as an introduction, and looking forward to the "body of the Book."[70]

Byron was little bothered by his increasing purpose. He had not acknowledged, previously, to how many cantos his poem might extend, or whether he should ever finish it.[71] No such definite number as twenty-four could he have taken seriously. His worries and apologies over splitting the third

canto into two, were financial, not artistic. If at setting off, he
had thought two dozen cantos would do, he had soon extended his reach to include a hundred.[72] He was amused at
writing an epic. It gave him pleasure to see it grow beneath
his hands, and take on new frills or new flourishes. It had
gained a life of its own, and developed almost independently
of its creator. He displayed the same interest in watching it
that a father might take in his young son, and was just as
delighted at its pranks. He was taking the Rules no more
to heart than anything else. For this was a humorous epic,
of no worth if not free—that is, with a reasonable amount of
freedom.

The combination of freedom and purpose is the key to
Don Juan. Freedom is its obvious characteristic. Byron
interrupts the narrative to talk about himself; "word or text,
I never know the word which will come next"; his digressions almost overtop the narration. But the story somehow
gets ahead. It is said that a man blindfolded will advance
for half a hundred paces, then spiral in decreasing circles toward an imaginary centre. *Don Juan* goes forward with the
directness of one who sees. Since it was not completed, to pass
final judgment on its form is impossible. Part by part,
however, it hangs together. Its arrangement seems accidental, a mere rough dovetailing of sections, until we con-
template rearranging the order of its incidents and find that
any change we may make in that direction is for the worse.
The narrative, to recollect the famous criticism of Swinburne,
has a sort of magnificent rhythm in the large. After Donna
Julia, Juan meets Haidée, after Haidée Gulbeyaz, after
Gulbeyaz he rescues Leila; he is next possessed by Catherine,
and escapes her to be received by a bevy of women in the
fashionable society of England. A first passion is followed
by shipwreck, shipwreck by romantic love, romantic love by
the slave market, the slave market by the Sultan's harem, the

harem by the battlefield, the battlefield by Catherine's court, barbaric Russia by slow-moving Germany and then by pseudo-cultured England. The epic goes forward not in a flow but in great strides;—Seven-League-Boot strides—at each of which the story is advanced into another region and a contrasting atmosphere. The epic, though a picaresque epic, has not an utter inconsequence of design.

Weaknesses in technique are almost intrinsic with the better qualities. There is a carelessness over minute points, as if minor matters were not worth bothering about. Juan's escape from the harem, with Johnson, Gulbeyaz, and Dudû, is left to the reader to explain. After the start of the siege, the two women are permanently forgotten. Juan is whisked from the battlefield to the Russian court as if on a magic carpet, without a glance at the country between. The gaps, however, play their own part in the narrative. They help the antithesis of parts; they balance one event with another, as no gradual transition could accomplish. And the omissions are confined, for the most part, to that period when Byron, resuming the composition of *Juan* after a spell at the drama, was having difficulty in getting back into the spirit of composing, weighted down as he was by his mass of unfamiliar facts. Flaws or virtues, the poem is strong enough to carry them all on its back.

That *Don Juan* is Byron's masterpiece has seldom if ever been disputed. If it has more glaring faults than some of his other compositions, it has equally or in a greater degree than they the supreme qualities of sincerity and strength, and in addition paints, on a vaster scale and in fuller outline, the author and the times. It has usually been said, and on the whole with truth, that Byron was at last finally satisfied, as he had never seemed to be before with any work. Such is a comforting reflection on one who had a perverse way of preferring his poorer productions. But it is after all only an approximation, and a little misleading as to the true significance of the poem.

Byron's independence was not a sudden flourishing, nor did it result entirely from the excellence of *Don Juan*. It must be remembered that he was also for a time independent about his dramas in the face of a deadlier discouragement than disapproval—lack of interest, silence. The opposition to the epic, moreover, on moral grounds, was of a kind to provoke his obstinacy, not to deaden his purpose—as Augusta pointed out to his critics.[73] The furore created in England by its publication was less great than that precipitated by *Cain*, and in the latter circumstance he stuck to his guns. To talk prudery and prudence to him in reproof was to flaunt a red handkerchief at a bull. Criticism, in its way, did as much to stimulate composition as to discourage the author from composing. And it must not be forgotten, that for nearly two years, in the midst of writing *Don Juan*, he transferred his attention entirely to his dramas.

As a matter of fact Byron, at least once, called one canto, the third, "dull, damned dull,"[74] and the two preceding and the two following, only tolerable. His plea was against "the Cant of the day . . . absurd half and half prudery."[75] As to the art of the poem, he appealed from the rather *a priori* criticisms of his contemporaries, to common sense: "If the poem has poetry, it would stand; if not, fall: the rest is 'leather and prunella,' and has never yet affected any human production 'pro or con.' Dullness is the only annihilator in such cases."[76] "I care nothing for what may be said, or thought, or written, on the Subject. If the poem is, or appears, dull, it will fail; if not, it will succeed."[77]

An *ex cathedra* answer to criticisms hardly fitted the humorous tone of the work. His serious claim to have composed serious poetry is but an incident in his correspondence and may be attributed to the encouragement of Shelley. The latter had, on October 21, 1821, written Byron in ecstasy, stating that "This poem carries with it at once the stamp of originality and a defiance of imitation," that nothing would ever be written like it in English, "without carrying upon it the mark of a secondary and borrowed light," and that "this sort of writing . . . is what I wished you to do when I made my vows for an epic."[78] Shelley believed the poem largely due to his suggestion that Byron should "come out of the abysmal 'wood of error' into the sun, [and] write something new and cheerful." He considered its poetry superior to that of *Childe Harold*,[79] and its scope a happy opportunity for Byron's powers. His enthusiasm overflowed: "Every word has the stamp of originality . . . something wholly new and relative to the age, yet surpassingly beautiful."[80] Byron's enthusiasm, in comparison, is but a restrained reflection of Shelley's: "I tell you, it will be long before you see any thing half so good, as poetry or writing. . . . I have read over the poem carefully, and I tell you, *it is poetry*. Your little envious knot of parson-poets may say what they please: time will show that I am not in this instance mistaken."[81] Byron's ordinary tone, however, in speaking of his epic, was not so flamboyant. His reserve, common sense, and humor checked his pride; though he might be elated with the work, and though he defended stoutly its moral obliquities, he did not rhapsodize.

In one important respect only he is noticeably more independent than in the case of his tragedies. Though he caused to be omitted the attacks on Castlereagh[82] and Southey,[83] from a sense of fair play, and still at times allowed Gifford to choose from alternative passages,[84] in the main he resented efforts to amend his text. From good-natured evasion on the plea of laziness,[85] his mood varied to fits of acerbation at well-meaning meddlers: "There shall be *no mutilations* . . . *nor omissions*, except such as I have already indicated. . . .

You shan't make *Canticles* of my Cantos. . . . I will have none of your damned cutting and slashing."[86] "I appeal not 'to Philip fasting,' but to Alexander drunk; I appeal to Murray at his ledger, to the people, in short, Don Juan shall be an entire horse, or none."[87] Byron's protest was both moral and artistic. He objected to toning down his language and his strictures to suit the cant prudery of the day. Furthermore, for once he was a better critic of his style than were his friends. In serious verse, in the heroic couplet, even in the drama, his taste had been uncertain. He could not choose between words that had almost the same application; he could not always distinguish aesthetic subtleties that meant so much to the critic of letters. But in his humor he was thoroughly at home. It was just this one quality, which none of his friends seems thoroughly to have appreciated, that marked him as apart. Their criticisms of *Don Juan* were inapt for not being in the spirit of *Don Juan*. In the last analysis, they were clumsy because they did not understand.

It was misunderstanding that must have been most discouraging to the poet. He early began to fret, either at criticisms or at inattentions. He took it ill that Gifford was not prompt with criticism;[88] fell "into a damned passion at the bad taste of the times,"[89] and became pettish over his friends' half-heartedness. "You ask me if I mean to continue *D. J.*, etc.," he demanded. "How should I know? what encouragement do you give me, all of you, with your nonsensical prudery? publish the two cantos, and then you will see."[90] The general outcry disheartened him. He wrote to a public, and when that public did not respond, much of his zest departed. He could not compose for some time after hearing that a Mr. Saunders had considered the poem "all Grubstreet," though he retaliated on the latter by calling him "nothing but a d-d saltfish seller."[91] To his diminishing enthusiasm Moore attributes his lower estimation for each succeeding canto.[92] He began to fear that the public was tired of his compositions,[93] and the sense of failure became an obsession with him, which he could only much later take with a grain of humor:

> Juan was my Moscow, and Faliero
> My Leipsic, and my Mont Saint Jean seems Cain.[94]

Teresa's remonstrance is the oft-repeated excuse for abandoning the poem at the end of the fifth canto.[95] There was also some fear that it might antagonize his daughter,[96] or at least weaken or destroy his legal hold upon her. But the fears intruded because he was in a mood for them. There was no talk, in any other case, of preferring his child to a poem.[97] When La Guiccioli objected, and friends hinted, he was already heartsick over his production and glad enough of an excuse to turn to the tragedies.

Teresa likewise was the technical excuse for resuming the poem, but again the excuse is not to be accepted entire, since with her permission went the condition that Juan should be a more moral person,[98] and the continuation "more guarded and decorous and sentimental ... than the commencement!"[99] A stronger urge was the admiration of Goethe and the Germans for the poem,[100] and the good news that *Juan* was the most popular of all his works, especially among women.[101] The return to the epic is coincident with the decline of interest in the dramas. The peak of the tragedies had been reached with or by the production of *Cain*; thereafter there was not so much a falling off as a complete failure to compose. Of the three remaining dramas, but one was finished, and that one was *Werner*—the product of an interest in a moral theme, and a final acknowledgement of the defeat of his aims, or the wearing out of his purposes for the theatre.

The unpopularity of his tragedies and the growing popularity of *Don Juan,* or at least a feeling in the poet that such was the case, might be sufficient to explain the transformation. Except *Don Juan,* after the composition of *Cain,* each succeeding work was of the nature of a potboiler, or, when it showed signs of a deeper purpose, showed likewise that the poetic will was not equal to the demands upon it. *Heaven and Earth, Werner, The Deformed Transformed, The Age of Bronze,* and *The Island,* all tell the same story. Byron was proud of none of them, and was right not to be. They were secondary explosions of poetizing power, during a time when his mind was mainly taken up with *Don Juan.* It is convincing proof of his creative energy, that in the short year stretching from June, 1822, through March, 1823, he composed not only ten cantos of his epic, but *The Age of Bronze, The Island,* and probably what part of *The Deformed Transformed* was finished. And yet the mood of the period is distinctly Juanesque. *The Island* reflects it in the character and speech of Ben Bunting—in the midst of a romantic paradise, a realism of tone and dialect that might have marred a more beautiful poem. The composition of these long poems in the midst of the writing of *Don Juan,* while denying the complete absorption of the poet in his masterpiece, contradicts also any assumption that the influence of his popular reputation upon him was overwhelming.

Byron, with all the intentness of his nature, was definitely committed to the Juanesque mood. Proud of his attitude or no, he realized in his "epic satire" a release for the teeming life of his mind. In its informal tone, its easy intimacies, its swift transition from one subject or one mood to another, its refusal to look ahead to the following word or to purge itself of the unallowable—in short, in its complete liberty of style, it satisfied the fluctuations of his temperament. The poem reflects Byron, on a vaster scale than any work or any group of works before. In it may be found a more intimate spiritual biography of the poet than he himself could have been aware of. Intruding upon the poem is the man, but the man not merely in his whims, his tricks, his prejudices; he develops before our eyes. *Paradise Lost*, the *Aeneid*, the *Iliad*, so far as they reflect anyone, mirror each a fully matured character with assured beliefs; *Don Juan*, as surely as the plays of Shakespeare, pictures a mind in the making. The later epic increases less in cynicism than in cynical tolerance. What was, in the episode of Haidée, but an interruption or conscious bathos to reverse the effect of sentiment, is in the later cantos a comment or further explanation of the action. It is true that as the narrative progresses there is less and less story and more and more soliloquizing. And yet the poet talks less about himself—or less personally. Part of the change consists of a maturing artistic mastery of the digression. Then, too, the digression has meanwhile come to signify differently. The love of Haidée and Juan, in the early cantos, is the outgrowth of a feeling that

> Man, being reasonable, must get drunk;
> The best of life is but intoxication.[102]

Comment, digression, and humorous letdown are a return to reason—the headachy, bad-tasting, disillusioned reason of the morning after. Byron in the first part of his poem throws himself into intoxication, with the inevitable revulsion. The later cantos differ from the earlier in their comparative sobriety. In describing the banquet, in Canto XV, Byron lets himself go, but as a Sybarite in his perfect senses. Aurora Raby, perhaps a later Haidée, is part of an English and social setting, not the unfulfilled dream of a poet's imagination. There is more wisdom, if less sadness, in these later cantos. They come to depict less and less an individual than a civilization—hence comment increases and the story dwindles.

In this losing himself while remaining himself, Byron may have unconsciously felt to lie the real triumph of his

Don Juan. The epic is less classic, perhaps, than some of the tragedies, in form if not in content. And yet it is linked closely with the tradition of the eighteenth century. If it has its bursts of romantic intoxication, it reflects more scrupulously, as the story proceeds, the sober light of the reasonable. In its mood, it grows steadily closer to what we may offer as one definition of the classic—a contentment with seeking beauty and adventure in the world of men. Even its licentiousness links it with Pope, Johnson, and Fielding,[103] and opposes it to the newer and more finicky school. Disillusioned its last cantos may be, but not bitter. And while the first reflect Byron, they do so in a far different way from the romances or *Childe Harold*. With good reason Byron contended that to publish the authorship was in large measure to spoil the fun.[104] Donna Inez, Don José, Don Alfonso's attorney, Juan's upbringing, all have their originals in his experience. But the first canto is his experience thrown on a screen—the screen of his humor. It is an objectification in a way different, because it is not a *cri du coeur*, from that of *Manfred*. To admit authorship was to deprive the poem of its impersonality, to reduce it to being but another confession in verse. Donna Inez, who, before the authorship is known, might be taken as a splendid and rather abstractly conceived caricature, becomes in relation to Byron's life another attack on Lady Byron.

Byron has been treated not altogether fairly by the nineteenth century. He is admittedly not the supreme poet that he was acclaimed by his contemporaries, but he is a more magnanimous man. His habitual use of the pronoun "I" has created the impression that he was only the petty egotist, deeply immersed in himself and unable to see a subject except through the haze of his prejudices. *Don Juan*, for all its autobiography, contradicts that assumption. As the tragedies had fitted individuals of Byron's temperament into concrete environments and had judged their actions by their effectiveness, so *Don Juan* parades before the reader all of Byron's sentiments, ideals, and weaknesses and judges them humorously, often harshly. *Don Juan* displays the personality of its creator more intimately than any other similarly great poem has ever done. Happily, too, it has an impersonality in its egotism. It includes in its scope a critique of the modern world, and an underlying respect for the great men of the past which, for all the humor, is part and parcel of it. No wonder that Byron, looking back on its first sixteen cantos, could conceive them as a mere introduction, and could plan, in jest or earnest, on a hundred more.[105] He had nothing now, except a Greek war, to prevent him.

NOTES

CHAPTER I

[1] "Lady Hester Stanhope was ... capital mimic. ... The first whom she crucified in my presence was poor Lord Byron. She had seen him, it appears, I know not where, soon after his arrival in the East, and was vastly amused at his little affectations. He had picked up a few sentences of the Romaic and with these he affected to give orders to his Greek servant in a *ton d'apameibomenos* style. ... She attributed to him a curious coxcomical lisp."—Alexander William Kinglake, *Eothen*, p. 123.

[2] Quoted in Ethel C. Mayne, *Byron*, p. 260.

[3] Leigh Hunt, *Lord Byron and Some of His Contemporaries*, p. 43.

[4] George E. Woodberry, *Heart of Man*, p. 192.

[5] *The Works of Lord Byron: Letters and Journals* (ed. Rowland E. Prothero), V, 446. Hereafter cited as *L. and J.*

[6] *Lord Byron's Correspondence* (ed. John Murray), II, 23. Hereafter cited as *L. B. C.*

[7] *Conversations of Lord Byron with the Countess of Blessington*, p. 165. Hereafter cited as Blessington.

[8] *L. B. C.*, I, 104.

[9] *L. and J.*, IV, 349.

[10] *Ibid.*, V, 571.

[11] *L. B. C.*, II, 123.

[12] *L. and J.*, II, 401.

[13] John Galt, *The Life of Lord Byron*, p. 131.

[14] *L. and J.*, VI, 196.

[15] Blessington, p. 302.

[16] *L. and J.*, III, 86-87.

[17] Blessington, p. 135.

[18] J. Kennedy, *Conversations on Religion with Lord Byron and Others*, p. 189.

[19] *L. and J.*, V, 451.

[20] "Never has pen or paper revealed more sharply how stationary was Byron's soul."—André Maurois, *Byron* (tr. Hamish Miles), p. 236.

[21] Hunt, *op. cit.*, p. 220.

[22] Maurois, *op. cit.*, p. 145.

[23] Hunt, *op. cit.*, p. 278.

[24] *Ibid.*, pp. 70, 71.

[25] J. D. Symon, *Byron in Perspective*, p. 122.

[26] *L. B. C.*, I, 162.

[27] *Ibid.*, II, 121.

[28] Paraphrased, with apologies, from Irving Babbitt's *The New Laokoön*, p. 97.

[211]

[29] *L. and J.*, VI, 253 n.
[30] *Ibid.*, V, 370.
[31] *Ibid.*, IV, 157.
[32] "I cannot *keep* my *resentments*, though violent enough in their onset."—*L. and J.*, VI, 35.
[33] *L. B. C.*, I, 44.
[34] *L. and J.*, II, 45.
[35] *Ibid.*, V, 425.
[36] *Ibid.*, IV, 10, 44.
[37] "I have seen the expression of his countenance on greater occasions, absolutely festered with ill-temper . . . his voice at the same time being soft, and struggling to keep itself in, as if on the very edge of endurance."—Hunt, *op. cit.*, p. 141.
[38] *L. and J.*, V, 155-56.
[39] Blessington, p. 302.
[40] "What is the matter with Byron is that superstition shadows all his thinking. . . . The fear of himself is audible in his poetry. . . . There is, indeed, no end to the medievalism of this most modern of men. If he did not believe in God, he believed in ghosts."—H. W. Garrod, *The Profession of Poetry and Other Lectures*, p. 58.
[41] Thomas Moore, *Letters and Journals of Lord Byron with Notices of His Life*, I, 80.
[42] Maurois, *op. cit.*, p. 288.
[43] *American Criticism*, p. xv.
[44] Maurois, *op. cit.*, p. 337.
[45] "There is a cure for love; there is none for poetry. Poets are all mad."—*Poems and Letters of Lord Byron, Edited from the Original MSS in the Possession of W. K. Bixby of St. Louis* (ed. W. N. C. Carlton), p. 36.
[46] *Op. cit.*, p. 60.

CHAPTER II

[1] According to Bacon, the purpose of poetry is "to give some shadowe of satisfaction to the minde of Man in those points wherein the Nature of things doth denie it . . . by submitting the shewes of things to the desires of the Mind."—J. E. Spingarn, *Critical Essays of the Seventeenth Century*, I, xi.
[2] "A Letter to the Publisher," by William Cleland, prefixed to the *Dunciad*.
[3] Spingarn, *op. cit.*, I, lxv. The greater part of my criticism of the seventeenth century has been distilled from Mr. Spingarn's brilliant introduction to his *Critical Essays*, to which and to whom I am sincerely grateful.
[4] *Ibid.*, I, lxx.
[5] *Ibid.*, p. lxxiii.
[6] *Ibid.*, p. lxxvi.
[7] *Ibid.*, p. xcviii.
[8] Samuel Johnson, *Alexander Pope*, p. 170. Hereafter cited as Johnson's *Pope*.
[9] Samuel Johnson, *Lives of the English Poets*, I, 100. Hereafter cited as Johnson's *Lives*.
[10] Joseph Addison, *The Works of Joseph Addison*, III, 170.

NOTES

[11] Johnson's *Pope*, p. 87.
[12] *Ibid.*, p. 156.
[13] Ll. 530 ff.
[14] "Epistle to Dr. Arbuthnot," ll. 340-41.
[15] Johnson's *Lives*, I, 175; III, 240.
[16] *Ibid.*, I, 183.
[17] *Essay on Criticism*, ll. 239-42.
[18] *Ibid.*, 115.
[19] "Aristotle's rules for epic poetry . . . cannot be supposed to square exactly with the heroic poems which have been made since his time, since it is evident to every impartial judge, his rules would still have been more perfect, could he have perused the *Aeneid*."—Addison, *Works*, III, 185.
[20] *Ibid.*, pp. 187-88.
[21] Johnson's *Pope*, p. 174.
[22] Addison, *Works*, III, 244.
[23] *Ibid.*, p. 417.
[24] *Ibid.*, p. 203.
[25] Johnson's *Lives*, I, 163.
[26] *Works*, III, 191.
[27] From the translation of Bossu's "A View of the Epick Poem," prefixed to the Popean *Odyssey*.
[28] "Epic poetry undertakes to teach the most important truths by the most pleasing precepts, and therefore relates some great event in the most affecting manner."—Johnson's *Lives*, I, 170.
[29] *Ibid.*
[30] Pope's Preface to the *Iliad*.
[31] Spingarn, *op. cit.*, I, ci.
[32] Nos. 262, 267, 273, 279, 285, 291, 297, 303, 309, etc.
[33] Ll. 152-60. Order of couplets inverted, we trust without violence to meaning.
[34] *Works*, III, 201.
[35] *Ibid.*, p. 204.
[36] This, with the succeeding treatment of Shakespeare, is taken from the Preface to the *Plays* (Pope's edition). Criticisms of Homer occur in the Introduction to the *Iliad*.
[37] I am indebted for much of this treatment of Johnson's critical views to Mr. P. H. Houston's excellent work on the subject. When the information is the result of my own investigation, I have indicated as much by references to Johnson's works.
[38] "Preface to Shakespeare."
[39] Johnson's *Lives*, I, 162.
[40] *Ibid.*, p. 163.
[41] *Ibid.*, p. 177.
[42] *Ibid.*, p. 194.
[43] *Essay on Criticism*, ll. 161, 163.
[44] *Ibid.*, ll. 213-14.

CHAPTER III

[1] Hunt, *op. cit.*, p. 52.
[2] "An Occasional Prologue," *The Works of Lord Byron: Poetry* (ed. Ernest Hartley Coleridge), I, 45, ll. 1-8. Hereafter cited as *Poetry*.
[3] Cf. *Childe Harold*, can. IV, st. 77; *L. and J.*, IV, 103-4.
[4] *Childe Harold*, can. IV, st. 38.
[5] *L. and J.*, IV, 385.
[6] *Ibid.*, V, 564.
[7] *Ibid.*, p. 374.
[8] Countess Guiccioli, *Lord Byron jugé par les témoins de sa vie* (tr. H. E. H. Jerningham, *My Recollections of Lord Byron*), p. 171. Hereafter cited as Guiccioli.
[9] *Poetry*, I, 377 n.
[10] *Ibid.*, VII, 47.
[11] *Ibid.*, II, 79-81.
[12] *L. and J.*, IV, 89; *Poetry*, I, 361 n.
[13] Cf. "rough Johnson, the great moralist," *Don Juan*, can. XIII, st. 7.
[14] *Poetry*, II, 78.
[15] *L. and J.*, V, 575.
[16] Thomas Medwin, *Journal of the Conversations of Lord Byron*, pp. 110-11. Hereafter cited as Medwin.
[17] Note to *Don Juan*, can. XII, st. 19.
[18] *L. and J.*, IV, 93.
[19] *Ibid.*, V, 559.
[20] *Ibid.*, p. 37. Cf. Johnson's approving quotation from Dryden: "Translation, therefore, is not so loose as paraphrase, nor so close as metaphrase."—*Lives*, I, 422.
[21] *L. and J.*, V, 42.
[22] *Ibid.*, p. 95.
[23] *L. B. C.*, II, 43, 119.
[24] *L. and J.*, V, 166.
[25] W. P. Ker, *The Eighteenth Century*, p. 13.
[26] *L. and J.*, IV, 238.
[27] Blessington, p. 170.
[28] *Ibid.*, pp. 226, 237.
[29] *L. and J.*, II, 124.
[30] *Ibid.*, IV, 230.
[31] *Ibid.*, I, 299.
[32] *Ibid.*, IV, 304.
[33] Blessington, p. 81.
[34] Medwin, p. 196.
[35] Blessington, pp. 264-65.
[36] *Ibid.*, pp. 349-50.
[37] *Ibid.*, p. 329.
[38] *Poetry*, I, 83, st. 4.
[39] Medwin, p. 211.
[40] *L. and J.*, II, 80.
[41] Blessington, p. 116.

⁴² Cf. *ibid.*, p. 42.
⁴³ *Poetry*, I, 183 n.
⁴⁴ *L. and J.*, V, 168.
⁴⁵ *Poetry*, III, 224.
⁴⁶ Medwin, p. 133.
⁴⁷ *L. and J.*, IV, 218.
⁴⁸ *Ibid.*, V, 55.
⁴⁹ *Ibid.*, III, 47.
⁵⁰ *Poetry*, I, 381 n.
⁵¹ *L. and J.*, III, 77.
⁵² Blessington, p. 261.
⁵³ Leslie Stephen, *English Literature and Society in the Eighteenth Century*, p. 207.
⁵⁴ *L. and J.*, IV, 169.
⁵⁵ *Ibid.*, pp. 196-97.
⁵⁶ *Ibid.*, V, 559.
⁵⁷ *Letters of Percy Bysshe Shelley* (ed. Roger Ingpen), p. 839. Hereafter cited as Shelley, *Letters*.
⁵⁸ *L. and J.*, IV, 485.
⁵⁹ *Ibid.*, V, 18.
⁶⁰ *Ibid.*, IV, 494.
⁶¹ *Ibid.*, V, 589 n.
⁶² *Ibid.*, p. 588.
⁶³ Shelley, *Letters*, p. 860.
⁶⁴ *L. and J.*, V, 557.
⁶⁵ "Es sind keine Flickwörter im Gedichte." Crabbe Robinson's *Diary*, II, 434-37, quoted in *L. and J.*, V, 517.
⁶⁶ *L. and J.*, V, 591.
⁶⁷ *Ibid.*, p. 82.
⁶⁸ *Autobiography of Leigh Hunt* (ed. Roger Ingpen), I, 210.
⁶⁹ *L. and J.*, IV, 237.
⁷⁰ *Ibid.*, V, 75.
⁷¹ *Ibid.*, II, 338.
⁷² *Ibid.*, V, 94.
⁷³ *Ibid.*, p. 93.
⁷⁴ *Ibid.*, p. 96.
⁷⁵ Medwin, p. 294.
⁷⁶ *L. and J.*, IV, 491-92.
⁷⁷ Shelley, *Letters*, p. 838.
⁷⁸ *L. and J.*, V, 559.
⁷⁹ "*Descriptive* poetry, the *lowest* department of the art."—*L. and J.*, IV, 493 n.
⁸⁰ *Ibid.*, V, 273.
⁸¹ *Ibid.*, p. 274.
⁸² Medwin, p. 242.
⁸³ *L. and J.*, IV, 426.
⁸⁴ *L.B.C.*, II, 139.
⁸⁵ *Ibid.*, V, 75.

[86] Medwin, p. 242.
[87] Ll., 369-84.
[88] *L. and J.*, V, 559.
[89] *Ibid.*, p. 568.
[90] *Ibid.*, p. 560.
[91] *Ibid.*
[92] *Ibid.*, p. 554.
[93] *Ibid.*, p. 543.
[94] *Ibid.*, p. 536.
[95] *Ibid.*, p. 550.
[96] *Ibid.*
[97] *Ibid.*, p. 546.
[98] *Ibid.*, p. 548.
[99] *Ibid.*, pp. 591-92.

CHAPTER IV

[1] It has no bearing upon the conclusion in this and the next paragraph that much of the preface is an almost verbatim recollection of the preface affixed by Moore to *Little's Poems*.
[2] Cf. *Poetry*, I, 210.
[3] "Answer to Some Elegant Verses, etc."
[4] Ll. 37-42, 52-66.
[5] *L. and J.*, I, 117-18.
[6] *Ibid.*, pp. 121-22.
[7] *Ibid.*, p. 103.
[8] *Ibid.*, p. 140.
[9] *Ibid.*, p. 124. The italics are all Byron's.
[10] *Ibid.*, p. 142.
[11] *Ibid.* Aug. 2, 1807.
[12] *Ibid.*, p. 144. Aug. 11, 1807.
[13] *Ibid.*, p. 147. Oct. 26, 1807.
[14] *Ibid.*
[15] *Ibid.*, II, 25.
[16] Edward Trelawny, *Records of Shelley, Byron, and the Author*, p. 32.
[17] Ralph Milbanke, Earl of Lovelace, *Astarte*, p. 313. Hereafter cited as *Astarte*.
[18] *Poetry*, II, 366 n.
[19] Medwin, p. 290.
[20] *L. and J.*, II, 283.
[21] Blessington, p. 197.
[22] Kennedy, *op. cit.*, p. 237.
[23] *L. and J.*, V, 132.
[24] Cf. Moore, *op. cit.*, II, 252.
[25] *L. B. C.*, I, 58-59.
[26] *L. and J.*, V, 435.
[27] *Ibid.*, II, 402.
[28] *L. B. C.*, I, 72.

NOTES 217

[29] *L. and J.*, III, 59.
[30] *Ibid.*, p. 64.
[31] *Ibid.*, VI, 336.
[32] Count Peter Gamba, *A Narrative of Lord Byron's Last Journey to Greece*, p. 138.
[33] *Ibid.*, p. 3.
[34] *L. and J.*, III, 405.
[35] Guiccioli, p. 226.
[36] *L. and J.*, II, 338.
[37] *Ibid.*, p. 343.
[38] *Ibid.*, p. 345.
[39] *Ibid.*, pp. 346-47.
[40] Blessington, p. 260.
[41] *L. and J.*, III, 263.
[42] St. 75.
[43] Ll. 219-20, 272, 336-43.
[44] *L. and J.*, IV, 129.
[45] Quoted in Johnson's *Pope*, pp. 131-32 n.
[46] *L. and J.*, IV, 285.
[47] *Ibid.*, V, 209.
[48] Colonel Leicester Stanhope, *Greece in 1823 and 1824—and Reminiscences of Lord Byron*, p. 538.
[49] V, 215.
[50] *Ibid.*, p. 143.
[51] Blessington, pp. 359-60.
[52] *L. and J.*, III, 405.
[53] Moore, *op. cit.*, I, 35.
[54] Blessington, pp. 261-62.
[55] Medwin, p. 69.
[56] *L. and J.*, V, 422.
[57] Trelawny, *op. cit.*, p. 32.
[58] *L. and J.*, V, 318.
[59] *Ibid.*, p. 189.
[60] *Ibid.*, III, 92.
[61] *Ibid.*, IV, 375 n.
[62] Stanhope, *op. cit.*, p. 539.
[63] *Ibid.*, p. 540.
[64] Blessington, pp. 219-20.
[65] *L. and J.*, V, 196.
[66] Shelley, *Letters*, p. 873.
[67] *L. and J.*, III, 248.
[68] Blessington, p. 195.
[69] Moore, *op. cit.*, I, 90.
[70] *L. and J.*, V, 173-74.
[71] *Ibid.*, p. 409.
[72] *Ibid.*, VI, 430 n.
[73] Cf. *ibid.*, pp. 76-77.
[74] Guiccioli, p. 50.

[75] *Ibid.*, p. 68.
[76] *L. and J.*, V, 479.
[77] Trelawny, *op. cit.*, p. 22.
[78] *L. and J.*, V, 215. See also *ibid.*, VI, 249, 448.
[79] See *ibid.*, p. 76.
[80] Karl Koenig, *Die Entstehung von Byrons English Bards and Scotch Reviewers*, p. 48.
[81] *L. and J.*, V, 113. See also *ibid.*, II, 359.
[82] *Poetry*, I, 387.
[83] Quoted in *Byron the Poet* (ed. Walter Briscoe), p. 32.
[84] Byron liked this simile so well that he repeated it, *L. and J.*, V, 471.
[85] *Ibid.*, p. 120.
[86] Medwin, p. 333.
[87] Quoted in *Poetry*, V, 474 n.
[88] Koenig, *op. cit.*, pp. 21-22.
[89] *L. and J.*, II, 149.
[90] Blessington, p. 224.
[91] *L. and J.*, I, 107.
[92] *Ibid.*, II, 337.
[93] *Ibid.*, p. 151.
[94] "I can't look over that *Giaour* again."—*Ibid.*, p. 340.
[95] *Ibid.*, p. 305.
[96] *Ibid.*, p. 150.
[97] *Ibid.*, p. 252.
[98] R. C. Dallas, *Recollections of the Life of Lord Byron*, pp. 26, 30.
[99] *L. and J.*, I, 123.
[100] *Ibid.*, III, 330 n.
[101] *Ibid.*, II, 254 n.
[102] *Ibid.*, V, 261.
[103] *Ibid.*, p. 366.
[104] See, e.g., *ibid.*, pp. 130, 235.
[105] As, e.g., "I leave this to your discretion; if any one thinks the old line a good one, don't accept either."—*Ibid.*, II, 274.
[106] *Ibid.*, IV, 418.
[107] Cf. *L. B. C.*, II, 176, for the omission of the "courser-courier" passage in *Don Juan.*
[108] *L. and J.*, II, 26.
[109] Blessington, p. 255.
[110] *L. and J.*, IV, 248; Medwin, p. 195.
[111] "I have never written but for the solitary reader."—*L. and J.*, V, 257.
[112] *Ibid.*, III, 75.
[113] *Ibid.*, IV, 248.
[114] *Ibid.*, V, 39-40.

CHAPTER V

[1] This subject has been treated penetratingly by Karl Koenig in his excellent dissertation, already cited, *Die Entstehung von Byrons English Bards and Scotch Reviewers*. To repeat it at greater length than a short summary would be an unnecessary impertinence.

NOTES

[2] Cf., e.g., "written when I was very young and very angry."—*L. and J.*, III, 192.

[3] *Ibid.*, I, 183.

[4] *Letters and Journals of Lord Byron with Notices of His Life*, I, 208.

[5] *L. B. C.*, I, 20.

[6] *Ibid.*, p. 21.

[7] *L. and J.*, IV, 177.

[8] *Ibid.*, I, 309-10.

[9] *L.B.C.*, I, 31.

[10] *The Pilgrim of Eternity: Byron—A Conflict*, p. 163.

[11] *L. and J.*, I, 320.

[12] *The Recollections of a Long Life*, I, 19. Hereafter cited as Hobhouse.

[13] *Op. cit.*, p. 163.

[14] Anna Ticknor, *Life, Letters, and Journals of George Ticknor*, I, 67. Hereafter cited as *Life of Ticknor*.

[15] "The publication of *Childe Harold* was urged, but not the suppression of the Satire."—*Westminster Review*, January, 1825, p. 12.

[16] *L. B. C.*, I, 60.

[17] See *L. and J.*, II, 43, for a substantiation of the assertion.

[18] *Ibid.*, III, 77.

[19] Dallas, *op. cit.*, p. 265.

[20] *Life of Ticknor*, I, 67.

[21] *L. and J.*, V, 450.

[22] *Ibid.*, I, 335.

[23] *Lara*, ll. 313-42.

[24] *Every Man His Own Poet*, by a Newdigate Prizeman (London, 1873).

[25] *L. and J.*, VI, 114 n.

[26] Moore, *op. cit.*, II, 261-62.

[27] Dallas, *op. cit.*, pp. 284-85.

[28] *L. and J.*, II, 268.

[29] *Ibid.*, p. 204 n.

[30] *Corsair*, III, 1170-1200.

[31] *L. and J.*, II, 220.

[32] Blessington, p. 138.

[33] *L. and J.*, III, 47-48.

[34] *L. B. C.*, I, 214.

[35] *L. and J.*, II, 293.

[36] *L. B. C.*, I, 238.

[37] *L. and J.*, II, 278.

[38] *Ibid.*, p. 293.

[39] *Ibid.*, p. 337.

[40] *Ibid.*, pp. 361-62.

[41] *Ibid.*, p. 351.

[42] *Memoirs and Correspondence of John Murray* (ed. Samuel Smiles), I, 357-58.

[43] Note to *Parisina*, I, 336.—*Poetry*, III, 519.

[44] Aug. 26, Sept. 1, Sept. 8, 1813.

[45] *L. and J.*, III, 40.

[46] *Ibid.*, p. 158.
[47] See *Poetry*, III, 235, 251, 296.
[48] Hobhouse, I, 99-100.
[49] *L. and J.*, III, 274.

CHAPTER VI

[1] *L. and J.*, IV, 37.
[2] *Ibid.*, p. 62.
[3] *Ibid.*, III, 251.
[4] *Letters and Journals of Lord Byron with Notices of His Life*, I, 90.
[5] II, 30.
[6] II, 611.
[7] *The Diary of Dr. John William Polidori* (ed. W. M. Rossetti), p. 121. Hereafter cited as Polidori's *Diary*.
[8] Trelawny, *op. cit.*, p. 25.
[9] Lady Blessington, *Idler in Italy*, p. 26.
[10] *L. and J.*, III, 442.
[11] Blessington, *Idler in Italy*, p. 26.
[12] Trelawny, *op. cit.*, p. 40.
[13] *L. and J.*, III, 442.
[14] P. 333.
[15] *Childe Harold*, can. iv, st. 9.
[16] *L. and J.*, V, 375.
[17] Can. iv, ll. 11-15, 20-25.
[18] Can. iv, ll. 1-5.
[19] *L. and J.*, VI, 24.
[20] *L. B. C.*, II, 205.
[21] *L. and J.*, VI, 41.
[22] *L. B. C.*, II, 202.
[23] *L. and J.*, V, 376.
[24] *Ibid.*, p. 375.
[25] *Ibid.*, VI, 41.
[26] *Ibid.*, IV, 230.
[27] *L. B. C.*, II, 69.
[28] Trelawny, *op. cit.*, p. 9.
[29] Kennedy, *op. cit.*, p. 198.
[30] Shelley, *Letters*, p. 931.
[31] *Ibid.*, pp. 650-51.
[32] *Ibid.*, p. 888.
[33] *L. B. C.*, II, 172.
[34] Shelley, *Letters*, p. 721.
[35] *Ibid.*, p. 912.
[36] *L. and J.*, IV, 138.
[37] Samuel C. Chew, *The Dramas of Lord Byron*, p. 67.
[38] *L. B. C.*, II, 43.
[39] *Ibid.*, p. 50.
[40] *Ibid.*, p. 43.
[41] For these parallels in detail, see Chew, *op. cit.*, pp. 60-66.

NOTES

[42] *Ibid.*, p. 60.
[43] *Works*, p. 323 n.
[44] Chew, *op. cit.*, p. 36.
[45] *Ibid.*, p. 69.
[46] Quoted in *Astarte*, p. 117.
[47] *L. and J.*, IV, 54-55.
[48] *Ibid.*, p. 66.
[49] *Ibid.*, p. 71.
[50] *Ibid.*, p. 80.
[51] *Ibid.*, p. 100.
[52] *Ibid.*, p. 110.
[53] *Ibid.*, p. 157.
[54] *Ibid.*, VI, 157.
[55] Trelawny, *op. cit.*, p. 203.
[56] *Ibid.*, p. 208.
[57] Hobhouse, II, 11.
[58] Note to *Childe Harold*, can. III, st. 99.
[59] Shelley, *Letters*, pp. 490-91.
[60] *Ibid.*, pp. 496-97.
[61] *Ibid.*, p. 500.
[62] *Childe Harold*, can. III, st. 6.
[63] *L. and J.*, IV, 155.
[64] Sts. 5-7.
[65] *L. and J.*, VI, 164.
[66] *Astarte*, p. 281.
[67] Quoted in Chew, *op. cit.*, p. 160.
[68] As he did in *L. and J.*, IV, 284.
[69] Quoted in André Maurois, *Ariel, ou la vie de Shelley*, p. 212.
[70] John Drinkwater, *The Pilgrim of Eternity*, pp. 270-271.

CHAPTER VII

[1] In speaking of "the dramas," I have reference mainly to the trio, *Marino Faliero, Sardanapalus*, and *The Two Foscari*.
[2] *L. and J.*, III, 195.
[3] *L. B. C.*, I, 105.
[4] *Ibid.*, II, 301.
[5] *L. and J.*, III, 81.
[6] *Life of Ticknor*, I, 66.
[7] Galt, *op. cit.*, p. 333.
[8] *L. B. C.*, II, 198.
[9] *L. and J.*, IV, 55.
[10] *Ibid.*, pp. 71-72.
[11] *Ibid.*, p. 137.
[12] Medwin, p. 104.
[13] *L. B. C.*, II, 202.
[14] *L. and J.*, V, 230-31.
[15] Johnson's *Lives*, I, 146.

[16] *Life of Ticknor*, I, 67.
[17] *L. and J.*, V, 268.
[18] *Byron the Poet* (ed. Walter Briscoe), p. 177.
[19] *L. and J.*, V, 347.
[20] *Ibid.*, pp. 217-18.
[21] *Ibid.*, pp. 243-44.
[22] *Ibid.*, p. 347.
[23] *Ibid.*, p. 372.
[24] Medwin, p. 108.
[25] *Poetry*, V, 474 n.
[26] *L. and J.*, V, 244.
[27] *Ibid.*, p. 372.
[28] *Ibid.*, p. 218.
[29] I. e., Johnson.
[30] *L. and J.*, V, 284.
[31] *Ibid.*, p. 167.
[32] *Ibid.*, p. 229.
[33] *Ibid.*, p. 325.
[34] *Ibid.*, p. 221.
[35] Shelley in a letter to Byron, *L. B. C.*, II, 172.
[36] *L. and J.*, VI, 25.
[37] *L. B. C.*, II, 201.
[38] *L. and J.*, V, 326-27.
[39] *Ibid.*, p. 195.
[40] *Ibid.*, IV, 91-92.
[41] *Marino Faliero*, Preface.
[42] Medwin, pp. 139-40.
[43] "Parere . . . sul Don Garzia."
[44] *L. and J.*, V, 361.
[45] Chew, *op. cit.*, p. 121.
[46] *Ibid.*, p. 120.
[47] *L. and J.*, V, 189.
[48] *Ibid.*, VI, 38.
[49] Medwin, p. 151.
[50] III, 5.
[51] *L. and J.*, VI, 16.
[52] Cf. *ibid.*, V, 470; VI, 24; Kennedy, *op. cit.*, p. 162.
[53] *L. and J.*, VI, 32.
[54] *L. B. C.*, II, 201-2.
[55] *L. and J.*, V, 372.
[56] *Ibid.*, VI, 67.
[57] Shelley, *Letters*, p. 912.
[58] Trelawny, *op. cit.*, p. 9.
[59] *L. and J.*, VI, 67.
[60] *Ibid.*, p. 172.
[61] *Ibid.*, p. 173.
[62] *Ibid.*, V, 474.
[63] *Ibid.*, p. 313.

[64] *Ibid.*, VI, 120.
[65] *Ibid.*, p. 93.
[66] "Our author ventures to think that Lord Byron failed in the drama. His Lordship had a shrewd suspicion of it himself. . . . I was quite sure I had no faculty for the drama. He reflected upon this; and observed in an undertone between question and no-question,—'Perhaps I have not succeeded in the drama myself.' "—Hunt, *op. cit.*, pp. 202, 203.
[67] Kennedy, *op. cit.*, p. 277.
[68] "Parere sulla Merope."
[69] Chew, *op. cit.*, p. 56.
[70] *L. and J.*, V, 75.
[71] "Parere sulla Congiura de' Pazzi."
[72] Chew, *op. cit.*, p. 30.
[73] *L. and J.*, V, 67.
[74] *Ibid.*, p. 232.

CHAPTER VIII

[1] William Parry, *Last Days of Lord Byron*, p. 163.
[2] *L. and J.*, IV, 260.
[3] "Lines to Mr. Hodgson," *Poetry*, VII, 6.
[4] *Op. cit.*, p. 6.
[5] Claude N. Fuess, *Byron as a Satirist in Verse*, p. 146.
[6] Can. I, st. 9.
[7] Can. II, st. 51.
[8] According to Lady Blessington, probably this and other passages were so intended.
[9] *L. and J.*, V, 482.
[10] *Ibid.*, p. 155.
[11] *Byron in England; His Fame and After-Fame*, p. 68.
[12] *L. and J.*, VII, 101.
[13] *Don Juan.*, can. VII, st. 2.
[14] Kennedy, *op. cit.*, pp. 163-64.
[15] Blessington, p. 46.
[16] *Ibid.*, p. 353.
[17] *L. and J.*, V, 96-97.
[18] *Ibid.*, VI, 155-56.
[19] *Ibid.*, V, 582.
[20] *The Vision of Judgment*, st. 54.
[21] *Don Juan*, can. XVI, st. 2.
[22] *Ibid.*, can. VIII, st. 89.
[23] "I detest all fiction, even in song."—*Ibid.*, can. vi, st. 8. "My Muse by no means deals in fiction."—*Ibid.*, can. xiv, st. 13. "'Tis the part of a true poet to escape from fiction whene'er he can."—*Ibid.*, can. VIII, st. 86.
[24] *L. and J.*, V, 347.
[25] *Don Juan*, can. XIV, st. 13.
[26] *L. and J.*, V, 347.
[27] See *Poetry*, VI, 304-372, and notes.

[28] *Don Juan*, can. VIII, st. 74.
[29] *Ibid.*, can. II, st. 60 n.
[30] Hobhouse, II, 57.
[31] *Don Juan.* "Dedication," st. 8.
[32] *Poetics*, IX, 1.
[33] *Don Juan*, can. VII, st. 2.
[34] *Ibid.*, can. XV, st. 19.
[35] *Memoirs . . . of John Murray*, p. 414.
[36] "To the Earl of Clare," l. 72.
[37] Chew, *Byron in England*, p. 68.
[38] Shelley, *Letters*, p. 839.
[39] *L. and J.*, IV, 341.
[40] *Don Juan*, can. IV, st. 117.
[41] *Ibid.*, can. V, st. 77; can. VI, st. 18.
[42] *Ibid.*, can. IX, st. 41.
[43] *Ibid.*, can. IV, st. 107.
[44] *Ibid.*, can. I, sts. 200-12.
[45] *Ibid.*, can. I, st. 6; can. V, st. 101.
[46] *Ibid.*
[47] *Ibid.*, can. VII, st. 80.
[48] *Ibid.*, can. V, st. 159.
[49] *Ibid.*, can. VII, st. 86.
[50] *Ibid.*, can. III, st. 111.
[51] *Ibid.*, can. I, st. 120.
[52] *Ibid.*, can. V, st. 159.
[53] *Ibid.*, can. I, sts. 6-7.
[54] *Ibid.*, can. XII, st. 45.
[55] *Ibid.*, can. XIII, st. 73.
[56] *Ibid.*, can. XV, st. 25.
[57] Medwin, pp. 202-3.
[58] *Ibid.*, p. 200.
[59] *Don Juan.*, can. XV, st. 25.
[60] *Ibid.*, can. IX, st. 41.
[61] *L. and J.*, IV, 342.
[62] *Don Juan*, can. I, st. 203. Cf. also Leigh Hunt, *Lord Byron and Some of His Contemporaries*, pp. 128-29: "Speaking of 'Don Juan,' I will here observe that he had no plan with regard to that poem; that he did not know how long he should make it, nor what to do with his hero. He had a great mind to make him die a Methodist—a catastrophe which he sometimes anticipated for himself."
[63] *L. and J.*, V, 242.
[64] *Ibid.*
[65] Medwin, pp. 201-3.
[66] *Don Juan*, can. XII, st. 87.
[67] *L. and J.*, V, 242.
[68] *Don Juan*, can. VIII, st. 138.
[69] *Ibid.*, st. 139.
[70] *Ibid.*, can. XII, st. 87.
[71] *L. and J.*, V, 242.

[72] *Don Juan*, can. XII, st. 55.
[73] *L. and J.*, IV, 276 n.
[74] *L. B. C.*, II, 132.
[75] *L. and J.*, IV, 277-78. Cf. also Hobhouse, III, 39.
[76] *L. and J.*, IV, 281.
[77] *Ibid.*, p. 281.
[78] *Ibid.*, V, 389.
[79] Trelawny, *op. cit.*, p. 79.
[80] *L. and J.*, V, 339-40 n.
[81] *Ibid.*, pp. 551-52.
[82] *Ibid.*, IV, 277.
[83] *Ibid.*, p. 281.
[84] *Ibid.*, V, 71.
[85] *Ibid.*, IV, 341.
[86] *Ibid.*, pp. 281-83.
[87] *L. B. C.*, II, 97.
[88] *L. and J.*, V, 77.
[89] *Ibid.*, IV, 371.
[90] *Ibid.*, p. 321.
[91] Moore, *op. cit.*, II, 270.
[92] *Ibid.*
[93] Gamba, *op. cit.*, p. 3.
[94] *Don Juan*, can. XI, st. 56.
[95] *L. and J.*, V, 320-1; *L. B. C.*, II, 176; Blessington, pp. 27, 93, 209.
[96] *Ibid.*, p. 362.
[97] *L. and J.*, V, 92.
[98] Blessington, p. 209.
[99] *L. and J.*, VI, 95.
[100] *Ibid.*, p. 74.
[101] *L. B. C.*, II, 244.
[102] *Don Juan*, can. II, st. 179.
[103] *L. and J.*, IV, 278.
[104] *Ibid.*, p. 348.
[105] *Ibid.*, VI, 429.

SELECTED BIBLIOGRAPHY

The following list includes only those works of which intimate use has been made.

Addison, Joseph. *The Works of Joseph Addison.* London, 1880. (Bohn Library Edition.)

Alfieri, Vittoria. *Tragedie.* Milano, Casa Editrice Sonzogno.

Astarte. See Milbanke, Ralph, Earl of Lovelace.

Babbitt, Irving. *The New Laokoön.* Boston, 1910.

Bell, Clive. *Civilization.* New York, 1928.

Blessington, Marguerite, Countess of. *Idler in Italy.* Paris, 1841.

——— *Conversations of Lord Byron with the Countess of Blessington.* Boston, 1859.

Briscoe, Walter (ed.) *Byron the Poet.* London, 1924.

Byron, George Gordon. *Letters and Journals of Lord Byron,* etc. See Moore, Thomas.

——— *Lord Byron's Correspondence.* Edited by John Murray. London, 1922.

——— *Poems and Letters of Lord Byron, Edited from the Original MSS in the Possession of W. K. Bixby of St. Louis, by W. N. C. Carlton, M.A., Published by the Society of the Dofobs.* Chicago, 1912.

——— *The Works of Lord Byron: Letters and Journals.* Edited by Rowland E. Prothero. 6 vols. London, 1898-1901.

——— *The Works of Lord Byron: Poetry.* Edited by Ernest Hartley Coleridge. 7 vols. London, 1898-1904.

Byron, Lord. *A Descriptive Catalogue of an Exhibition of Manuscripts and First Editions of Lord Byron Held in the Library of the University of Texas,* etc. Austin, Texas.

Chew, Samuel C. *Byron in England: His Fame and After-Fame.* London, 1924.

——— *The Dramas of Lord Byron.* Baltimore, 1915.

SELECTED BIBLIOGRAPHY

Dallas, R. C. *Recollections of the Life of Lord Byron.* Philadelphia, 1825.
Drinkwater, John. *The Pilgrim of Eternity: Byron—A Conflict.* New York, 1925.
Foerster, Norman. *American Criticism.* Boston, 1928.
Fuess, Claude N. *Lord Byron as a Satirist in Verse.* New York, 1912.
Galt, John. *Life of Lord Byron.* London, 1830.
Gamba, Count Peter. *A Narrative of Lord Byron's Last Journey to Greece.* London, 1825.
Garrod, H. W. *The Profession of Poetry and Other Lectures.* London, 1929.
Graves, Robert. *Good-Bye to All That.* New York, 1930.
Guiccioli, Countess. *Lord Byron jugé par les témoins de sa vie.* Translated by H. A. H. Jerningham, *My Recollections of Lord Byron.* New York, 1867.
Hobhouse, John Cam, Lord Broughton. *The Recollections of a Long Life.* London, 1909-1910.
Hunt, Leigh. *Autobiography of Leigh Hunt.* Edited by Roger Ingpen. Westminster, 1903.
────── *Lord Byron and Some of His Contemporaries.* London, 1828.
Johnson, Samuel. *Alexander Pope.* New York, 1897.
────── *Lives of the English Poets.* Oxford, 1905.
Kennedy, James. *Conversations on Religion with Lord Byron and Others.* London, 1830.
Ker, W. P. *The Eighteenth Century* (English Association Pamphlet, No. 35).
Kinglake, A. W. *Eothen.* Edinburgh and London, 1885.
Koenig, Karl. *Die Entstehung von Byrons English Bards and Scotch Reviewers.* Freiburg, 1913.
Lewis, Wyndham. *The Lion and the Fox.* New York, 1927.
Maurois, André. *Ariel, ou la vie de Shelley.* Paris, 1923.
────── *Byron.* Translated by Hamish Miles. New York, 1930.
Mayne, Ethel C. *Byron.* London, 1912.
Medwin, Thomas. *Journal of the Conversations of Lord Byron.* London, 1824.

Milbanke, Ralph, Earl of Lovelace. *Astarte.* London, 1921.
Moore, Thomas. *Letters and Journals of Lord Byron with Notices of His Life.* 2 vols. London, 1830.
Murray, John. *Memoirs and Correspondence of John Murray.* Edited by Samuel Smiles. London, 1896.
Parry, William. *Last Days of Lord Byron.* Philadelphia, 1825.
Peacock, T. L. *Works.* London, 1875.
Polidori, Dr. John William. *The Diary of Dr. John William Polidori.* Edited by W. M. Rossetti. London, 1911.
Pope, Alexander. *Complete Poetical Works.* Boston, 1903. (Cambridge Edition.)
——— ed. *Works of Mr. William Shakespeare.* Edited by Mr. Pope and Dr. Rewell. London, 1728.
Shelley, Percy Bysshe. *Letters of Percy Bysshe Shelley.* Edited by Roger Ingpen. London, 1914.
Spectator, The. London and Toronto, 1907. (Everyman's Library Edition.)
Spingarn, J. E. *Critical Essays of the Seventeenth Century.* Oxford, 1908.
Stanhope, Colonel Leicester. *Greece in 1823-1824—and Reminiscences of Lord Byron.* London, 1825.
Stephen, Leslie. *English Literature and Society in the Eighteenth Century.* London, 1904.
Symon, J. D. *Byron in Perspective.* London, 1924.
Ticknor, Anna. *Life, Letters and Journals of George Ticknor.* 2 vols. Boston, 1877.
Trelawny, Edward J. *Records of Shelley, Byron, and the Author.* New York, 1867.
Woodberry, G. E. *Heart of Man.* New York, 1920.

INDEX

ABERDEEN, Lord, 43.
Addison, Joseph, 23, 26, 27, 28, 31; review of Milton by, 32-33; spokesman for his age, 24.
Aeneid. See Virgil.
Aeschylus, 28, 172; *Prometheus Bound*, 168.
Age of Bronze, The. See Byron.
Alastor. See Shelley.
Alfieri, Vittorio, 55, 72, 73, 158, 159, 164, 170, 171, 172, 179, 181; comparison of with Byron, 161-63.
Ariosto, Ludovico, 109, 116, 191; *Orlando Furioso*, 193.
Aristotle, 22, 27, 35, 63, 158, 167, 189, 194, 195, 196.
Ars Poetica. See Horace.
Astarte, vi, viii, ix, 139.
Aucher, Father: *English-Armenian Grammar*, 17.

BACON, Sir Francis, 14, 22.
Bankes, William, 99.
Baviad. See Gifford.
Beattie, James, 103, 109.
Becher, Rev. John T., 77.
Beckford, William: *Vathek*, 140.
Berni, Francesco, 182, 192.
Bertram. See Maturin.
Blessington, Lady, 9, 11, 54, 67, 82, 88, 91, 116, 126, 128.
Blues, The. See Byron.
Boiardo, 182.
Boileau, Nicolas, 22, 45, 63; *Lutrin*, 25.
Bossu, René le: thesis prefixed to Pope's *Odyssey*, 22; on epic poetry, 28.
Bosworth Field. See Byron.
Bowles, William Lisle, 65, 158; controversy of with Byron, 67-72, 78,
159; edition of Pope, 45, 69; *Invariable Principles of Poetry*, 67, 69.
Braham, John, 155.
Bride of Abydos, The. See Byron.
British Bards. See Byron.
Brougham, Henry, Lord, 43.
Bunyan, John, 8.
Burns, Robert, 36-37, 40, 53, 65, 72, 73, 76; "Farewell to Ayrshire," 77.
Butler, Samuel: *Hudibras*, 46.
Byron, George Gordon, and Alfieri, 161-63; on art, artificial *versus* natural, 70-71; and the *Astarte* problem, viii-ix; artistic morality of, 50-52; attitude of toward his art, 128 ff.; and Bowles controversy, 66-70, 78; and the Byronic hero, 111-15, 121-22, 124; "Byronic pose" of, 5; Calvinism of, 6-13; classicism of, 52-58; departure of from England, 123-25; and the drama, 83, 86, 152-58, 176-78, 178-81; Eastern travels of, 167; emendations by, 98-101; fame and after-fame of, vi; on glory, 102; irritability of, 16-19; in Italy, 125 ff.; neoclassic taste of, 49-50, 128; on nobility of style, 72; personality of, 3-5; poetic composition of, 90, 98, 127-28; on poets and poetry, 80-86; and the Pope problem, viii; self-confession by, 20; and Shelley, 132-36; skepticism of, 13-16; and the theatre, 83, 86, 152-58, 176-78, 178-81.
Works:
  Age of Bronze, The, 207.
  Beppo, 81, 93, 94, 126, 131, 136, 138, 166, 172, 182, 189.
  Blues, The, 50.
  Bosworth Field (projected epic), 80.

[229]

INDEX

Works *(con.)*
  Bride of Abydos, The, 116, 118; composition of, 93.
  British Bards, 105.
  Cain, 158, 163, 167, 169, 178, 181, 206, 207; Calvinism in, 7; characteristics of 174-76.
  Childe Harold, 1, 12, 21, 57, 61, 62, 64, 96, 103, 120, 129, 132, 133, 135, 136, 138, 152, 153, 179, 186, 187, 192, 199, 209; reverence for old in, 5-6; preface to, 50-51; genesis of, 108-10; Dallas's part in, 110; identification of Byron with Childe, 111-13, 121-22; comparison of with *Manfred,* 138-39; return to composition of, 144-46; Cantos III and IV, 144-51; Byron's opinion of last canto of, 150.
  Corsair, The. 118, 120, 122, 123, 145, 149.
  Curse of Minerva, The, 115.
  Deformed Transformed, The, 166, 169, 176, 207.
  Don Juan, 12, 81, 84, 91, 92, 93, 94, 97, 123, 128, 135, 137, 138, 145, 149, 152, 162, 171, 172, 180, 182-210; anti-climaxes in, 7; preface to Canto I, 59; aim of, 182-84; satire on sentimentalism in, 184-87; effort at verisimilitude in, 188-89; style of, 189-93; adaptation of the Rules, 193-98; plan of, 198-202; Byron's attitude toward, 203-9.
  Dream, The, 141.
  Drury Lane Address, 49, 137, 153.
  English Bards and Scotch Reviewers, 38, 41, 46, 72, 78, 80, 95-96, 99, 108, 109, 136, 153, 192; analysis of, 42-45; composition of, 105-6; reaction against, 57-59, 106-7.
  "Epistle to the Corinthians," Byron's translation of, 17.
  Francesca of Rimini (projected drama), 175.

Works *(con.)*
  Giaour, The, 115, 116, 117, 119, 122, 137, 145.
  Heaven and Earth, 103, 135, 155, 169, 176, 178, 207; Calvinism in, 7.
  Hints from Horace, 42, 57, 72, 108, 110, 136, 153; analyzed, 45-47.
  Hours of Idleness, 54, 105, 107, 153; analysis of, 74-78; preface to, 74-76; references to, 76-77; reception of, 79.
  "Farewell to the Muse," 79.
  "Fragment Written Shortly after the Marriage of Miss Chaworth," 77.
  "Occasional Prologue," 153.
  "On a Distant View . . . of Harrow on the Hill," 153.
  "To the Earl of Clare," 77.
  Island, The, 149.
  Lament of Tasso, The, 129, 135, 138, 192.
  Lara, 6, 116, 123; description of Lara in, 113-14.
  Manfred, 21, 136, 138, 146, 148, 156, 158, 163, 169, 170, 176, 181, 209; connected with Calvinism, 7; comparison of with *Childe Harold,* 138-39; problem of, 139-44; comparison of with *Marino Faliero,* 173; comparison of with *Cain,* 174.
  Marino Faliero, 134, 158, 162, 167, 168, 169, 172, 175, 179, 180, 181, 206; analysis of, 169-72; and *Manfred,* 173.
  Mazeppa, 131.
  Morgante Maggiore, translation of first canto of, 137.
  Parisina, 115, 116, 119, 137.
  Prisoner of Chillon, The, 131.
  Prophecy of Dante, The, 129, 135, 138, 192.
  Romances, The, 115-22: composition of, 117-19; dissatisfaction with, 119-22.

INDEX

Works *(con.)*
  Sardanapalus, 162-67, 172, 175, 178, 180, 181; preface to, 173.
  "She Walks in Beauty," 90.
  Siege of Corinth, The, 86, 116, 119.
  Tiberius (projected drama), 175.
  Two Foscari, The, 162, 167, 169, 172.
  Vision of Judgment, The, 67, 138, 149, 187.
  Waltz, The, 108.
  Werner, 137, 149, 155, 157, 169, 170, 176, 206, 207.
Byron, Lady, 16, 123, 184, 209.

CAIN. *See* Byron.
Campbell, Thomas, 44, 46, 53, 61, 110, 154.
Carlisle, Lord, Frederick Howard, 6, 99.
Carlyle, Thomas, comparison of with Byron, 6-7, 18.
Castelnau: *Essai sur l'histoire de la nouvelle Russie,* 188.
Casti, Abbate Giovanni Battista, 191, 192.
Castlereagh, Lord, 59, 184, 204.
Cervantes, 189, 191.
"Characters of Women." *See* Pope.
Chatterton, Thomas, 65.
Chaucer, Geoffrey, 26, 31, 47.
Chesterton, G. K., 184.
Chew, Samuel C., 140.
Childe Harold. See Byron.
Christabel. See Coleridge, S. T.
Churchill, Charles, 184, 192.
Claudian, 27, 28, 62.
"Cockney School," 65, 66, 68, 71.
Codrus, 63.
Coleridge, Ernest H., 81, 96, 188.
Coleridge, S. T., 43, 57, 59, 154, 155, 165; *Christabel,* 55, 102, 116; *Remorse,* 140.
Collier, Jeremy, 24.
Colman, George, 43, 154.
Congreve, William, 23, 164.
Cooke, G. F., 155.
"Cornwall, Barry." *See* Procter.

Corsair, The. See Byron.
Cowper, William, 8, 64.
Crabbe, George, 44, 53, 61, 99, 101, 195.
Croker, John W., 74, 190.
Cumberland, Richard, 43.
Curse of Kehama. See Southey.
Curse of Minerva, The. See Byron.

DALLAS, R. C., 43, 99, 124, 144; on publication of *Childe Harold,* 110-11.
Dante, 54, 72, 73, 123.
Darwin, Erasmus, 44.
Deformed Transformed, The. See Byron.
Della Cruscans, the, 40.
Dennis, John, 25, 30.
Don Juan. See Byron.
Dream, The. See Byron.
Drinkwater, John: *Pilgrim of Eternity,* 87, 108, 110, 124, 161.
Drummond, Sir William: *Odin,* 55.
Drury Lane, Byron's contact with, 83, 86.
Drury Lane Address. See Byron.
Dryden, John, 22, 26, 44, 87, 175, 184, 195.
Dunciad. See Pope.

EDINBURGH Review, 6, 43, 104, 105, 175, 177.
Edwards, Jonathan, 18.
"Elegy on the Death of an Unfortunate Lady." *See* Pope.
Elizabethans, 36, 105; criticized in eighteenth century, 26; by Johnson, 34; Byron's opinion of, 159-61, 171.
Elliston, Robert William, 168.
Emerson, R. W., 14.
Endymion. See Keats.
English-Armenian Grammar. See Aucher, Father.
English Bards and Scotch Reviewers. See Byron.
Epistle to Dr. Arbuthnot. See Pope.
Essay on Criticism. See Pope.

INDEX

"FAREWELL to Ayrshire." *See* Burns.
"Farewell to the Muse." *See* Byron, *Hours of Idleness.*
Faust. See Goethe.
Fielding, Henry, 24, 29, 47, 209.
"Fragment Written Shortly after the Marriage of Miss Chaworth." *See* Byron, *Hours of Idleness.*
Francesca da Rimini. See Hunt.
Francesca of Rimini. See Byron.
Frere, John H., 100; *Monks and the Giants, The,* 136, 193; *Whistlecraft,* 192.
Fudge Family in Paris. See Moore.
Fuess, Claude N.: *Lord Byron as a Satirist in Verse,* 193.

GALT, John, 11.
Gamba, Count Pietro, 84, 126.
Garrod, H. W., 20.
Giaour, The. See Byron.
Gifford, William, 44, 49, 57, 59, 81, 100, 101, 110, 119, 177, 192, 204; influence on *English Bards,* 38-42, 48; *Baviad,* 38, 39, 40, 68, 136; *Maeviad,* 38, 68.
Godwin, William, 124.
Goethe, 52, 64, 123, 163, 206; *Faust,* 140, 142; *Werther,* 140, 199.
Goldsmith, Oliver, 62.
Grahame, Mr., 43.

"HAFIZ," 44.
Hallam, Henry, 43.
Hamlet. See Shakespeare.
Harris, Harry, 168.
Harvey, Gabriel, 22.
Hayley, William, 44.
Heaven and Earth. See Byron.
Hemans, Mrs. Felicia Dorothea, 64.
Henry IV. See Shakespeare.
Herbert, Helga, 43, 103.
Hints from Horace. See Byron.
Hobhouse, John Cam, 11, 100, 109, 110, 120, 175.
Hodgson, Rev. Francis, 44, 53, 99.
Holland, Lord, 43, 98.
Homer, 29, 31, 35, 44, 49-50, 52, 155, 195, 197, 199; criticized by Pope, 33-34; *Iliad,* 27, 168, 194, 208; *Odyssey,* 30, 198.
Hook, Theodore, 43.
Horace, 62, 63, 195; model in eighteenth century, 26; *Arts Poetica,* 31; imitated in *Hints from Horace,* 45.
Hours of Idleness. See Byron.
Hudibras. See Butler.
Hunt, Leigh, 4, 14, 51, 65, 66, 178; *Francesca da Rimini,* 63, 65.
Hyperion. See Keats.

IBSEN, Henrik, 178.
Iliad. See Homer.
Iliad, translation of. *See* Pope.
Invariable Principles of Poetry. See Bowles.
Island, The. See Byron.

JEFFREY, Francis, 43, 45, 47, 49, 57, 105.
Jerusalem Delivered. See Tasso.
Johnson, Samuel, 22, 23, 26, 27, 28, 29, 30, 38, 39, 50, 51, 52, 53, 68, 79, 130, 151, 165, 167, 197, 198, 209, on original genius, 34; Shakespeare, preface to, 35.
Jonson, Ben, 22, 47, 164.
Julian and Maddalo. See Shelley.
Juvenal, 63.

KEAN, Edmund, 155.
Keats, John, vii, 97, 133; Byron's criticism of, 65-66, 72; *Endymion,* 65; *Hyperion,* 66; "Sleep and Poetry," 66.
Kemble, John, 155.
Kennedy, James, 178.
Kenney, James, 43.
Ker, W. P., 52.
Koenig, Karl, study of *English Bards,* 95, 97.

LA BRUYÈRE, 23.
La Guiccioli, Teresa, 49, 90, 206.
Lake School, 54, 59, 65, 68, 86, 195.
Lamb, Lady Caroline, 112.

INDEX

Lambe, 43.
Lament of Tasso, The. See Byron.
Lara. See Byron.
Lear. See Shakespeare.
Lee, Nathaniel, 28, 141.
Lewis, Matthew Gregory, 43, 44, 113, 140.
Licensing Act, 47.
"Little, Thomas." See Moore.
Lockhart, J. G., 38.
Longinus, 31, 34.
Lucan, 27.
Lutrin. See Boileau.
Lycidas. See Milton.
Lyrical Ballads, 105; preface, 38.

*M*ACBETH. See Shakespeare.
Maeviad. See Gifford.
Mahomet, 70.
Mallock, Mr., 114.
Manfred. See Byron.
Marino Faliero. See Byron.
Marmion. See Scott.
"Martinus Scriblerus." See Pope, *Dunciad.*
Massinger, Philip, 44.
Maturin, Charles Robert, 155; *Bertram,* 140.
Maurois, André, 12.
Mazeppa. See Byron.
Medwin, Thomas, 67, 68, 81, 96, 128, 200.
Milman, Henry Hart, 169.
Milton, John, 27, 29, 31, 40, 44, 46, 56, 69, 70, 143, 195; *Lycidas,* 28; *Paradise Lost,* 26, 32, 33, 176, 208; *Samson Agonistes,* 157, 164.
Monks and the Giants, The. See Frere.
Montgomery, James, 43.
Moore, Thomas ("Thomas Little"), 43, 44, 54, 56, 57, 61, 68, 76, 77, 82, 99, 109, 121, 154, 186, 205; *Zeluco,* 113, 144; *Fudge Family in Paris,* 115; *Letters and Journals of Lord Byron,* 106, 125.
Morgante Maggiore. See Pulci; translation of first canto of. See Byron.
Morley, Lord, 150.
Muir, Dr. Henry, 94.

Munden, 155.
Murray, John, 50, 72, 94, 100, 119, 130, 143, 177, 205.
Mysterious Mother. See Walpole.

*N*APOLEON, 9, 146.
Nicholson, Howard, 84.

"*O*CCASIONAL Prologue." See Byron, *Hours of Idleness.*
Odyssey. See Homer.
"On a Distant View . . . of Harrow on the Hill." See Byron, *Hours of Idleness.*
Orlando Furioso. See Ariosto.
Ossian, 56, 76.
Othello. See Shakespeare.
Otway, Thomas, 44.
Ovid, 27.

*P*ARADISE *Lost.* See Milton.
Parisina. See Byron.
Parker, Miss Margaret, 89.
Peacock, Thomas Love, 1, 140.
Pilgrim of Eternity. See Drinkwater.
Pillans, 43.
Plato, 51.
Polidori, John W., 50, 127.
Pope, Alexander, 22, 24, 27, 40, 44, 45, 46, 49, 50, 51, 57, 60, 61, 73, 76, 77, 87, 134, 151, 161, 184, 192, 195, 198, 209; Byron's devotion to, viii; on original genius, 34-36; Byron-Bowles controversy, 61-72; "Characters of Women," 120; *Dunciad,* 39; preface to ("Martinus Scriblerus"), 29-30, 50, 194; "Elegy on the Death of an Unfortunate Lady," 120; *Epistle to Dr. Arbuthnot,* 39, 44, 86; *Essay on Criticism,* 25, 31, 39, 44; *Iliad,* translation of, 32, 109, 116; *Rape of the Lock,* 25, 120; Shakespeare, edition of, 32.
Prisoner of Chillon, The. See Byron.
Procter, Bryan Waller ("Barry Cornwall"), 63, 163, 169.
Prophecy of Dante, The. See Byron.

Pulci, Luigi; *Morgante Maggiore*, 51, 183, 191, 192.

Q*UEEN Mab.* See Shelley.

R*ADCLIFFE*, Mrs. Ann, 113.
Rape of the Lock. See Pope.
Remorse. See Coleridge.
René, 140.
Reynolds, Frederick, 43.
Richard III. See Shakespeare.
Richards, 44.
Richardson, Samuel, 24.
Rogers, Samuel, 44, 50, 53, 61, 101; *Voyage of Columbus*, 116.
Romances, The. See Byron.
Rosa Matilda, 44.
Rose, William Stewart, 100.
Rousseau, Jean Jacques, 56, 146, 147, 186.
Rules, The, 27, 29, 35, 49, 50; adaptation of in *Don Juan*, 193-98. *See also* Aristotle.
Rymer, Thomas, 30, 167; belligerent rationalism of, 23.

S*T. Irvyne.* See Shelley.
Samson Agonistes. See Milton.
Sardanapalus. See Byron.
Scott, Walter, 43, 44, 46, 53, 56, 57, 61, 68, 82, 84, 109; *Marmion*, 76, 113.
Shakespeare, William, 26, 31, 32, 44, 69, 70, 72, 73, 154, 159, 160, 192; criticized by Pope, 33-35; admired by Byron, 46-47; *Hamlet*, 180, 198; *Henry V*, 159, 165; *Lear*, 153; *Macbeth*, 155; *Othello*, 153; *Richard III*, 155, 180; *Winter's Tale*, 165; *Works*, editions of. See Pope; Johnson.
Shaw, Bernard, 174; *You Never Can Tell*, 4.
Shelley, Mary, 96, 97, 167.
Shelley, Percy Bysshe, vii, 11, 14, 15, 55, 59, 62, 63, 66, 82, 92, 126, 127, 130, 147, 150, 177, 176; relations of with Byron, 132-36, 147-48; praise of *Don Juan* by 203-4; *Alastor*, 140; *Julian and Maddalo*, 133; *Queen Mab*, 140; *St. Irvyne*, 140, 141.
Shenstone, William, 36, 109.
Sheridan, R. B., 43, 44, 160, 164.
"She Walks in Beauty." See Byron.
Siddons, Mrs. Henry, 155.
Siege of Corinth, The. See Byron.
Skeffington, 43.
"Sleep and Poetry." See Keats.
Smith, Sydney, 43.
Socrates, 70.
Sophocles, 28, 70.
Sotheby, William, 82, 155.
Southey, Robert, 43, 46, 57, 59, 61, 66, 90, 184, 204; *Curse of Kehama*, 103.
Spencer, William, 53.
Spenser, Edmund, 26, 31; model of good English, 34.
Staël, Madame de, 186.
Stanhope, Colonel Leicester, 84, 88.
Stanhope, Lady Hester, 1.
Statius, 27, 28.
Steele, Richard, 24.
Strangford, Lord, 43, 109.
Swift, Jonathan, 30, 46, 47; comparison of with Byron, 5, 14, 194.
Swinburne, Algernon C., 201.
Symon, J. D., 14.

T*ASSO*, 27, 44, 116; *Jerusalem Delivered*, 193.
Thomson, James, 56, 103, 109.
Tiberius. See Byron.
Ticknor, George, 110, 155, 157.
"To the Earl of Clare." See Byron, *Hours of Idleness*.
Trelawny, Edward J., 67, 126, 133.
Tully, Richard, *Tripoli*, 188.
Two Foscari, The. See Byron.

U*NITIES*, the, 22, 163, 168, 173, 174, 176; defense of, 165-67.

V*ATHEK.* See Beckford.
Vida, Marco Girolamo, 63.
Virgil, 27, 29, 31, 44, 199, 208; *Aeneid*, 196, 198.

INDEX

Vision of Judgment, The. See Byron.
Voltaire, 51; *Candide,* 140.
Voyage of Columbus. See Rogers.

WALLER'S preface to *The Monks and the Giants,* 193.
Walpole, Horace: *Mysterious Mother,* 140.
Waltz, The. See Byron.
Warton, Joseph, 38.
Warton, Thomas: *History of English Poetry,* 174.
Werner. See Byron.

Werther. See Goethe.
Wheel of Fortune, The, 153.
Whistlecraft. See Frere, J. H.
Windham, William, 85.
Winter's Tale. See Shakespeare.
Wordsworth, William, vii, 43, 44, 46, 57, 59, 60, 61, 65, 66, 89, 133, 147, 150.
Wycherley, William, 23.

"**X**. Y. Z.," 44.

YOU *Never Can Tell.* See Shaw.

www.ingramcontent.com/pod-product-compliance
Lightning Source LLC
Chambersburg PA
CBHW021400290426
44108CB00010B/326